GULF WAR SYNDROME

Legacy of a Perfect War

GULF WAR SYNDROME

Legacy of a Perfect War

Alison Johnson

With a foreword by
James J. Tuite, III

MCS Information Exchange
Brunswick, Maine

MCS Information Exchange
2 Oakland Street
Brunswick, ME 04011

ISBN 0-9675619-7-3

Printed in the United States of America

To the veterans who for a brief period faced great danger in the Persian Gulf and for ten long years have faced pain, illness, and abandonment by those for whom they fought.

Contents

Part II

Foreword

In 1993, I began working for then U.S. Senator Donald W. Riegle (D-MI) as a Legislative Fellow on defense and foreign policy matters. I had just completed my doctoral comprehensive examinations in World Politics. I also brought to my fellowship a background as an Army combat medic in Vietnam and a twenty-year career as a Secret Service Agent. My assignments as a Secret Service Agent included periods spent working on protective intelligence related to the Middle East and, later, as the Forensic Science Research Coordinator (and chemical hygiene officer). It is an unusual background, to be sure, but it put me in a natural position to be called upon to look into the complaints coming into Senator Riegle's office from Michigan's Gulf War veterans. Thus was I lured, reluctantly, into conducting an investigation into Persian Gulf War veterans' health issues and then into an investigation of the U.S. role in arming Iraq prior to the 1991 Gulf War. As the scope of the initial inquiry expanded, I was asked to direct the investigation as a member of the professional staff of the U.S. Senate Committee on Banking, Housing and Urban Affairs.

My investigations led me to two inescapable conclusions: veterans of the Gulf War had likely been exposed to chemical warfare agents and other environmental toxins and the U.S. had played a significant role in arming Iraq with chemical and biological weapons. My investigations also fueled a nascent but coordinated campaign by the Departments of Defense and Veterans Affairs to deny that there had been any incidents in which U.S. troops were exposed to chemical warfare agents and further to deny that there was any illness in U.S. veterans that could be linked to their service in the Gulf. Subsequent events continue to prove the fallacy of the government's original assertions.

Denial after denial by the Department of Defense has unraveled. Some of the classified reports obtained by the Committee outside official channels were said not to have existed. Over time, however, they surfaced as the Pentagon continued to backpedal on this issue. Other documents, including most of the chemical and biological warfare incident logs, disappeared from secure locations about the time they were requested by Congress.

Working with Senator Riegle before he retired in 1995, I directed the production of three investigative reports. Other Members of Congress have produced additional reports and have sponsored further medical research over the subsequent years. I, too, have continued to work on this issue. Although additional information has come to light to refine our knowledge, the basic conclusions have remained the same: soldiers in the Gulf were exposed to a chemical soup to varying degrees, exposures to low levels of chemical warfare agents occurred, and the U.S. role in arming Iraq was extensive. U.S. decisions prior to, during, and subsequent to the war had significant impact upon the number of troops exposed. Since 1996, the Department of Defense has reluctantly admitted that over 100,000 troops might have been exposed in just a single incident at Khamisiyah. The Department of Veterans Affairs, though armed since 1998 with the legislation that will allow it to act on behalf of Gulf War veterans, continues to stint them the care and compensation that they merit.

The veterans' accounting of their experience is corroborated by the telling of similar events by unrelated co-combatants from many of the nations that supported the military coalition formed to defeat Saddam Hussein. Unfortunately, scientists are ill prepared to conduct research that may involve dynamic variations among multiple exposures. Yet dozens of peer-reviewed articles published in highly reputable scientific and medical journals have confirmed evidence of abnormal rates of undiagnosed symptoms as well as evidence of neurological and genetic damage among veterans deployed to the Persian Gulf during the 1991 war. In the final analysis we may never be able to say which veterans were exposed to which toxins and in what amounts. We can, however, address the issue that the veterans were exposed to many toxic substances that by themselves or in combination can lead to the types of symptoms and illnesses being reported.

The Department of Veterans Affairs needs to focus on identifying the underlying pathologies of these illnesses and focus on attempting to treat these veterans. The Department of Defense must stop meddling in veterans affairs and address the technology and doctrinal shortcomings that led to these exposures being dismissed as insignificant. The Department of Defense should also take a hard look at the ethical conduct of their senior leadership responsible for the mishandling of this issue.

Alison Johnson has ably brought together the voluminous official record that exists on the issue of Persian Gulf War Syndrome and possible and potential exposures that may be affecting Gulf War veterans' health. She has brought this official record to life by collecting the haunting individual stories of Gulf War veterans. Her chronicle also folds in the startling medical research conducted by others and myself, which shows the very real and physical damage suffered by these veterans.

Based upon her previous works addressing the medical conditions of individuals afflicted with multiple chemical sensitivity syndrome—*Casualties of Progress: Personal Histories from the Chemically Sensitive,* and several well-produced videos—Alison Johnson provides a special insight into the torment being suffered by those who are stricken with these poorly understood but nevertheless real and debilitating complex illnesses. She makes a compelling case for the Gulf War veterans' cause in *Gulf War Syndrome: Aftermath of a Toxic Battlefield,* a video she produced and directed, and in the chapters that follow. Her book should find a wide audience among veterans, their families, their doctors, and the general public. If those who may be called upon to serve, and those who are so well protected, do not take up this cause, the commitment made by President Abraham Lincoln in 1865, which forms the creed of the Department of Veterans Affairs, "To care for him who shall have borne the battle, and for his widow, and his orphan," may be irrevocably harmed.

James J. Tuite, III
Chronic Illness Research Foundation

Preface

Ten years ago, like so many other Americans, I watched CNN hour by hour and day by day as the drama of the Gulf War unfolded. I have never forgotten that visceral feeling of the great danger the young men and women in our Armed Forces were facing in a confrontation with a dictator who possessed a vast arsenal of chemical weapons and had not hesitated to use them on earlier occasions.

As the war was drawing to a successful close and I watched on the evening news the images of oil well fires burning throughout Kuwait, I realized that the soldiers who were breathing for weeks the toxic fumes from this vast inferno were at risk for developing sensitivity to a wide array of chemicals. At that point, I was not yet aware of the myriad of other toxins to which our troops were exposed during the Gulf War.

The danger from exposure to the smoke from the oil well fires was apparent to me because of my background in the field of chemical sensitivity. My knowledge of the condition know as multiple chemical sensitivity, or MCS, was gathered over many years, first from my own experience, then from that of my daughters, and later from my involvement as a national advocate for the chemically sensitive. In the latter role, I conducted a survey of 351 patients concerning their experience with various therapies they had tried. Sadly, as my survey shows, there is no quick fix for the chemically sensitive. I subsequently produced a video entitled *Multiple Chemical Sensitivity: How Chemical Exposures May Be Affecting Your Health*, which contained an eight-minute section on Gulf War syndrome. That project then led to a book, *Casualties of Progress: Personal Histories from the Chemically Sensitive*, which included stories from six Gulf War veterans. Several of these veterans thanked me for publicizing their health problems. I found their gratitude to be almost embarrassing—it was I who owed a huge debt of gratitude to them for facing grave danger during Desert Storm on behalf of all of us.

In February 2000, I attended a hearing on Gulf War syndrome held by the Human Resources Subcommittee of the House Committee on Government Reform, chaired by Congressman Christopher Shays (R-CT). Several members of the committee obviously understood the relationship between chemical sensitivity and Gulf War syndrome, but it was clear that the officials from the Department of Defense (DOD) and the Department of Veterans Affairs (VA) who testified that day just didn't get it. I was also sorry to see that although over

100,000 Gulf War veterans are now sick, only two attended that hearing. I realized, however, that many of them were just too ill to travel to Washington and others had been financially devastated by their illness and could not afford the trip. Still others had probably given up trying to get anyone to listen to their plight, having been worn down by years of DOD and VA neglect and denial of their problems. The summary to the 1997 report of the Shays subcommittee indicates what sick veterans have faced for years: "Sadly, when it comes to diagnosis, treatment and research for Gulf War veterans, we find the Federal Government too often has a tin ear, a cold heart and a closed mind."

The need was all too clear, and a few days later I decided to make a video to try to show what was happening to the Gulf War veterans. It was released in October 2000 under the title *Gulf War Syndrome: Aftermath of a Toxic Battlefield*. Once again one project led to another. The enormously complex issues that must be considered in any attempt to begin unraveling Gulf War syndrome could not be covered in sufficient depth in a 78-minute video. The present book is my attempt to shed a little more light on the various toxic exposures that have led to long-term, devastating consequences for the men and women who risked their lives in the Gulf War and lost their health.

About the Author

Alison Johnson, B.A., M.A., is a graduate of Carleton College and studied mathematics at the Sorbonne on a National Science Foundation Fellowship. She received a master's degree in mathematics from the University of Wisconsin, where she studied on a Woodrow Wilson Fellowship, and she is currently a freelance editor for university presses. She has produced and directed three videos on multiple chemical sensitivity, as well as a video titled *Gulf War Syndrome: Aftermath of a Toxic Battlefield.* She has also edited a book titled *Casualties of Progress: Personal Histories from the Chemically Sensitive.* Johnson and her daughters have multiple chemical sensitivity, but through avoidance of chemical exposures, they are now able to function well in normal life circumstances.

For information on ordering Alison Johnson's videos, books, or survey of therapies, see the website <<http://www.conceptmed.com/Johnson>> or the Appendix.

Acknowledgments

I wish to express my appreciation to several people who read extensive portions of the manuscript: Guy Emery, Betsey Grobe, Gail Johnson, Wells Johnson, Ann McCampbell, Jeanne Mayo, Jim Moss, and Bob Weggel. Thanks also to Roxane Bates, Tom Donnelly, Meryl Nass, Larry Plumlee, Jennifer Rickard, Gerald Ross, Craig Stead, Kelly Seibert, and Jim Tuite for providing useful information. I wish to express my special gratitude to graphic artist Zi Pinsley, who designed the cover, and Jayson Askan, a Gulf War veteran who provided the cover photographs. One other person deserves great credit for his efforts that have been instrumental to my work, and that is Richard Startzman, the cinematographer who made the videos with me. Those projects were possible only because he was willing to serve important and neglected causes.

Nothing in this book should in any way be construed as medical advice. It is important to consult your physician concerning any health problem.

Note to the Reader

This book consists of two parts. Part I contains a discussion of the various major toxic exposures in the Persian Gulf that may have contributed to the development of Gulf War syndrome. Part II contains personal histories from twenty-four veterans of Desert Storm, who describe their war experience and its effect upon their health and lives. Some readers may find that they prefer to skip back and forth between the expository material of Part I and the narratives of Part II, a procedure that may make reading the book a more meaningful experience.

The following abbreviations will be used for frequently cited sources:

Riegle report—"U.S. Chemical and Biological Warfare-Related Dual Use Exports to Iraq and Their Possible Impact on the Health Consequences of the Persian Gulf War," Senate Committee on Banking, Housing, and Urban Affairs, chaired by Senator Donald W. Riegle, Jr. (D-MI), May 25, 1994.

Shays report—"Gulf War Illnesses: VA, DOD Continue to Resist Strong Evidence Linking Toxic Causes to Chronic Health Effects." Second Report by the House Committee on Government Reform and Oversight, Subcommittee on Human Resources, chaired by Congressman Christopher Shays (R-CT), November 7, 1997.

SIU report—"Report of the Special Investigation Unit on Gulf War Illnesses," Senate Committee on Veterans' Affairs, chaired by Senator Arlen Specter (R-PA), 1998.

GWS video footage—video interviews from our video *Gulf War Syndrome: Aftermath of a Toxic Battlefield*, including not only passages from the video itself but other passages from the raw footage.

Part II—Material from the personal histories in the second section of the present book.

Several online reports from the RAND Corporation and the DOD are used extensively, and for these reports a notation like (RAND *DU,* 3:8) indicates section or chapter 3, page 8.

List of Abbreviations

ACh—acetylcholine

AChE—acetylcholinesterase

ALS—amyotrophic lateral sclerosis

ANG—Army National Guard or Air National Guard

AVIP—Anthrax Vaccine Immunization Program

CARC—chemical agent resistant coating

CCEP—Comprehensive Clinical Evaluation Program

CDC—Centers for Disease Control and Prevention

CFS—chronic fatigue syndrome

DEET—N,N-diethyl-m-toluamide

DOD—Department of Defense

DU—depleted uranium

EPA—Environmental Protection Agency

FDA—Food and Drug Administration

IND—investigational new drug

IOM—Institute of Medicine

MOPP-4—mission-oriented protective posture, level 4

MCS—multiple chemical sensitivity

NAPP—nerve agent pretreatment pack

NBC—nuclear/biological/chemical

NCO—non-commissioned officer

NIH—National Institutes of Health

OPIDN—organophosphate-induced delayed neuropathy

OPIDP—organophosphate-induced delayed polyneuropathy

OSAGWI—Office of the Special Assistant for Gulf War Illness

PB—pyridostigimine bromide

PGW—Persian Gulf War

PTSD—post-traumatic stress syndrome

VA—Department of Veterans Affairs

VOC—volatile organic compound

PART I

Introduction

On August 2, 1990, Saddam Hussein moved the troops he had been massing along the Iraqi border with oil-rich Kuwait across that line in the sand, thereby setting in motion a chain of events that would bring almost 700,000 U.S. soldiers to the Persian Gulf. During the next few months, as President George Bush was hastily putting together a coalition to oppose Saddam, troops and materiel were quickly ferried to Saudi Arabia. U.S. military planners were so apprehensive about Saddam's capacity and willingness to wage chemical and biological warfare that supplies sent to the Gulf included 100,000 body bags.

On January 17, the air war began with massive air strikes against Baghdad and the Iraqi chemical weapons factories. All across America, people watched as missiles streaked across the night sky of Baghdad and General Norman Schwarzkopf presented impressive footage of high-tech missile attacks on Iraqi targets. Then on February 24 the ground war began, and to the great surprise of all concerned, the war ended only a hundred hours later, on February 28. The 100,000 body bags remained in storage because only 148 soldiers died in the conflict. The number of wounded was also very low—only 467.

The war was more than just a victory over Saddam Hussein, however. It was a victory over the lingering malaise regarding military actions that had gripped America since the Vietnam debacle. In comparison to Vietnam, Desert Storm seemed like the perfect war—quick and efficient, with very few U.S. casualties.

Our troops were welcomed home as heroes, and in the euphoria of those heady days, soldiers who had already begun having health problems in the Persian Gulf hoped they would soon feel better because they had left behind them the harsh desert atmosphere and the battlefield exposures. As the months passed, however, more and more of them began to experience a deterioration in their health. They had gone to the Gulf in peak physical condition, but now they were plagued by a variety of symptoms that often seemed minor at first but soon became more troublesome as they persisted and intensified. These symptoms included joint and muscle pain, muscle twitching, headaches, extreme fatigue, diarrhea, rectal incontinence, urinary frequency and urgency, insomnia, persistent rashes, memory loss, confusion, and dizziness. Many veterans described their illness as a flu that never went away.

As time passed, various veterans begin to compare notes and learn that others too were now sick, even though their health had been excellent when they left for Desert Storm. This information sharing may well have been discouraged by the military, if the experience of Cpl. Larry Perry is any example. On November 19, 1998, he testified to the Presidential Special Oversight Board chaired by former Senator Warren Rudman concerning his experience:

> I am here today to tell you what happens to those that tell what happened in the Gulf. In other words, those that go public or tell others what experience they had in the Gulf to media or investigation teams . . .
> I was the assistant officer in charge of . . . a Navy CB detachment.
> . . . We were hit with two direct SCUD missile attacks that Mr. Rostker's office says is now back to a sonic boom. When fireballs are in the sky, it's not a sonic boom. Our skin was on fire . . . we were starting to show immediate signs of flu-like symptoms and the longer we stayed in Saudi Arabia, the worse some of us got.
> When we came home, so many of my men were sick and being the assistant officer in charge, I tried to help them. When I tried to help them, all officers in charge and assistant officers in charge were called to the headquarters in Huntsville, Alabama. We were told that if anyone was dissatisfied with the way things were going, they could just get the hell out.
> When I kept helping my men, I was put on report and put on restriction to the chief's quarters at the reserve center and given a direct order not to talk to my men anymore. This happened two months in a row. I was given a 2(a) [2.8] evaluation and put out of the Reserves, ending a 22-year career.
> I went from a 4-0 [4.0] Chief Petty Officer, being assistant officer in charge, to a prisoner with a 2(a) [2.8] evaluation. I have never been so humiliated in all my life.[1]

When veterans like Corporal Perry approached the DOD and VA to suggest that they had perhaps been exposed to nerve agents during the war, their suggestions were dismissed. Thus began a conflict between the DOD and VA on one side and a steadily growing number of sick veterans on the other, a conflict that is still going on ten years after the end of the war. From

[1] Proceedings, Public Hearing, Presidential Special Oversight Board for Department of Defense Investigations of Gulf War Chemical and Biological Incidents, November 19, 1998, 20-21.

the beginning, it was a hugely unequal battle. A veteran with debilitating health problems often was too ill and too short of money to contend with the powerful bureaucracies that controlled almost all the relevant information about possible toxic exposures in the Gulf War, much of it in classified documents. The men and women in our Armed Forces had been trained to fight wars, not political and legal battles.

A party line seems to have been disseminated throughout the VA system. Why else would ill veterans who went to VA hospitals in various areas of the country so frequently see the same language appearing in their medical evaluations, language like "Patient is malingering for secondary gain"? Webster's defines "malinger" as "to pretend incapacity (as illness) so as to avoid duty or work"—a cruel charge to level at soldiers whose sense of duty led them to face great danger and harsh conditions in the Persian Gulf. The term "secondary gain" is not so common that one would expect it to be rolling off the tongue of VA doctors from Oregon to Texas. According to secondary gain theorists, patients with chronic, ill-defined illnesses are engaging in certain behavior patterns in order to get special attention or because they want others to take care of them. Sfc. Sherrie McGahee, who served as an intelligence analyst in the Gulf War, faced this attitude from Army psychologists to whom she was referred when she sought help for her increasing health problems. Her 1994 report stated:

> Patients with this type of response style tend to overreport their symptoms in an attempt to elicit assistance. . . .
> Some consideration of the secondary gains that this individual may derive from an increasing role as a patient (whether psychiatric or orthopedic) is encouraged. There is some possibility that the longer she is allowed to be dysfunctional on the job, the more ingrained a "patient" identity will become.
>
> (GWS video footage)

When we filmed Sergeant McGahee in June 2000 for our video *Gulf War Syndrome: Aftermath of a Toxic Battlefield*, the damage that her service during the war had wreaked upon her body could hardly be doubted by even the most obdurate of psychologists. To listen to Sergeant McGahee speak and to watch her as she slowly and with great effort struggles to find words is to see brain damage made visible. There is no secondary gain here, only a devastating loss of mental and physical function. To move any distance now, she must use a wheelchair. She walks with great difficulty, her balance obviously precarious. Lurching from side to side, she leans on a cane as she tries to steady herself by placing her other hand against the wall. Sergeant McGahee finally won an action against her Army psychologists for misdiagnosis and obtained 100 percent disability, but it was a long battle. This single mother struggles to support herself and the three of her five children who are still living with her.

When I showed our video to the September 2000 convention of the National Gulf War Resource Center, the section containing quotations from Sergeant McGahee's psychological report superimposed upon footage of her struggling to walk struck an obvious chord with the veterans in the audience. Almost all of them had met with the same skeptical attitudes when they had sought help. One veteran who encountered similar skepticism is Sgt. James Green, who had been scheduled to go to the Gulf War but ended up in Germany on an antiterrorist mission at the time his Air Force unit was deploying. In anticipation of his imminent departure for the Middle East, he had been given an anthrax vaccination and had started taking PB pills (an anti–nerve agent medication discussed in Chapter 5). He began to feel ill almost immediately, and since that time his health has steadily deteriorated. His many symptoms include terrible headaches, severe diarrhea, chronic lung obstruction, muscle and joint pain, extreme fatigue, and serious memory problems. Sergeant Green's situation illustrates the danger of simply concluding that the symptoms of Gulf veterans have a psychological origin or are related to stress. In his story in Part II, he reports the problems he encountered when he sought assistance from the VA: "I repeatedly went to see the VA doctors about a lump in my throat. For over a year, I complained to them about this lump, but they ignored it, trying to say I was just having psychological problems. Finally when the lump grew, I was diagnosed with thyroid cancer and I had to have half of my thyroid removed" (Part II, 223).

When I called Sergeant Green during the summer of 2000 to see if he could send me a picture for possible inclusion in our video, he had recently undergone surgery to have the rest of his thyroid removed. His other health problems continue unabated. When I asked if he would look sick in a photo, he summarized his current health status in two words: "I'm dead."

In a 1999 Gulf War syndrome special produced by Eddie Rollins of Alabama PBS, the wife of an ill Gulf War veteran describes the attitudes that she and her husband encountered: "They told me that I was an enabler because I was allowing and supporting and encouraging him to be sick and that if I was just a stronger wife I would go in there and convince him that he was better, and he would be better."

Col. Herbert Smith, the highest-ranking Army officer who has acknowledged having Gulf War syndrome, also ran into the same maddening attitudes when he sought help from Army physicians. While he was still in the Persian Gulf, he had begun having serious health problems. His legs were so swollen that he could not lace up his boots, and eventually he could not even put them on. His lymph nodes were swollen, and he had terrible pains in his joints.

Colonel Smith reports: "I was sent to Walter Reed Army Medical Center, and I maintained my relationship with Walter Reed until I got to the point where . . . not only did [a doctor] tell me that I had somatoform disorder and that everything was in my head, but he also accused me of bleeding myself so that I would fake my anemia" (GWS video footage).

Colonel Smith's daughter has told me that at first she too did not believe her father was really sick. Her attitude was shared by far too many family members of Gulf War veterans who began suffering from a wide variety of troubling symptoms during and shortly after the war. This disbelief from family members and friends was an added burden for these men and women who were already trying to deal with the loss of their health. But it is hardly surprising that many family members reacted in this way when the DOD and the VA were releasing a steady stream of statements questioning whether there were any real health problems associated with service in Desert Storm.

As the years have passed, however, and the physical deterioration of many veterans has become all too apparent, the standard phrases used by VA doctors have changed. No longer is there so much talk of "malingering" and "secondary gain." The new buzz phrase is "somatoform disorder."[2] Colonel Smith ran into this diagnosis early on at Walter Reed, and by now word seems to have spread throughout the VA system that if you don't understand these baffling illnesses, try calling them a somatoform disorder, or a functional somatic syndrome. Applying these terms to ill veterans amounts to saying

---

[2] Drs. Arthur J. Barsky and Jonathan F. Borus, psychiatrists at Brigham and Women's Hospital in Boston, are the authors of an article titled "Functional Somatic Syndromes" that appeared in *Annals of Internal Medicine* on June 1, 1999. Barsky and Borus state: "The term functional somatic syndrome refers to several related syndromes that are characterized more by symptoms, suffering, and disability than by disease-specific, demonstrable abnormalities of structure or function." The authors note that physicians are "increasingly confronted by patients who have disabling, medically unexplained, somatic symptoms. . . . These patients often have a strong sense of assertiveness and embattled advocacy . . . and they may devalue and dismiss medical authority and epidemiologic evidence that conflicts with their beliefs." Barsky and Borus's statement offers an excellent example of how people with chronic illnesses such as Gulf War syndrome, multiple chemical sensitivity, chronic fatigue syndrome, fibromyalgia, and sick building syndrome are viewed by physicians who do not like to have their authority questioned. (These conditions, which may well all be variants of the same underlying condition, are listed in the beginning of the Barsky and Borus article as examples of functional somatic syndromes.) It is worth noting that Brigham and Women's Hospital was featured in a NOVA special on sick building syndrome that discussed how many nurses and other staff members of the hospital had developed chronic debilitating conditions like multiple chemical sensitivity. The hospital will have a substantial liability problem if multiple chemical sensitivity is recognized as a valid medical condition that can be precipitated by exposure to toxic chemicals.

that yes, they are sick, but the illness arises from their own psychological attitudes. This view of Gulf War syndrome blames the victim and ties nicely back to the stress theory, which has always been at the core of DOD and VA beliefs about what is wrong with suffering Gulf War veterans. Like the term "secondary gain," the term "somatoform" is unusual enough that it is hard to believe that VA physicians all around the country spontaneously came up with this term on their own.

There is one notable case of a VA physician who refused to follow the party line—Dr. Victor Gordan of the VA hospital in Manchester, New Hampshire. And perhaps there is a reason why Dr. Gordan has taken such an independent course. He refused to accept the party line in his native Romania and instead fled to the United States in 1976. That was fortunate for the more than 700 Gulf War veterans who have traveled from all over the country to consult with him. While Dr. Gordan cannot eliminate their health problems—he has stated that it is very difficult to treat Gulf War syndrome—he has offered these ailing veterans his conviction that they are indeed sick as the result of their service in the Persian Gulf. Dr. Gordan has testified to committees of Congress on four occasions and was one of the first experts to suggest that toxic exposures were responsible for Gulf War syndrome.

From time to time, government officials have considered the possibility that chemical sensitivity plays a role in Gulf War syndrome, but such consideration has tended to be cursory. In 1995, Maj. Gen. Ronald R. Blanck, then surgeon general of the U.S. Army, stated that "researchers should take a closer look at multiple chemical sensitivity as a possible cause of some of the symptoms [of Gulf War syndrome]."[3] In a report to Congress in January 1998, the Acting Assistant Secretary of the Department of Health and Human Resources, John Eisenberg, M.D., stated: "One of the first activities to be undertaken in fiscal year 1998 is to convene a consensus-building conference. This conference will strive to fully characterize the nature of multiple chemical exposures within the Gulf War veterans population and to relate this characterization to what is known about multiple chemical sensitivity and related conditions and disorders within civilian populations." The RAND report on PB pills that was commissioned by the DOD (see Chapter 5) discusses the relationship of MCS to Gulf War syndrome; the first section of chapter 11 is titled, "Can PB Lead to MCS?"

In Chapter 13, I will discuss how the umbrella view offered by MCS could enhance our understanding of Gulf War syndrome. This is more than a question of nomenclature because the condition of MCS has been around for decades. There is a significant body of information and experience that has

---

[3] *Maine Sunday Telegram,* July 9, 1995, A7.

been accumulated by those unfortunate enough to have developed this condition and by the physicians who have attempted to help them—not always effectively, because this is such a difficult condition to treat, but almost always with a genuine concern for these patients too often scorned or dismissed by the medical establishment. From my experience with multiple chemical sensitivity and Gulf War syndrome, I have the impression that while many MCS patients can remain relatively symptom free so long as they avoid toxic exposures, far too many veterans with Gulf War syndrome feel terrible every day and are continually coping with a significant level of pain. Several veterans I interviewed are taking over 25 pills a day, despite the fact that chemically sensitive people usually have trouble tolerating medications, which are, after all, chemicals. Claudia Miller, M.D., who has served for many years as a consultant to the Houston VA's regional referral center, has noted that among the veterans she has interviewed, "nearly 40 percent reported adverse reactions to medications."[4] It is possible that if physicians were to focus not only on medicating these veterans but also on teaching them how to reduce their day-to-day exposures to toxic chemicals, they might see more improvement in their health.

In the following chapters, I will discuss the various toxic exposures our soldiers encountered in the Persian Gulf. U.S. decision makers faced no easy choices in this war, and there may have been no way to avoid most of these toxic exposures. But it is now important for government officials to assume responsibility for the damage done to the bodies of over 100,000 suffering veterans. The DOD and VA must go beyond the present policy stated by spokesperson Col. Dian Lahon:

> Many of the veterans that we've met and talked to have chronic health problems that prevent them from working and providing for themselves and their families. Unfortunately, if they cannot prove to the Department of Veterans Affairs that this health, chronic health problem, is directly tied to this military service, there is no health care or benefits program that is available to them from the Department of Veterans Affairs.
>
> (GWS video footage)

"Service connection" is the operative phrase. If veterans cannot prove that their health problems arose from service in the Gulf, then they must not only cope with constant pain and suffering and large medical bills, but they must

---

[4] Claudia Miller, prepared testimony submitted to the Committee on Government Reform, Subcommittee on National Security, Veterans Affairs, and International Affairs, U.S. House of Representatives, February 2, 2000, p.2.

also live with the ever-present worry about how they can provide for themselves and their families. Too many veterans are in the position of Sergeant Green, who agonizes at the age of 34 about what the future will bring for his wife and children: "I wonder now if I will live many more years, and my main concern is worrying about my family. If I die from Gulf War syndrome and the VA hasn't recognized the condition as being service connected, then my family will get only a one-time death benefit of $800" (Part II, 224).

A major event in the effort to understand Gulf War syndrome and link it to service in the Gulf War occurred in November 2000, when Lea Steele, Ph.D., published in the *American Journal of Epidemiology* a comprehensive study on the prevalence and patterns of Gulf War illness. Dr. Steele is the director of the Kansas Persian Gulf War Veterans Health Initiative, one of a handful of state programs in the country established to focus upon Gulf War–related illnesses. In 1998, Dr. Steele directed a study comparing the health problems of 1,548 Gulf veterans (PGW) with those of 482 veterans of the same era who did not serve in the Gulf War (non-PGW). For the purposes of this study, Gulf War illness was defined to be having chronic symptoms in three of six areas: (1) fatigue/sleep, (2) pain, (3) neurologic/cognitive/mood, (4) gastrointestinal, (5) respiratory, and (6) skin. Using this definition, Gulf War illness occurred in 34% of PGW veterans and 8% of non-PGW veterans surveyed in the Kansas study.[5]

The prevalence statistics from the Kansas study thus indicate that far more than 100,000 Gulf veterans are suffering from Gulf War syndrome. (The conservative figure of 100,000, which is often cited, is obtained by adding together the numbers of soldiers who have registered with either the DOD or the VA registries for Gulf War illnesses.) The prevalence rate of 34% found in the Kansas study suggests that the problem is far greater and that over 200,000 of the 697,000 veterans who served in Desert Storm may now be ill.

Dr. Steele compared her results with those obtained in two other studies: the CDC study of four Air National Guard Units in Pennsylvania and the British Unwin study. In the CDC study, 45 percent of PGW veterans and 15 percent of non-PGW veterans met the CDC definition of chronic multisymptom illness.[6] In the British Unwin study, which used different

---

[5] Lea Steele, "Prevalence and Patterns of Gulf War Illness in Kansas Veterans: Association of Symptoms with Characteristics of Person, Place, and Time of Military Service," *American Journal of Epidemiology* 152, no. 10 (2000): 993.

[6] "We defined a case as having 1 or more chronic symptoms . . . from at least 2 of the following categories: fatigue; mood and cognition (symptoms of feeling depressed, difficulty remembering or concentrating, feeling moody, feeling anxious, trouble

criteria to determine a case, 62 percent of PGW veterans and 36 percent of non-PGW veterans met the criteria for Gulf War illness.[7] Dr. Steele points out that when one considers what she terms "the excess burden of illness associated with deployment to the Gulf War," which is the difference in each study between the rates of illness for PGW veterans and non-PGW veterans, then the excess burden of illness is consistent across the studies: 30 percent in the CDC study, 26 percent in the Unwin study, 27 percent in the Kansas veterans using the CDC criteria, and 26 percent in the Kansas veterans using the more restrictive Kansas definition for Gulf War illness. (When the Kansas veterans are evaluated using the CDC definition, 47 percent of the PGW veterans and 20 percent of the non-PGW veterans have Gulf War illness.)[8]

The Kansas study also presents statistics for the prevalence in both groups of various chronic symptoms that started after the end of the Gulf War. Fatigue was a problem in 36 percent of the PGW veterans but only 12 percent of the non-PGW veterans. In the PGW veterans, 17 percent reported that they felt unwell after exercise or exertion, compared to only 4 percent of the non-PGW veterans. Diarrhea was a problem in 19 percent of the PGW veterans compared to 6 percent of the non-PGW veterans. Difficulty breathing was reported in 18 percent of the PGW veterans but only 4 percent of the non-PGW veterans. Nausea was a problem for 17 percent of the PGW veterans compared to 4 percent of the non-PGW veterans. Short-term memory problems were reported by 32 percent of the PGW veterans but only 8 percent of the non-PGW veterans. Many other symptoms were surveyed, and in general PGW veterans suffer from these various symptoms at two, three, or four times the rate of non-PGW veterans.

One of the most interesting aspects of Dr. Steele's study is her finding that the rate of Gulf War illness among the Kansas veterans differed depending upon where they served in the Persian Gulf theater. The rate of illness was 21 percent among those serving on a ship, 31 percent among those serving in Saudi Arabia or Bahrain who did not enter Iraq or Kuwait, and 42 percent among those veterans who did enter Iraq or Kuwait.

---

finding words, or difficulty sleeping); and musculoskeletal (symptoms of joint pain, joint stiffness, or muscle pain)." Keiji Fukuda et al., "Chronic Multisymptom Illness Affecting Air Force Veterans of the Gulf War," *Journal of the American Medical Association* 280, no. 11 (September 16, 1998): 983.

[7] C. Unwin et al., "Health of UK Servicemen Who Served in the Persian Gulf War," *Lancet* 353(1999):169-78.

[8] Steele,"Prevalence," 997.

Of particular interest is Dr. Steele's finding that among those veterans who were present during the air and ground wars (January 17-February 28), the time of departure from the Persian Gulf was a relevant variable. Veterans who left in March 1991 had a Gulf War illness rate of 25 percent, those leaving in April or May had a 36 percent rate, and those leaving in June or July had an illness rate of 43 percent.[9]

It is important to note that the ground war ended on February 28, and things were relatively quiet thereafter. If stress were a key factor in Gulf War syndrome, one would not expect to see a far higher rate of illness among those veterans who stayed until June or July than in those who left in March. The increase in the rate of illness with a later departure from the Persian Gulf would also seem to suggest that the anthrax vaccine is not the sole culprit. The vaccine was in very short supply, so only 150,000 soldiers could be vaccinated, and virtually all of them would have received the vaccine before the end of the war. The higher rate of Gulf War illnesses for those departing later would seem instead to point to the influence of toxic chemicals from the oil well fires and heavy pesticide use. (Veterans report that even during the winter months, flies and other insects were a major problem in the desert.) It is also of interest to consider how PB pills might fit into this picture. Virtually everyone who took the PB pills did so in January or February, so that variable did not change with varying departure dates. But if the PB pills caused the soldiers to develop chemical sensitivity, as the RAND report on PB suggests may have been the case, then the longer they were exposed to the oil well fires and pesticides, the more their health would have deteriorated.

---

[9] Ibid., Table 6, p. 99.

Chapter 1

Exposure to Nerve Agents

One of the greatest dangers facing the Coalition forces in the Gulf War was the large stocks of nerve agents that Saddam Hussein had accumulated. During the war between Iran and Iraq, the world had seen that he did not hesitate to use these horrific weapons on the battlefield. Many Iranian soldiers died or suffered terrible physical injury as the result of the chemical attacks that Saddam Hussein unleashed upon his adversaries. Even some of his own people, the Kurds, fell victim to nerve agent attacks, and television cameras flashed around the world pictures of the bodies of Kurds who had died in agony, coughing blood. According to Amnesty International, "Some 5,000 Kurds were killed within an hour" during one attack in 1988 (Riegle, 54).

As Coalition forces were assembling in Saudi Arabia in late 1990 in response to Iraq's August 2 invasion of Kuwait, the problem of defending troops against chemical and biological attacks was uppermost in the minds of Coalition commanders. Among the first targets hit during the air war were 28 chemical weapons factories where deadly nerve agents like sarin, tabun, and VX were being produced.[1] One of the main areas attacked by Coalition bombers was a huge complex in the desert 65 miles northwest of Baghdad in an area called Muthanna. The Riegle report notes that according to UN inspectors, Muthanna had the capability of producing two tons of sarin and five tons of mustard gas a day, as well as VX, one of the most lethal nerve chemicals ever developed (Riegle, 22). The UN inspectors found at Muthanna the following chemical warfare agents:

- 13,000 155-mm artillery shells loaded with mustard gas;
- 6,200 rockets loaded with nerve agent;
- 800 nerve agent aerial bombs;
- 28 SCUD warheads loaded with sarin;
- 75 tons of the nerve agent sarin;
- 60-70 tons of the nerve agent tabun;
- 250 tons of mustard gas and stocks of thiodiglycol, a precursor chemical for mustard gas.

                                                    (Riegle, 22)

---

[1] Jim Tuite, GWS video footage.

The vast extent of Iraq's chemical warfare program becomes apparent when one realizes that despite hundreds of Coalition bombing raids at Muthanna and other sites, the weapons listed above still remained at Muthanna or had been moved there after the war. According to the Riegle report, "Coalition bombing against these facilities involved hundreds—if not thousands—of tons of bulk chemical nerve agents, mustard gas" (Riegle, 24). Even small amounts of these deadly gases can kill large numbers of exposed troops. When terrorists attacked commuters on the Tokyo subway with sarin nerve gas, 11 people died and 5,550 others were injured. The U.S. Army Chemical Research, Development and Engineering Center at the Aberdeen Proving Grounds in Maryland has stated in a material safety data sheet (MSDS) for the nerve agents sarin and soman:

The inhibition of cholinesterase enzymes throughout the body by nerve agents is more or less irreversible so that their effects are prolonged. Until the tissue cholinesterase enzymes are restored to normal activity, probably by very slow regeneration over a period of weeks or 2 to 3 months if damage is severe, there is a period of increased susceptibility to the effects of another exposure to any nerve agent. During this period the effects of repeated exposures are cumulative; after a single exposure, daily exposure to concentrations of nerve agent insufficient to produce symptoms may result in the onset of symptoms after several days. Continued daily exposure may be followed by increasingly severe effects. After symptoms subside, increased susceptibility persists for one to several days. *The degree of exposure required to produce recurrence of symptoms, and the severity of these symptoms depend on duration of exposure and time required to produce recurrence of symptoms, and the severity of these symptoms depend on the duration of exposure and the time intervals between exposures. Increased susceptibility is not specific to the particular nerve agent initially absorbed* [original italics].
(Riegle, 26)

The Riegle report also provides a long list of symptoms that could result from exposure to a nerve agent:

Tightness in chest, wheezing, anorexia, nausea, vomiting, abdominal cramps, epigastric and substernal tightness, heartburn, diarrhea, involuntary defecation, increased sweating, increased salivation, increased tearing, slight bradycardia [slow heartbeat], myosis [pinpoint pupils], blurring vision, urinary urgency and frequency, fatigue, mild weakness, muscular twitching, cramps, generalized weakness, including muscles of respiration, with dyspnea and cyanosis, pallor and occasional elevation of blood pressure; giddiness, tension, anxiety,

jitteriness, restlessness, emotional lability, excessive dreaming, insomnia, nightmares, headaches, tremors, withdrawal and depression; ... drowsiness, difficulty concentrating, slowness on recall, confusion, slurred speech, ataxia [uncoordinated muscular movements], coma (with absence of reflexes) . . . convulsions, depression of the respiratory and circulatory centers . . . fall in blood pressure.
(Riegle, 26-27)

The MSDS for sulfur mustard gas (HD) provided by the U.S. Army Chemical Research, Development and Engineering Center states: "Chronic exposure to HD can cause skin sensitization, chronic lung impairment, cough, shortness of breath, chest pain, and cancer of the mouth, throat, respiratory tract, skin, and leukemia. It may also cause birth defects" (Riegle, 31).

Since the end of Desert Storm, there has been an ongoing debate about whether Iraq actually used any chemical weapons during the war. A *Washington Post* article appearing on March 7, 1991, stated that U.S. intelligence sources said that these weapons had never been moved from storage depots north of the Euphrates River down to the battlefield areas. The Riegle report quotes a U.S. military intelligence source as saying in March 1991: "It was a matter of not deploying chemical weapons, rather than not having them. . . . My guess . . . is they never managed to get it down to division level" (Riegle, 18). Information received by the committee suggests otherwise, however:

Dale Glover, of the 1165th Military Police Company, was with the 7th Corps, approximately 75 miles inside Iraq, when they came upon a destroyed artillery site. They entered a bunker that was half uncovered by the bombing. Inside there was a very strong ammonia smell. They discovered leaking chemical munitions inserts packed inside aluminum casings. A test confirmed a blister agent. They went back to their unit and reported what they had found. Mr. Glover recalled that "they didn't get back to us for 2-3 hours, then told us it was a false positive, nothing to be concerned about." However, he said, within hours they were ordered to move from the location where they were camped, about three miles from the bunker. Mr. Glover recalled that they had been at that position only a couple of weeks and had not expected to move that soon. When questioned if the site they discovered was south of the Euphrates, he confirmed that it was.
(Riegle, 18)

A similar story involves another soldier serving in the 7th Corps in southern Iraq:

Somewhere between As Salman and Bashra (in a position south of the Euphrates River), his unit came upon bunkers containing crates of substances that "made you choke, made you want to throw up, burned

your eyes. It smelled like ammonia, only a lot stronger." He could not approach the crates without experiencing immediate breathing problems. He said these crates were leaking.
(Riegle, 19)

The London *Sunday Times* reported on January 27, 1991, ten days into the air war, that "an unnamed Pentagon source had said that Hussein had given frontline commanders permission to use these chemical weapons at their discretion, and that 'it was no longer a question of if, but when'" (Riegle, 20). Iraqi commanders would have had to use these weapons carefully, however, because in the case of any short-range use, weapons carrying nerve agents or mustard gas would have to be fired only when the wind would blow the resulting toxic vapors away from Iraq's own troops. According to the Riegle report, "Soviet doctrine questions the utility of initiating chemical warfare, since chemical weapons produce secondary effects that could obstruct troop advances. *U.S. military doctrine warns that . . . the use of a nerve agent against a target area of no more than a dozen hectares (a hectare is about 2.47 acres) can, under certain weather conditions, create a hazard zone downwind of up to 100 kilometers in length. Within this downwind area, friendly military units would have to take protective measures*" (Riegle, 24; original italics).

The dilemma that Coalition forces faced was clear. They could leave the chemical weapons factories and storage sites intact and hope that a U.S. ultimatum warning Saddam Hussein of massive retaliation (read: nuclear) if he used nerve agents would deter him from using these dreaded weapons. Alternatively, they could bomb these factories and destroy the stocks of nerve agents. But what would happen when the nerve agents were blown up? Would they become aerosolized and eventually drift over Coalition forces that were massing to the south?

U.S.A. Today reported in a front-page story on August 14, 1997: "The Lawrence Livermore National Laboratory had in a 1990 study informed the U.S. Air Force—three months before the Gulf War began—that bombing of Iraqi chemical weapons manufacturing facilities would release deadly nerve agents over U.S. troops who were massing several hundred miles to the south. This report predicted a dispersion of chemical warfare agents over an area 10 times greater than subsequent DOD and CIA studies would show" (Shays, 23). The choice for Coalition commanders was indeed difficult. They could either risk having our forces on the receiving end of full-strength attacks with nerve agents if they left the chemical factories and depots in place, or they could take the chance that when they bombed the factories the low levels of nerve agents that might drift over the troops would not be strong enough to cause serious injury to large numbers of soldiers. The fears that haunted U.S. commanders can perhaps best be indicated by the fact that our forces took huge numbers of body bags to the Persian Gulf because of the very real possibility of an Iraqi attack with chemical or biological weapons. Few would deny that our commanders made the right decision when they decided the risk of leaving Saddam Hussein's chemical weapons in place was too great to bear.

On January 17 the air war began, and during the next few weeks Coalition bombers flew hundreds of sorties, attacking all the major Iraqi facilities where chemical or biological weapons were known to be manufactured or stored. From this point on, there would be continuing controversy over the extent to which low levels of chemical agents may have drifted over the troops massing to the south in preparation for an eventual ground war.

At the heart of this controversy are the Czech chemical detection teams that monitored for nerve agents and mustard gas during the war. An extensive report on their activities appeared in the *New York Times* on October 19, 1996. These teams, which consisted of 269 soldiers, included 58 specialists who had a minimum of four years of training in the field. Because the Czech army was renowned for the excellence of its chemical weapon detection capabilities, Saudi Arabia contracted with the Czechs to provide this detection service for the Saudi forces during the Gulf War.

On January 19, 1991, two days after the air war had begun and the Coalition had started bombing Iraq's chemical weapons facilities, Czech units detected mustard gas and sarin in an area close to the Kuwaiti border. That same day French chemical units also detected low levels of nerve agent in the same general region, about 19 miles from King Khalid Military City, the huge base in northern Saudi Arabia used as a staging area. It was not until August 1996 that the Defense Department at last announced that five years earlier both the French and the Czech chemical troops had detected nerve agents (*NYT*, 10).

Reporters for the *New York Times* conducted interviews in Prague to learn more about the activities of the Czech teams. The Czechs related that when they detected sarin and mustard gas on January 19 they immediately concluded that these substances had been released by the Coalition bombing of Iraqi chemical sites that had begun just two days earlier. They recalled that Czech troops had donned their protective suits in response to the detections, but to their surprise American troops nearby did not put on their MOPP-4 suits. (U.S. soldiers were issued various levels of protective clothing—MOPP-4, "mission oriented protective posture four," was the highest level of protection and included not only a full-body suit but a hooded mask and gloves.) According to the *Times*, the combat logs kept by senior American officers under General Schwarzkopf show that the Czech warning was indeed passed to the Americans, who chose to ignore it.

A Gulf War veteran who spoke on a confidential basis to the staff of Senator Riegle's committee reported that on one occasion between January 20 and February 1, "he was located about 40 miles east of King Khalid Military City (KKMC), when at one position, every M-8 alarm [a chemical agent detection alarm] went off—over 30 at once.... The NBC [nuclear/biological/chemical] NCO radioed in that a nerve agent plant had been bombed about

150 miles away. The source recalled that they were told to take no action and they did not" (Riegle, 97-98).

Brian Martin, who served in the 37th Airborne Combat Engineer Battalion, was stationed only six miles from the Iraqi border in late January. He noted in his journal during this period that what were called "false alarms" were going off very frequently. The troops were first told that the alarms were caused by vapors arising from the sand. Eventually when this explanation failed to satisfy anyone, "Martin said he was informed by both his battalion commander and the battalion NBC NCO that the alarms were sounding because of 'minute' quantities of nerve agent in the air, released by the Coalition bombing of Iraqi chemical weapons facilities. The troops were assured that there was no danger" (Riegle, 96-97).

Troy Albuck, an anti-tank platoon leader, reported to the staff of the Riegle committee that "his unit was told that the chemical alarms were going off because of what was drifting down from the Coalition bombings" (Riegle, 97).

Although the Czech troops did don their protective suits whenever they detected nerve agent or mustard gas in the air, this precaution apparently did not suffice to protect them from the ill effects of these extremely poisonous substances. The former Czech defense minister, Antonin Baudys, stated to a *New York Times* interviewer that Czech officials had notified American officials that dozens of Czech veterans were reporting mysterious illnesses that had plagued them since their return from the war. According to the *Times* article, however, "As recently as last August [1996], the Defense Department reported to Gulf War veterans that Czech soldiers were not complaining of unusual health problems—evidence, Pentagon officials suggested, that chemical exposures were not responsible for the health problems of American soldiers." Interviews conducted by the *Times,* however, presented a far different story. Vaclac Hlavac, a former warrant officer, reported that he had been experiencing respiratory problems since the war and had lost almost all of his upper teeth within two years of his return from the Persian Gulf although he had had no serious dental problems prior to the war. Jan Huzan, another Gulf War veteran who served with the Czech troops, reportedly also lost almost all his teeth after he returned. (Mr. Huzan died in 1995 of cancer of the digestive tract and had told friends that he thought this cancer was the result of chemical exposures during the war.)

Large numbers of American veterans have also reported unusual dental problems since the war. Among the many cases from soldiers whose stories appear in Part II are Pat Browning, a truck driver in the war who had to have dentures after she returned, even though she was only 32, and Bob Jones, who has had nine root canals since the war.[2] Col. Herbert Smith didn't realize until he watched our video on Gulf War syndrome that the extensive dental

---

[2] Bob Jones, personal communication to author, June 2000.

problems he had experienced since the war were part of that condition. Dr. Victor Gordan, a VA physician in Manchester, New Hampshire, who has treated over 700 Gulf War veterans from all over the country, has seen large numbers of these veterans with what he describes as "brittle teeth" (GWS video footage).

The Czech Defense Ministry set up a health monitoring program for the chemical detection troops after the war when reports of illness began to surface. According to the *New York Times* article, "An estimated 30 to 40 Czech troops—or about 11 to 15 percent of the soldiers who had served in the Gulf—had sought medical help for symptoms they attributed to the Gulf War, including chronic fatigue, digestive ailments, rashes and joint pains," symptoms very similar to those affecting ill American Gulf veterans. Unfortunately, the Czech government closed down this monitoring program in 1994, so there is no way of knowing how many more Czech veterans may now be ill or the current condition of those who previously reported health problems.

Czech soldiers who turned to their military for help with their deteriorating health encountered attitudes frustratingly similar to those faced by American veterans. Dr. Frantisek Sedlak, a physician at the Czech Central Military Hospital who examined many of the ill Czech veterans, has stated, "In my opinion, these problems are 80 percent psychological." The treatment he suggested to these veterans was psychotherapy and tranquilizers. In a statement that is indeed ironic, he said that his proposed treatment must have worked because none of the veterans returned to him. Using words that sound as if they might have been scripted by the Pentagon, Dr. Sedlak asserted, "These chemicals either kill you or they leave you alone, without any consequences" (*NYT*, 10).

But as the *New York Times* noted, only three months before its article on the Czech detection teams was published, the Pentagon had announced: "According to the Czech Defense Ministry, 'no members of the former Czechoslovak contingent showed symptoms during or after the detections were made in Saudi Arabia. . . . No evidence of physical effects from exposure to harsh climatic conditions or chemical agents was found among any of the soldiers.'"

The DOD's initial denial of health problems among the Czech chemical teams was just part of its general pattern of minimizing the possibility that toxic exposures in the Gulf War had led to long-term illness for Gulf veterans. This attempted DOD coverup was circumvented, however, by Jim Tuite, the principal investigator on the Senate Banking Committee chaired by Senator Donald Riegle, Jr., which held hearings on Gulf War syndrome in the early 1990s. In testimony before the House Committee on Government Reform, Subcommittee on Human Resources, which was chaired by Christopher Shays and held extensive hearings on the issue of Gulf War syndrome, Tuite stated:

Up to now, the missing element . . . has been the mystery of how the [chemical] agents were transported from the research, production and storage sites in Iraq to [Coalition] troops. . . . The report I submit today [I believe] solves the mystery of the [chemical] detections that occurred after the initial wave of Coalition bombings of these chemical warfare agent storage facilities during the first two days of the air war. Using available visible and infrared meteorological satellite imagery from NOAA [National Oceanic and Atmospheric Administration], which was available to military planners [but not used] during the war—a war before which they expressed deep concern over the fallout effects from these bombings—I have been able to determine that a thermal plume rose into the atmosphere over the largest Iraqi chemical warfare agent research, production, and storage facility at Muthanna after Coalition aircraft and missile bombardment.

Seventeen metric tons of sarin were reportedly destroyed during these attacks, which began on January 17, 1991. These thermal and visual plumes extended [southerly] directly toward the areas where those same chemical warfare agents were detected and confirmed by Czechoslovak chemical specialists. Hundreds of thousands of U.S. servicemen and women were in the area where these detections occurred, assembling for the upcoming ground invasion of Iraq and the liberation of Kuwait.

(Shays, 24)

Once Jim Tuite realized why the chemical detection alarms had sounded so frequently after the Coalition bombing began, he began to focus his attention on these alarms that the Pentagon insisted were all the result of malfunctioning equipment:

During the congressional investigation into this issue, we found that logs had been kept of chemical detections and chemical activity in the Gulf. We requested these logs, and we were told by the Pentagon in writing that these logs did not exist. Later we found out that in fact these logs did exist. They existed in two secure locations—one in Maryland and one in Florida—and they disappeared from these locations about the time we requested them. These are secure locations intended for security of classified information, and at the time these logs were classified secret. These are secret documents that disappeared from two separate locations simultaneously at the same time that Congress showed an interest in this issue.

(GWS video footage)

Chapter 2

SCUD Missile Attacks

When the air war began, Iraq started firing large numbers of SCUD missiles at Coalition forces. Although one of these missiles hit a barracks and killed several American soldiers, most of the SCUD missiles were either blown up by Patriot anti-missile missiles or exploded in midair before they ever reached their target. The question remains whether some of these missiles were carrying nerve agents. In 1993 the UN inspectors who visited the vast arsenal at Muthanna, a primary target of Coalition bombing, found chemical warheads on SCUD missiles that each held five gallons of sarin. According to the Riegle report, these weapons had been deployed elsewhere during the bombing of Muthanna and were moved back to Muthanna after the war.

Staff investigators for the Riegle committee interviewed many soldiers who believed SCUD missiles had been blown up above their units by Patriot missiles. The Riegle report that summarizes the committee's findings states:

> Not every detail can be verified by multiple sources to date, but additional data from unofficial and unrelated sources continue to bolster initial accounts of events best explained as missile and rocket attacks or aerial explosions. Units located in areas where these events occurred are reporting high rates of illnesses. The areas in which these events occurred were key logistic and staging areas, as well as those areas which were breached during the liberation of Kuwait. Many veterans of these units have reported seeing large numbers of dead or dying animals in the area after the attacks; one veteran noted that "all the insects were dead too."
>
> (Riegle, 58)

One veteran who vividly recalls the dead animals is S.Sgt. Tim Smith, who served in a National Guard unit:

> Once when I was driving an officer at night, taking him to a meeting, we came upon a pile of dead sheep in the middle of the desert, not

knowing what had caused it or how many there were. We didn't stop, we just turned the lights on and saw the sheep piled on both sides of this dirt road. The way that it caught our sight was that we saw the eyes of the desert rats reflected in our headlights, and we said, "What are all these things?" And then when we got close enough, we could see that they were eating the sheep. The night that we saw the dead sheep was the night of the first air offensive, and I was coming back from the medical facility, where I had taken somebody who had fallen, and en route back, we had gotten off the road that we usually took. That's when we came upon the dead sheep, and we didn't know if they were diseased or if there had been a chemical attack.

(GWS video footage)

The Riegle report contains many interesting accounts of SCUD attacks provided by Gulf veterans testifying before the committee. Since the DOD has always denied that there was any Iraqi use of nerve agents during Desert Storm, I have included a large number of these eyewitness accounts. One may doubt what a handful of people say, but when dozens of Gulf veterans all offer consistent accounts, it suggests that something other than a sonic boom occurred. The next several pages consist entirely of material quoted directly from the Riegle report (59-84):

Event 1:

January 17, 1991, early morning hours, Cement City

Staff Sergeant [Willie] Hicks . . . has testified . . . that, at about 2:30 a.m. on January 17, 1991, he heard a loud explosion, which was followed by a sounding of alarms. As Hicks was running to the bunker, his face began to burn. One member of the unit "just dropped." About ten minutes later, according to Hicks, the unit's first sergeant came by and told members of the unit to go to the highest level of alert. The unit remained at that level for 24 hours.

Two or three days later, Hicks began feeling ill and noticed blood in his urine. Several other members of the unit began experiencing "problems" with their rectums. Hicks testified that when members of the unit began to question what had happened, they were ordered by their commanding officer not to discuss it. Of the unit's 100 soldiers, 85 now suffer from medical problems, and one, Staff Sergeant Bayle, who Hicks described as having been in good physical shape, has inexplicably died. Hicks described another member of the unit, Staff Sergeant Heal, as being seriously incapacitated.

Hicks, a former teacher and Vietnam veteran, carries a notebook with him everywhere. He claims to have a severe problem with memory loss. He quit his job because he kept passing out and getting lost on the way to work. Other symptoms being suffered by Mr. Hicks include headaches, blood in his urine, insomnia, joint and muscle pain, deteriorating vision, loss of mobility in his left arm, night sweats, and diarrhea (sometimes bloody). His illness has been classified by the Veterans Administration as post traumatic stress disorder.

Event 2:

January 19, 1991, early morning hours, Camp 13, 6-7 miles west of Port of Jubayl, Kingdom of Saudi Arabia. (Although some individuals reported this event as taking place on January 20, documentary evidence indicates that it took place on the 19th.)

Witness 1: Petty Officer Sterling Symms, then assigned to the Naval Reserve Construction Battalion 24, in an area south of the Kuwait border, testified before the Senate Armed Services Committee that between 2:00 a.m. and 3:00 a.m. on January 20, 1991, there was a "real bad explosion" overhead. The alarms went off and everybody started running towards their bunkers. Petty Officer Symms said there was a sharp odor of ammonia in the air. His eyes burned and his skin stung. His unit donned full chemical gear for nearly two hours until the "all clear" was given.

Later, according to Symms, members of the unit were advised that what they heard was a sonic boom. Petty Officer Symms said that he did not believe that it was a sonic boom because there was also a "fireball" associated with the explosion. Members of the unit were ordered not to discuss the incident. Petty Officer Symms says he has since experienced fatigue, sore joints, running nose, a chronic severe rash, and open sores which have been diagnosed as an "itching problem."

Witness 2: Mike Moore, assigned to the same unit as Symms, also reported that on January 20, 1991, at about 3 a.m., he was awakened by a double explosion. As the sound of the explosion faded, the alarms went off. The unit intercom announced "Go to MOPP level 4." Everyone in the tent put on their gas gear and went to the bunker. They stayed at MOPP level 4 until about 7 a.m. Later that day or the next, everyone's chemical suits and masks were collected and replaced. According to Mr. Moore, he was told the explosion was a sonic boom, to quit worrying about it, and to get back to work. Mr. Moore said that he later heard that what he heard was an incoming SCUD, but he also heard rumors that an Iraqi MIG was shot down in the area that night. . . .

Since returning home from the Gulf, he has suffered a severe thyroid problem, a heart attack, memory loss, tired and aching joints, rashes on his feet, nervousness, and muscle cramps.

Witness 3: Mr. William Larry Kay was an electrician assigned to Naval Mobile Construction Battalion 24. He was also assigned to Camp 13. On January 20, 1991, Mr. Kay heard two "booms," shaking the whole building. Sirens began going off. The camp intercom announced "confirmed mustard gas—go to MOPP level 4." . . . He went outside and put his gas mask on. It immediately filled with fumes. He recalls that it smelled like ammonia. . . . Mr. Kay was assigned to a decontamination team. There were other people assigned to test for chemical contamination. A radio call came in for these people to check for gas. Then, almost immediately, the intercom announced "all clear."

Mr. Kay said that after the incident, in response to questions from the unit as to what had occurred, the unit Commanding Officer said, "Have you ever heard of a sonic boom?" When members of the unit continued to question the unit commanders about what had occurred, they were ordered not to discuss the incident.

Witness 4: Mr. Terry Avery of Salem, Alabama worked on utilities for Naval Mobile Construction Battalion 24, and was also assigned to Camp 13. During the night of January 20, 1991, Mr. Avery said that he heard a double explosion. The alert siren went off. He put on his gas mask and went to the bunker. While in the bunker, his unit received the command to go to MOPP level 4 over the camp loudspeaker. He put on his chemical suit. Mr. Avery said he was almost completely dressed when they announced "all clear." . . .

Mr. Avery was later told by his Master Chief that the noise he heard was just a sonic boom. A veteran of Vietnam who had heard sonic booms before, Mr. Avery felt that it was not a sonic boom, but he never got a good answer about the explosion. He reported that the rumor going around the camp was that an enemy plane had been shot down over the desert.

Late in the summer of 1991, Mr. Avery began feeling tired and having headaches. He saw a private doctor, who said he was probably working too hard in the sun. He says he does not think he is as ill as the rest of the men in his unit (NMCB24). He feels that he has leveled out, but he still has good days and bad days. He currently suffers from fatigue, headaches, weight gain, itching, muscle and joint pains, and memory loss.

Witness 5: The following are excerpts from one of two letters written by a U.S. serviceman present at Camp 13 during the January 19, 1991 incident. This individual has been interviewed by U.S. Senate professional staff. These original letters confirm the actual events of that morning. This individual has requested confidentiality. The original letters have been retained as evidence.

8:00 pm
19 Jan 91

Dear Mom,

I just talked to you on the phone. I really didn't want to call you and tell you about the SCUD missile/gas attack so you wouldn't worry, but I really needed to hear a familiar voice. . . . I'm trying like hell to keep my mind off the fact that it's night time again, and we could get hit again.

Mom, I can deal with getting shot at, because I can fight back and even if I got hit, I can be put back together, a missile, on the other hand, doesn't work like that, but I can even accept that. But gas scares the hell out of me. I know how to put on the protective suits and gear, but it's the thought. Once the missile hit (without warning!) we were so busy getting dressed in our chemical suits we never had time for it to sink in and be scared. I was proud of all of us because no one froze up—we all responded like we'd been trained to, but after we got suited up, we had to sit there and force ourselves to breathe slow and try and cool down—the suits are very hot. It's hard to slow your breathing when your heart's beating a million times a minute. . . . [a] fire team [went] out and . . . patrolled the camp and checked all of the towers. The rest of the camp were in their bunkers except security and the chemical detection teams. I know they detected a cloud of dusty mustard gas because I was there with them, but today everyone denies it. I was there when they radioed the other camps north of us and warned them of the cloud. . . . I talked to the look-outs that saw the air burst and cloud and had to stay with them for a few minutes to try and calm them down even though I was just as scared (probably more!). Jubail is South East of us, and that's where the SCUD hit that was confirmed, but the air burst my guys saw was only 200+ yards west of us. I don't know what that was, but that's where most of the gas came from I think. But the wind was almost blowing due North. I probably won't sleep much tonight, but at least I'll be able to respond faster.

In the interview with Senate staff, this veteran said that during patrols around Camp 13 in the days just after the incident he wrote about, he observed many animals that were either sick or dead. He also confirmed that after the attack, their chemical protective gear was replaced.

Witness 6: Mr. Mike Tidd was assigned to perform security duties with Naval Mobile Construction Battalion 24. He currently suffers from joint aches and pains, sinus infections, diarrhea, urinary urgency and frequency, rashes, small mosquito bite-like sores, heartburn, dizziness, occasional low temperatures, occasional night sweats, and chronic fatigue. Mr. Tidd kept a log while in Saudi Arabia.

According to his log, on January 19, a little past 0330 hrs., Mr. Tidd was sitting on Tower 6 when all of a sudden, there was a double boom off to the northwest of the camp, accompanied by a bright flash of light. Within minutes, the general quarters alarm sounded. Mr. Tidd's unit first donned their gas masks and ponchos, and then minutes later, the call came to go to MOPP level 4. At about 0600 hrs., the "all clear" was sounded.

Event 3:

January 19, 1991, early morning hours (possibly January 20). King Abdul Aziz Naval Air Station (NMCB24-Air Det), 3 miles south of Port of Jubayl, Kingdom of Saudi Arabia

Witness 1: Mr. Larry Perry, of North Carolina, was a naval construction worker stationed near the port city of Al-Jubayl, at King Abdul Aziz Naval Air Station. He says the explosion on January 20, 1991 sent his entire unit running for the bomb shelter. When they emerged in their gas masks, they were enveloped by a mist.

Witness 2: Mr. Fred Willoughby of Columbus, Georgia was with Naval Mobile Construction Battalion 24-Air Det. He currently suffers from headaches, diarrhea, aching joints, blood shot eyes, bloat, intestinal problems, and chronic fatigue. He has had a polyp removed from his colon, and suffered from rectal bleeding in 1992.

Mr. Willoughby has reported that on January 20, 1991, at about 3-4 a.m., he was "hanging out" outside his tent when he heard a long, loud explosion. Shortly thereafter, a siren sounded and he went inside the tent to get his gas mask. By the time he came out, people were yelling "MOPP 4, MOPP 4, not a drill." Immediately, his mouth, lips, and face became numb all over, a sensation he likened to novocaine at the dentist's office. He was in the bunker for about an hour or an hour and a half. When he came out of the bunker, he and the others in the unit were told by the officers and chiefs that what they had heard was just a sonic boom. The next day, the unit was told not to talk about it. But the unit's MOPP gear was collected and replaced the next morning. Mr. Willoughby also heard that an enemy aircraft was shot down in the Gulf, not far from the base.

Witness 3: Roy Morrow of Phoenix City, Alabama was a builder with NMCB24 and was assigned to the Air Detachment at King Abdul Aziz Stadium. On January 20, 1991, he heard two explosions between 3:00-3:30 a.m. He was awakened and went to the bunker. The unit went to MOPP level 2 for 25-30 minutes. The "all clear" was then given. When he exited the bunker, Mr. Morrow noticed the Marines running and screaming "MOPP level 4." The siren sounded again. He began to feel a burning sensation on his arms, legs, the back of his neck, and on his ears and face. His lips felt numb. His unit went to full MOPP level 4. Right before he went to the bunker the second time, Mr. Morrow saw a flash at the commercial port of Al-Jubayl. He had a radio in the bunker, and heard a call for the decontamination teams to respond.

BU2 Edwards was the head of the decontamination team in Mr. Morrow's unit. According to Mr. Morrow, BU2 Edwards said the next day that mustard gas and lewisite had been detected. When they began to discuss it, according to Mr. Morrow, the unit was told that the two explosions were a sonic boom, and they were ordered not to talk about it any more. The next day, all of their chemical gear was collected and replaced with new equipment.

The numbness experienced by Mr. Morrow remained for at least a week. Within two to three days after the incident, unit members began to suffer from rashes, diarrhea, and fatigue. The aching joints began a couple of weeks later. Mr. Morrow's symptoms have been getting progressively worse until the present time. He currently suffers from swollen lymph nodes, fatigue, diarrhea, night sweats, low grade temperature, weight loss, aching joints, muscle cramps, rashes, (transient) blisters, welts (2-3 times a month), a permanent hand rash, and short-term memory loss.

Witness 4: Mr. Harold Jerome Edwards, the chemical NCO in charge of the Nuclear/Biological/Chemical team for the Naval Mobile Construction Battalion 24 Air Detachment at King Abdul Aziz Naval Air Station was interviewed by U.S. Senate staff on January 13, 1994. During that interview Mr. Edwards said that he conducted three M-256 tests for chemical agents on the evening of this event. According to Edwards, two of the three tests he conducted were positive for chemical blister agent. He said that the negative test was conducted in an area in between a number of rows of tents. He also said that he reported this information to his unit commander. In addition, Mr. Edwards said that a member of the unit, Tom Muse, blistered in the area under his watch during this event. The "all clear" was given from a higher command. Mr. Edwards was called out to serve on a chemical decontamination team that day. He said that the Mark 12 decontamination unit assigned to the team was inoperative and that he was assigned to take out a 500 gallon water truck and stand by to decontaminate incoming personnel. According to Mr. Edwards, no one was decontaminated by his team. He said that this was the only time he was called out on this type of mission throughout the entire war.

Event 4:

Late February 1991, "Log Base Charlie," 7 miles from the Iraqi border near Rafha

Witness 1: Ms. Valerie Sweatman from Columbia, South Carolina, was serving as a telecommunications specialist with the U.S. Army, assigned to the 2nd MASH Hospital. . . . One night in late February 1991, she was awakened by a sergeant and was told there was a chemical alert and to go to MOPP level 4. She put on her MOPP suit and mask and began going outside while she was still putting on her gloves. Her unit stayed at MOPP level 4 for 1-2 hours. That night, she heard that there was a SCUD alert that night. She did not, however, hear any explosion. The morning after this incident, Ms. Sweatman's hands were itching from the wrists on down. She had developed little blisters which went away about a week later. She was treated with ointments and Benadryl for a "skin condition."

Ms. Sweatman had heard the chemical alarms go off on other occasions prior to the incident reported above. She was the night telecommunications NCO for her unit, and heard alarms sounding during the first nights of the air war, when her unit was assigned to King Khalid Military City (KKMC). On one occasion during this period, she heard a blast and felt a mist in the same area. After this incident she experienced nausea, diarrhea, and bloody stools. Her unit began taking the nerve agent pre-treatment pills (NAPP) [PB pills] after these earlier alarms. Although the alarms sounded, the NBC NCO claimed that they were sounding because the alarm equipment had bad batteries and not because of chemicals.

Ms. Sweatman currently suffers from headaches, exhaustion, fatigue, memory loss, nausea, muscle and joint pains, rectal and vaginal bleeding, and rashes. She has been diagnosed as having arthritis, headaches, and post traumatic stress disorder (PTSD).

Event 5:

Early February 1991. In the desert between Jafir Al Batin and King Khalid Military City, northern Saudi Arabia

Witness 1: Ms. Michelle Hanlon of Killeen, Texas was assigned to the 1st Calvary Division as a communications specialist. On February 14, 1991, during lunch, she heard an explosion overhead. She thought at the time that it was a SCUD being intercepted by a Patriot missile and thought nothing more of it.

On another occasion, when her unit was assigned to a field base near Hafir Al Batin, she recalled that one night, the night air breeze made her eyes begin to water. She immediately put on her gas mask and thought nothing more of the incident. She also reported that on a number of days, she could actually smell sulfur from the Coalition bombings of Iraqi chemical plants during the air war.

She is currently suffering from intestinal problems, hemorrhoids, occasional fatigue, a rash on her finger (like little water blisters under the skin), cervical infections which coincide with intestinal problems, and some memory loss. She feels that she is becoming progressively more ill. Her rash has been diagnosed as eczema and has been treated with antibiotics. She is 23 years old.

Witness 2: Mr. Richard Voss was with the 207th Military Intelligence Brigade assigned to the 1st Infantry Division. Mr. Voss recalled witnessing what appeared to be a missile attack while stuck in slow-moving traffic heading west toward Hafir Al Batin on Tapline Road in early February 1991. Mr. Voss reports that sometime between noon and 4:00 p.m., he watched the missile, coming in from the north-northeast, impact to the east of Hafir Al Batin, about one mile away from his vehicle. He saw a large dark brown cloud rise up. Within two or three minutes, MPs came by giving the gas alert signal. He recalled that the wind was blowing from the north or northeast at the time of the incident.

Currently, Mr. Voss suffers from headaches, occasional fatigue, joint and muscle pain, memory loss/inability to concentrate, urinary urgency, dizziness, photosensitivity, shortness of breath, rashes, recurring walking pneumonia, chest pains, numbness, and severe joint pains in both wrists and hands.

Witness 3: Ms. Patricia Williams of Nolanville, Texas was assigned to the 1st Calvary Division, near Hafir Al Batin, as a civilian mechanic. One late afternoon in mid-February, she recalled an explosion somewhere in the desert. She described it as a very powerful explosion that she both heard and felt. To her knowledge, no chemical alarms had been set up. Coincidentally, her unit was told that they were going to have a chemical practice; they were told to put on their chemical gear. They were kept at MOPP level 4 for about twenty minutes, but told that this was just a practice. They were also told that the sound they had just heard was a sonic boom. Five civilians were so frightened that they departed that night. . . . Ms. Williams said that she did not get sick in the Persian Gulf until this incident. After this incident, she experienced headaches, diarrhea, and photosensitivity.

Ms. Williams currently suffers from headaches, fatigue, joint and muscle pain, memory loss, lumps on her arms and neck, night sweats, insomnia, urinary urgency, diarrhea, photosensitivity, gastrointestinal problems, deteriorating vision, shortness of breath, coughing, thyroid problems, abnormal hair loss, swollen lymph nodes, sinusitis, and chest pains.

Event 6:

Witness 1: Charlene Harmon Davis was a medical secretary with the 34th Aeromedical Patient Staging Station at KKMC. She reported that, on February 22, she was getting ready for work (her shift began at 7:00 p.m.) when three of what she believed to be SCUD missiles were intercepted over KKMC by Patriot missiles. Ms. Davis recalls that the chemical alarms went off. After these explosions, her face, eyes, and throat began to burn, her nose began to run, and she began to feel nauseous. There was a funny taste in her mouth. These immediate symptoms lasted for about twenty minutes, but she has gotten progressively more ill since that incident. . . .

Ms. Davis currently suffers from migraine headaches, patellar syndrome, seborrheic dermatitis, hip pain, hair loss, insomnia, night sweats, nightmares, numbness in toes, fatigue, joint and muscle pain, gastrointestinal problems, and dizziness. She also suffers recurring rashes which she says began after the first explosion, believed to be a SCUD missile attack, occurred near her location a few days after the beginning of the air war. Ms. Davis reports that these rashes continue to be a problem to this day. She has advised Senate staff that she is extremely concerned about her health as well as her prognosis. She is twenty-eight years old.

Event 7:

Approximately January 20, 1991, early morning (pre-dawn hours). Vicinity of King Fahd International Airport

Mr. Rocky Gallegos was a Lance Corporal with Bravo Battery, 2nd Light Anti- aircraft Missile Battalion. He observed what he believed to be a SCUD missile shot out of the sky almost directly overhead by a Patriot missile while on the midnight- 5:00 a.m. guard duty shift on approximately January 20. He reported that the explosion "blossomed like a flower." According to Mr. Gallegos, it exploded again when it hit the ground. Mr. Gallegos said that after the explosion he exper-ienced a "very strong raunchy taste, like very bitter burnt toast" in his mouth. He also began experiencing headaches, nausea, diarrhea, and sensitivity to bright lights almost immediately after the attack. He did not hear the chemical alarms go off immediately. Approximately 10 minutes later, however, the alert alarms sounded and they were ordered to put on their masks.

Mr. Gallegos remained at his post until approximately 4:00 a.m., when he along with a lieutenant, a staff sergeant, and three other enlisted personnel, went on a patrol to investigate the incident. They drove in the general direction of the explosion, but were not able to find evidence of impact.

Mr. Gallegos remained outside until daylight, when he noticed that his hands were tingling and looked as though they were sunburned. During the events of the early morning, his hands had been the only exposed area; his face was covered by a hood, scarf, and glasses, but he removed his gloves to smoke a cigarette.

Later that morning, about a half hour after they returned from the patrol, Mr. Gallegos was assigned to drive the NBC NCO to check all of the chemical detection units. At the fourth or fifth unit, the NBC NCO came back with something written on a piece of paper. He shoved the paper in his pocket and told Mr. Gallegos: "get me back to camp—Now!" Mr. Gallegos described him as "very excited about something," but when questioned the NBC NCO told Mr. Gallegos that it was none of his business.

Two days later, they again went out to patrol the area where the explosion occurred. According to Mr. Gallegos, they saw at least half a dozen dead sheep and a couple of camels that appeared to be very sick. . . .

Mr. Gallegos continued to suffer headaches, nausea, diarrhea, and photosensitivity during his tour of duty in Saudi Arabia. He became more seriously ill about two weeks before leaving Saudi Arabia. He also suffers from sinus infections (bleeding), narcolepsy, blackouts, dizziness, rashes, hair loss, joint pains in his knees, elbows, and hands, dental problems, muscle pains and spasms, fatigue, night sweats, insomnia, nightmares, and blurred vision.

Event 8:

Early in the "Air War"—approximately January 20, 1991. Dhahran, Kingdom of Saudi Arabia

Witness 1: Ms. Patricia Browning of New London, North Carolina, then a Staff Sergeant assigned to the 227th Transportation Company, was at Khobar Towers in Khahran when a Patriot missile intercepted what she believed to be a SCUD missile directly overhead. Her unit went to MOPP level 4 for 3½-4 hours. Ms. Browning said that her eyes began to burn, and she smelled a strong odor that reminded her of ammonia. Shortly afterwards she broke out in a rash and began experiencing headaches, nausea, vomiting, and sensitivity to bright lights.

Ms. Browning, who is thirty-seven years old, currently suffers from memory loss, severe recurring headaches, fatigue, joint and muscle pain, recurring rashes, night sweats, sleepiness, diarrhea, gastro-intestinal problems, dizziness, blurry vision and photosensitivity, coughing and shortness of breath, two duodenal ulcers, chest pains, heart arrhythmia, and erratic blood pressure. She said that many of these symptoms originated while she was still in Saudi Arabia.

Witness 2: Mr. Randall Vallee, a Sergeant with the 113th Transportation Company, was at the "Expo," just north of Dhahran on January 20. He said he remembers this incident well because it was the first time he came under attack. He heard two or three explosions and felt the concussion. . . . Officers began yelling at everyone to get back into the Expo center and go to MOPP level 4 immediately. . . . The air raid sirens went off after he got into the building. Once in the building, he put his chemical gear on and sat down. He recalled becoming nauseous, weak, dizzy, sweating profusely, his head throbbing, and becoming very, very thirsty, as though he were dehydrated. He stated that his vision became blurry, but at the time he thought it was either because of his mask or his sweating. The blurry vision didn't last long; the headache and nausea lasted about twenty minutes, and he continued to feel weak and dizzy for about forty-five minutes. When he went outside, after the all clear was given, he immediately noticed a "very suffocating smell, as though there wasn't enough air to breath, kind of like ammonia, but very strong." He recalled others commenting on the smell, which dissipated soon. . . .

Mr. Vallee recalled several attacks and the smell of ammonia several times while at Tent City. He said that the missiles were shot out of the sky so close to them that the fragments would land between the tents. Although his unit's chemical suits were used frequently, they were never replaced. He noticed as the days progressed that his chest "started getting tight," and he was getting flu symptoms. The nausea, fatigue, headaches, and respiratory problems continued off and on. Finally he became "so dizzy that he couldn't walk." He was diagnosed with an ear infection, and sent home on January 28.

Mr. Vallee currently suffers very severe recurring headaches, fatigue, respiratory problems, joint pain, memory loss, recurring rashes, depression and irritability, night sweats, insomnia, blood in his urine, constipation, nausea, dizziness, shortness of breath and coughing, thyroid problems, flu symptoms, sinus problems and sensitivity to smells. He always feels cold, and takes medication for pain.

. . .

Event 10:

Riyadh, date unknown

Mr. Michael Kingsbury was a driver/mechanic with the 601st Transportation Company during the Gulf War. . . . Mr. Kingsbury was in Riyadh for six hours rest and relaxation when the first SCUD missile attack took place. Although he does not remember the date of the attack, he was certain that it was the first SCUD attack on Riyadh. Mr. Kingbury reported that three SCUDs came in, the alarms went off, and they went to MOPP level 4. He immediately began to experience nausea and a sore throat. His nose began to run and his eyes burned a little. . . .

The symptoms that began with the attack never went away. In addition, he began to suffer skin irritation after the attack. He began having stomach problems when he returned from the Gulf and currently suffers from memory loss, rashes, aching joints, headaches, rectal bleeding, nausea, sensitivity to light, abnormal hair loss, high fevers, clammy skin, lumps, bloody oral/nasal mucous, night sweats, sore muscles, and fatigue.

Event 11:

January 18, 1991, around midnight (poss. very early on January 19) Log Base Alpha

Mr. William Brady was the Battalion Logistics NCO with the 217th Maintenance Battalion. Around midnight on January 18, or possibly very early on the 19th, Mr. Brady was awakened by what he believed to be a SCUD intercepted by a Patriot directly over his unit's position. He said there was a deafening sound, a flash of light, and everything shook. Chemical alarms were going off everywhere, and there was sheer panic. He remembered the chemical litmus paper turning red, and a positive reading from an M-256 kit. Mr. Brady said that his nose began to run, and he smelled and tasted sulfur. He began coughing up blood a couple of days after the attack, and continued to do so "the whole time we were there after the attack." They remained at MOPP level 4 for five or six hours. . . .

Beginning on January 22, Mr. Brady began getting too sick to work. He had been taking the nerve agent pre-treatment pills [PB pills] since about January 17, and had been getting severe headaches from them. Approximately three days after the attack, his eyes began to burn, he developed a high fever, and "taking a breath of air made his lungs feel like they were burning up." He also had diarrhea, sores, nausea, and a runny nose. On January 24, he went to the 13th Evacuation Hospital, which had no beds available for him. He described the hospital as completely filled with people that seemed to have the same illness that he had. His January 26 diary entry said: "I'd rather die than feel like this." . . .

Mr. Brady currently suffers from severe recurring headaches, chronic fatigue, joint and muscle pain, rashes, depression, night sweats, insomnia, urinary urgency, diarrhea, gastrointestinal problems, lightheadedness, photosensitivity, shortness of breath, coughing, abnormal hair loss, sensitivity in his teeth, burning and itching everywhere, arthritis, worsening leg cramps, "flu symptoms all of the time," a tingling in his arms, and a "bulging disc" in his neck. He had a heart attack in May 1993.

Event 12:

January 1991 (4-5 Days into the Air War). Near Ras Al Khafji

Mr. Norman Camp is a Staff Sergeant with the U.S. Marine Corps. He told Senate staff during an interview that he was near Ras Al Khafji several days into the air war when the chemical alarms went off, not only at their position, but also at their Division Supply Area, which was about 20 miles to their east. They went on 100% alert, but word was passed down from division not to go to MOPP. Sergeant Camp recalled that his whole platoon began falling ill the following night. He got headaches, nausea, and diarrhea for a day. Most others were sick for about a day and a half.

Sergeant Camp currently suffers from headaches, joint pain in knees and elbows, memory loss, night sweats, occasional insomnia, urinary urgency, dizziness, photosensitivity, shortness of breath, coughing, and heart problems.

*   *   *   *   *

The question of whether any of the SCUDs were actually carrying nerve agents is difficult to settle now that ten years have passed. Investigators for the Riegle committee were able, however, to conduct some interviews that offer tantalizing suggestions that some of the SCUDs did indeed carry a deadly payload. On October 8, 1993, the staff interviewed Joseph Boccardi, a tank crewmember in the 1st Cavalry Division. While he was recuperating in a medical facility from an injury sustained in a fall from his tank, he met a lieutenant assigned to the facility by the name of Lieutenant Babika. One day the lieutenant asked him to ride along to an area near King Khalid Military City that the Saudis had used as a training camp. Mr. Boccardi reported that the place he was taken to seemed to be like a palace and that his companion took him to a room where several of his friends were relaxing and playing cards. As it turned out, the men were part of a Czech NBC (nuclear/biological/chemical) team. According to the Riegle report:

> He [Mr. Boccardi] asked someone there "if we were kicking their butts so bad, why didn't they hit us with chemicals?" At that, everyone in the room got quiet and the Czech colonel spoke in "broken English" for the first time. He said, according to Mr. Boccardi, "they did hit us with chemicals." According to the Czech colonel, a SCUD hit where they were staying. As soon as they learned that the Patriot had missed the SCUD, they put on their chemical gear and went out onto a balcony near the railing. The Czech colonel said they detected traces of sarin and another gas which Mr. Boccardi believed began with the letter T [tabun?].
>
> According to Mr. Boccardi, the Czech colonel said that he called U.S. command officials about the result of their tests. He, the Czech colonel, said that he was told not to say anything about it. The colonel also said that he later heard that a number of the soldiers in the area developed skin rashes shortly after this incident.
>
> (Riegle, 93-94)

Over a year after the Riegle committee heard this account, a member of the 371st Chemical Company of Greenwood, South Carolina, stepped forward to give additional information about the Czech detections. In an account corroborated by several other soldiers in the same platoon, he reported that two days after a SCUD had exploded in the area of King Khalid Military City the platoon was sent to train with the Czech chemical team. According to the Riegle report, two members of the group stated that "the Czech colonel who commanded the unit had told them that his unit had detected measurable quantities of chemical nerve agent immediately after the Scud attack," which they believed had occurred in the latter part of January 1991. Like Joseph Boccardi, the members of this chemical platoon described the facility where the Czechs were headquartered as being like a palace. Of particular interest is this passage in the report:

> The unit Executive officer and first sergeant, while not present during the training mission, confirmed that they too were aware of the

training, the missile attack, and the reported detection of the chemicals. The unit first sergeant said that this information had been recorded in the unit's logs, but that he received a message to send the logs to Washington, D.C. for historical purposes shortly after they returned from the Persian Gulf. . . .

One member of the unit estimated that as many as 85% of the members of this unit are currently suffering from many of the symptoms associated with Gulf War Syndrome.

(Riegle, 95-96)

It would be interesting to know if this incident report in the logs was among those that disappeared when congressional committees began asking hard questions about whether U.S. forces had been exposed to nerve agents during the Gulf War. Of particular relevance are the comments of John Deutch, Deputy Secretary of the DOD at the time, who was interviewed by Ed Bradley on CBS News's *60 Minutes* on March 12, 1995. The Shays report quotes this interchange:

Mr. DEUTCH. Our most thorough and careful efforts to determine whether chemical agents were used in the Gulf lead us to conclude that there was *no widespread use* of chemicals against U.S. troops.
BRADLEY. Was there any use? Forget widespread.
Mr. DEUTCH. I—I do not believe . . .
BRADLEY. . . . was there any use?
Mr. DEUTCH. I do not believe there was *any offensive use* of chemical agents by Iraqi military troops. There was not . . .
BRADLEY. Was there any—any accidental use. Were our troops exposed in any way?
Mr. DEUTCH. I do not believe that our troops were exposed *in any widespread way* to chemical . . .
BRADLEY. In any narrow way? In any way?
Mr. DEUTCH. The Defense Science Board did an independent study of this matter and found, in their judgment, that there was *not confirmation of chemical weapon widespread use* in the Gulf. [italics added in report]

(Shays, 16)

Deutch's guarded comments clearly leave the door open both for exposure of the troops to the fallout from Coalition bombing of the Iraqi chemical factories and for limited offensive use of chemical agents by Iraq. As is so often the case in comments from officials of the DOD, the VA, and the CIA, Deutch escapes Bradley's attempt to pin him down by saying that there was "not confirmation" of the use of chemical weapons that so many soldiers believed they had encountered. His insistence on using the word "widespread" also suggests that the DOD may in fact be aware of isolated instances of the use of chemical warfare.

Dr. Jonathan Tucker, director of the chemical and biological nonproliferation project at the Monterey (California) Institute for International Studies, stated in a report to the Shays subcommittee that there were almost 14,000 chemical alarm systems used during the war and that each of them went off a couple of times a day on average. According to Tucker, "The alarms went off so frequently, day and night, that some commanders ordered their troops to disregard or even disable them because no obvious symptoms of nerve-agent poisoning had been observed. DOD officials contend that every one of the tens of thousands of chemical agent alerts during the Gulf War was a false alarm" (Shays, 18).

Two patterns seem to emerge from these events. First, soldier after soldier has described hearing tremendous explosions that they attributed to a SCUD missile being blown up by a Patriot missile. Sometimes they even saw an associated flash of light or fireball. Many of them smelled chemicals in the air, and almost all of them immediately developed strong physical symptoms. Most of the veterans who testified to committees of Congress about these events have seen their health decline significantly after returning from the Persian Gulf. The second clear pattern that emerges is that when such explosions occurred, commanding officers passed the word to their troops that the explosion had only been a sonic boom. It is especially suspect that the troops were told not to discuss the matter further. Now, years after the fact, the DOD and VA try to claim that there could not have been nerve agents involved because no one had acute symptoms at the time. But by insisting that these explosions were sonic booms, the commanding officers made it far less likely that any troops would report their nausea or diarrhea to the medics. Similarly, by forbidding the soldiers to discuss the explosions, the officers made it less likely that troops would compare notes about what symptoms they experienced after the explosion.

It is possible that when the first few SCUDs were intercepted and exploded and the chemical alarms sounded but no one developed a life-threatening reaction, senior officers made a judgment call that if the SCUDs were indeed carrying nerve agents, the amount reaching the troops after the SCUD was exploded high above them was small enough and dilute enough that it was causing no serious health problems. The commanders might also have worried that if their troops believed that the SCUDs were carrying sarin or other deadly nerve agents, general panic might greatly hamper military operations.

But the paramount reason why commanders downplayed these SCUD events may be the ultimatum the United States had issued to Saddam Hussein to the effect that if he used chemical weapons against Coalition forces, then he could expect a no-holds-barred retaliation. Most observers interpreted this ultimatum to mean we would hit Iraq with nuclear weapons. By issuing this threat, the United States placed itself in a difficult position. If Saddam did indeed unleash SCUD missiles carrying nerve agents, U.S. commanders would have to deny that the SCUDs were carrying nerve agents or drop nuclear bombs on Iraq. It is not surprising that they chose to deny that the SCUDs were carrying nerve agents. If Saddam had loaded some of the SCUDs with nerve agents, he knew that he had called our bluff, but the American public remained unaware of the high stakes poker game being played out in the Persian Gulf.

Chapter 3

Khamisiyah

After the ground war ended on February 28, U.S. commanders decided to blow up the Iraqi ammunition dumps that were scattered across southern Iraq. The demolition of the complex known as Khamisiyah was an event whose consequences are still being debated today. After years of denial that any troops were exposed to chemical weapons during the Gulf War, the DOD finally admitted in 1996 that large numbers of soldiers were in fact exposed to low levels of sarin when Khamisiyah was blown up. As the summary to the Shays committee report states: "With that first admission, the three pillars of Government denial—no credible detections, no exposures, no health effects—began to crumble" (Shays, 2).

The vast Khamisiyah complex consisted of about 100 bunkers in which were stored rockets and other weapons. These bunkers were spread over a main area covering about nine square kilometers and a second smaller area located in a depression that came to be known as "the pit" (SIU, 23). The task of destroying the bunkers at Khamisiyah fell to soldiers from the 37th Engineer Battalion and the 307th Engineer Brigade, which were part of the 82nd Airborne Division. These soldiers had been given no intelligence information that indicated the presence of chemical weapons at Khamisiyah. Nevertheless, they did use MA81 chemical detection alarms to check each bunker to see if there was any sign of chemical weapons (SIU, 22). An alarm would not have been expected to sound, however, if the rockets containing nerve agent were all intact. Nerve agents are so lethal in tiny amounts that Iraqis could not have handled these weapons safely if any nerve agent had been leaking from them.

The troops assigned to set the explosive charges had also received the impression that Iraqi chemical weapons would bear special markings. One message sent to the demolition units in February 1991 stated that chemical weapons could be identified by a distinctive color pattern or a certain number of rings. But on March 6, 1991, the CIA sent a message to DOD intelligence offices in Riyadh stating that the Iraqis had not in fact used special markings to identify weapons containing chemical agents. Unfortunately, the 37th Engineer Battalion never received this message and in any case had already started the demolition process when it was sent.

On March 4, the army engineer units destroyed 37 bunkers in the main area at Khamisiyah, but a few days later, on March 9, soldiers investigating the surrounding area discovered large quantities of rockets in the pit area. Since they were running out of some demolition supplies, the plan was not to totally destroy the rockets but to render them inoperable by breaking them apart. Had they realized that the rockets contained nerve agents, they would have known that it was essential to set large enough explosive charges to burn up the rockets and the chemicals they contained. As it was, they simply set off explosions on March 9 and 10 that broke open the weapons, enabling the nerve agents they contained to escape into the atmosphere or drain into the sand (SIU, 24).

Sgt. Brian Martin, one of the soldiers in the 37th Engineer Battalion who helped blow up Khamisiyah, provided a crucial videotape of the event to the Shays subcommittee and to the media in the summer of 1996. Had that video not suddenly appeared, the world might never have heard about Khamisiyah. The release of the tape once again focused attention on Gulf War syndrome and sent DOD officials scurrying to keep the coverup of Gulf War syndrome from unraveling. Sergeant Martin indicated in testimony to the Shays subcommittee that the troops withdrew three miles for the March 4 detonations. During the later detonations, they apparently withdrew twelve miles, probably because the explosions ignited many rockets, which went shooting off in all directions (SIU, 24). Sergeant Martin described the scene at Khamisiyah in his testimony:

> On March 4, 1991, we entered the depot area, placing explosives in and around 33 bunkers. We set time charges for detonation, then moved south three miles to what we considered a "safe zone." At no time whatsoever did we fear . . . chemical exposure. We were told . . . there were no chemicals in the area. Our commanders knew nothing about chemicals in the bunkers. Seven minutes later the destruction of Khamisiyah began.
>
> Witnessing these awesome explosions was a remarkable sight. The explosions blew straight into the air, then would spread at the top . . . the closest thing to a nuclear mushroom we would ever see. Our excitement quickly turned to fear when "cook offs" or fallout from the explosions began showering down on us. . . .
>
> Since Khamisiyah, I suffer from . . . blood in vomit and stools, blurred vision, shaking and trembling . . . muscles weakening . . . chest pounding like my heart was going to explode. . . . I suffer from excruciatingly painful headaches, memory loss, and severe diarrhea . . . mood swings . . . I violently vomit if I smell perfumes, vapors or chemicals. I get lost and forget where I am sometimes. I am an ex-paratrooper who needs a cane and wheelchair to get around. My joints . . . swell, burn and hurt.
>
> (Shays, 11)

Sergeant Martin's reactions suggest that despite DOD statements to the contrary, there were soldiers who quickly began to develop symptoms after the destruction of Khamisiyah.

Information about the kind of weapons that had actually been present at Khamisiyah eventually came from UNSCOM, the United Nations Special

Commission, whose teams traveled around Iraq after the war seeking out and destroying chemical weapons stores. According to the Riegle report: "At the first inspection in October of 1991, UNSCOM found rockets at the Khamisiyah pit and determined that they contained a mixture of sarin and cyclosarin. UNSCOM inspectors tested at least one chemical rocket at that time and also noted the presence of over 300 more leaking and damaged rockets." When UNSCOM teams returned in May of 1996, they found in the main Khamisiyah complex that had been blown up on March 4, 1991, several plastic burster tubes of the kind that would be used in chemical weapons (SIU, 25). UNSCOM succeeded in finding Iraqi records indicating that approximately 60 tons of sarin and cyclosarin had been placed in 8,000 122mm rockets and over 2,000 of these rockets had ended up at Khamisiyah, half in the main area and half in the pit.

Unfortunately, the DOD initially discounted the 1991 UNSCOM report, believing that the Iraqis might have deceived the inspectors by taking them to a nearby storage site at An Nasiriyah or that they might have moved chemical weapons to the site where they took the UNSCOM team in order to conceal true information about their chemical weapons program (Riegle, 27). Confusion of site names added to the problem from the beginning because U.S. intelligence sources originally called the Khamisiyah bunker complex by the name of Tall al Lahm, a town located on the other side of the complex. The units that blew up the bunkers referred to the site as Objective Gold.

But evidence indicates that whatever the complex was called, some people in the U.S. intelligence community and Armed Forces knew even before the war that there were probably chemical weapons stored at Khamisiyah. According to the Shays report:

> In April 1997, the CIA released 41 declassified documents, one of which stated the CIA had warnings starting in 1984 that thousands of chemical weapons were stored in Khamisiyah bunkers. According to news accounts, the CIA claims they notified the Pentagon before the war of the presence of these weapons at Khamisiyah. The DOD had denied it until February 25, 1997, when the Pentagon disclosed that the CIA had in fact warned the Army but it never reached commanders of the 37th Army Engineers Battalion that detonated the Khamisiyah depot.
> (Shays, 23)

Jim Tuite, principal investigator for the Senate Banking Committee study of Gulf War syndrome, is highly critical of the DOD's attitude toward the Khamisiyah affair:

> Khamisiyah is only one of hundreds of munition sites and depots that we destroyed after the war whose contents we never inventoried and we destroyed as though there were no risk to troops in the surrounding area. We don't know what was in these bunkers. We didn't know, according to the DOD, what was in Khamisiyah at the time, even though evidence

developed afterwards suggests the contrary. But bunker after bunker after bunker was destroyed without any inventory of the contents, without any knowledge of what was being blown up, without any effort to protect the troops in the area from the fallout that may have occurred from these detonations.

When we were conducting the Senate Banking Committee investigation and we first raised this inquiry, we were told by the Pentagon that the fallout couldn't have reached the troops because the wind was blowing in the wrong direction. But we looked at the satellite images and the plumes, the smoke plumes from all the bombing and from the oil well fires that were going on at the same time [which] suggested that the wind was blowing towards the troops. The Pentagon insisted that no chemical agent exposure occurred. In 1996, they admitted, well, maybe at Khamisiyah 185 soldiers may have been exposed, then a few months later, well maybe 400 had been exposed. Then it was 5000, then it was 20,000, then 100,000, then 120,000.

(GWS video footage)

In 1997 the Pentagon sent letters to almost 98,000 veterans, informing them that computer modeling studies indicated that they might have been exposed to sarin or cyclosarin when Khamisiyah was blown up. Computer models had indicated that the plumes resulting from the explosions could have carried as far as 300 miles to the south and extended over areas where almost 100,000 troops were stationed (Shays, 23). Three years later, in November of 2000, the Pentagon sent out letters to about 30,000 veterans to say that although they had been informed in 1997 that they had been exposed to these nerve agents, it now appeared that they had not in fact been exposed. Oddly enough, about the same number, 30,000, of new veterans got letters saying that they were probably exposed to sarin and cyclosarin when they were serving in the Khamisiyah region.

The Pentagon may be telling the veterans exposed to the fallout from the destruction of Khamisiyah not to worry, but these veterans would hardly be reassured by a passage in a book just published in December 2000. *Saddam's Bombmaker* was written by the bombmaker himself, Khidhir Hamza, with the assistance of Jeff Stein. Hamza worked for over two decades in Iraq's nuclear bomb program. In a chilling passage, he recounts how Saddam Hussein decided to bury chemical and biological weapons in bunkers in southern Iraq along the invasion routes that Coalition forces might follow: "His thinking was that the Allies, following U.S. tactical doctrine, would blow up the bunkers as they advanced, releasing plumes of invisible gas into the prevailing winds and ultimately onto themselves." According to this plan, Coalition forces wouldn't realize until weeks or months later what had happened. "The pattern of contamination would be so disparate, the symptoms so amorphous, the sources of illness couldn't be easily confirmed."[1] The last statement could hardly have been better phrased if it had been an internal memo circulated among DOD and VA officials attempting to coverup the reality of Gulf War syndrome.

---

[1] Khidhir Hamza, with Jeff Stein, *Saddam's Bombmaker* (New York: Scribner, 2000), 244.

Chapter 4

Low Level Exposure to Toxins

The release of the videotape of the destruction of Khamisiyah was a watershed event. This evidence was welcomed by the many observers who had been suggesting that U.S. forces might have been exposed to low levels of nerve agents as the result of the Coalition bombing of Saddam Hussein's chemical weapons factories and storage depots as well as possible offensive Iraqi use of nerve agents on SCUD missiles. DOD officials had repeatedly denied that any such exposures took place but were finally forced to admit that almost 100,000 U.S. soldiers had been exposed to low levels of sarin and cyclosarin when Khamisiyah was blown up. DOD officials continued to insist, however, as they had from the beginning of the Gulf War syndrome controversy, that in any case there is no danger from low level exposure to nerve agents. When Dr. Stephen Joseph, who until his resignation in March of 1997 was the DOD's assistant secretary for health affairs, testified to the Shays subcommittee, he asserted: "Current accepted medical knowledge is that chronic symptoms or physical manifestations do not later develop among persons exposed to low levels of chemical nerve agents who did not first exhibit acute symptoms of toxicity" (Shays, 37).

The DOD has always maintained that there were no acute symptoms coinciding with the possible exposures to fallout from the Coalition bombing of Iraqi chemical sites or the destruction of bunkers like Khamisiyah or with the possible exposures to nerve agents carried by SCUD missiles. Many veterans have, however, reported in their testimony to congressional committees and presidential advisory committees that they experienced various symptoms on these occasions. The DOD assertion that no acute symptoms occurred seems to be based upon a lack of such symptoms being recorded in the medical records of the various units serving in the war. Because some of the most common acute symptoms were intestinal cramps, diarrhea, vomiting, and headaches, it is hardly surprising that troops serving in theater did not rush to their medics to report these symptoms. Tracy Smith describes the typical soldier's attitude: "Going to the medics or the hospital was for people who had the luxury of time to go on sick call or were bleeding profusely. It wasn't an option for most of us. We were soldiers invincible to pain and death" (Part II, 169). If the officers in charge of the units had not continually denied that the chemical detection alarms were sounding for a reason, however, soldiers would have been far more likely to report their symptoms to the medics.

Civilian scientists testifying to the Shays subcommittee have disputed Dr. Joseph's conclusions about low level exposures to toxic chemicals. Claudia

Miller, M.D., a professor at the University of Texas Health Science Center in San Antonio, Texas, and a member of the Department of Veterans Affairs Gulf War Expert Scientific Advisory Committee, is a leading authority in the field of health consequences of exposure to low levels of toxic chemicals and is also a leading researcher in the field of chemical sensitivity. In her testimony to the Shays subcommittee, Dr. Miller disagrees with Dr. Joseph's assessment about low level exposures to nerve agents (which are organophosphates or related compounds) and their lack of health consequences:

> I think it is premature for anyone to say that low levels of organophosphates cannot cause chronic health problems. . . . There is a lot of literature now suggesting that is quite a possibility and there are ways to approach that question scientifically. . . . Sarin was not the only organophosphate-type exposure soldiers may have encountered in the Gulf: pesticides in this chemical class and pyridostigmine bromide [PB], a related carbamate drug, were also widely used. There are now several studies, in addition to our own, linking chronic, multi-system symptoms to [low level] organophosphate/carbamate exposure.
>
> (Shays, 37)

Also at odds with Dr. Joseph's dismissive attitude toward the risks of low level exposure to nerve agents is the testimony of Frank Duffy, M.D., an associate professor of neurology at Harvard Medical School. In the 1970s, Dr. Duffy studied a group of people who were exposed to low levels of nerve agents—employees at the U.S. Army's Rocky Mountain Arsenal near Denver, Colorado, where weapons containing nerve gas were stored. According to the Shays report, the Army physician at the facility had noticed that many employees were developing symptoms that included "fatigue, sleep difficulties, memory loss, trouble concentrating, irritability, loss of libido, among others," symptoms similar to those reported by many Gulf War veterans. In the case of these civilian employees, their symptoms had developed "much later following reported exposures to the nerve agent sarin, an organophosphate."

Dr. Duffy injected a group of rhesus monkeys with low doses of sarin and compared their symptoms after one year had passed with those experienced by the workers whose exposure to sarin had occurred a year or more earlier. According to his testimony:

> Low levels of exposure to the nerve agent sarin can produce long-lasting effects. It was perfectly clear that not only were people, after [low level sarin] exposure showing long-term effects, but it was widely accepted in the pesticide industry that exposure to related compounds like malathion and parrathion [sic] or the chlorinated hydrocarbon insecticides led to long-term consequence. . . .

It has been suggested that since Army personnel did not appear to suffer acute symptoms which could be clearly recognized as resulting from acute sarin exposure, that this explanation for Gulf War syndrome must be irrelevant. This is not necessarily a valid assumption. First, the low level exposure to the monkey group demonstrated no symptoms . . . And second, most of the exposed Army personnel at RMA [Rocky Mountain Arsenal] suffered relatively minor symptomatology.

(Shays, 38-39)

A December 10, 1996, article in the *New York Times* discussed the findings of Dr. Duffy and his colleagues: "Their research, which studied the effects of low doses of sarin on humans and primates, showed the exposure resulted in long-term or chronic, perhaps permanent, changes in brain waves, which could be connected with . . . symptoms common among Gulf veterans" (Shays, 39).

Of particular interest in view of the DOD's contention that Gulf War illnesses are the result of stress, not toxic exposures, is a passage from a letter that Dr. Duffy wrote in 1987 to Robert Hall of the Hawaii Institute for Biosocial Research:

I applaud your effort in raising the level of consciousness about the serious potential for long-term effects due to exposures to the [organophosphate] compounds. It has been our experience that the side effects of minimal but continual exposures to the compounds *mimic the symptoms associated with a stressful life* [emphasis added in report]. Accordingly, most individuals are unable to determine whether their irritability is related to a stressful life or to a recent organophosphate exposure. This is a serious issue.

(Shays, 39)

Seymour Antelman, M.D., a professor of psychiatry at the University of Pittsburgh Medical School, has been doing research for years in what is called "time dependent sensitization," a phenomenon closely related to multiple chemical sensitivity. Dr. Antelman has succeeded in producing a condition that resembles MCS in rodents by exposing them to low levels of toxic chemicals over an extended time period. In a November 15, 1996, letter to the *New York Times,* Dr. Antelman wrote: "[Dr. Joseph's] view . . . is almost certainly wrong. My research, published in leading scientific journals and the subject of a June 21, 1988, *Science Times* article, has shown that the effects of chemicals can develop and grow over time, and need not be present at the time of exposure. Such 'time dependent sensitization' is more likely after exposure to a low level stimulus" (Shays, 39-40).

K. Husain et al. have reported on an experiment in which they gave mice a daily low level dose of sarin by inhalation for ten days.[1] The level of exposure was low enough that no cholinergic signs appeared, but the mice developed typical OPIDP, organophosphate-induced delayed polyneuropathy. (This condition will be discussed in Chapter 7.) Fourteen days after the mice were first exposed to sarin, they began to develop ataxia (uncoordinated movements) that tissue analysis showed was related to axonal degeneration of the spinal cord. The researchers later duplicated their findings in a study of hens that were given low-level subcutaneous injections of sarin for ten days.[2]

The research of Husain and his colleagues was considered in the reports issued by the Institute of Medicine (IOM) on September 7, 2000. The IOM was asked by the VA "to conduct a review of the scientific literature on the possible health effects of agents to which Gulf War veterans may have been exposed."[3] The IOM began by analyzing the four agents that veterans' groups had particularly implicated: sarin, PB, depleted uranium, and anthrax and botulinum vaccines. The conclusion for sarin was typical: "The committee concludes that there is inadequate/insufficient evidence to determine whether an association does or does not exist between exposure to sarin at low doses insufficient to cause acute cholinergic signs and symptoms and subsequent long-term adverse health effects."[4] The conclusions for PB and the vaccines were in effect the same: We can't tell if these substances contributed to Gulf War illnesses. In the case of depleted uranium, the committee reached a similar conclusion for health outcomes other than renal dysfunction or lung cancer. For the latter effects, they found "limited/suggestive evidence of no association."[5]

The RAND report titled *Chemical and Biological Warfare Agents* released in December 2000 also takes note of the research of Husain and others: "In summary, there is evidence of asymptomatic or unrecognized nerve agent (and organophosphate pesticde) exposure producing effects of various

---

[1] K. Husain et al., "Delayed Neurotoxic Effect of Sarin in Mice After Repeated Inhalation," *Journal of Applied Toxicology* 13, no. 2 (March-April 1993): 143-45.

[2] K. Husain et al., "A Comparative Study of Delayed Neurotoxicity in Hens Following Repeated Administration of Organophosphorus Compounds," *Indian Journal of Physiological Pharmacology* 39, no. 1 (January 1995): 47-50.

[3] "Gulf War and Health," Executive Summary, Institute of Medicine, September 7, 2000, 2.

[4] Ibid., 8.

[5] Ibid., 6.

durations in humans and animals. Alterations of mental function are the best-documented effect."[6]

Victor Gordan, M.D., the New Hampshire VA physician who has treated over 700 Gulf War veterans, testified to the Shays subcommittee that he is convinced that chemical exposures during the war have played a major role in Gulf War illnesses:

What is strikingly consistent in these veterans' stories are (1) a drastic change in their health status from very good to perfect, as it was before deployment to the Gulf War, to poor to fair after their return from the war; (2) the large variety and number of symptoms suggesting dys-function of more than one organ system in their bodies; and (3) the very consistent history of being exposed to chemicals in the Gulf, including the strong belief [by veterans] of being exposed to chemical warfare. These consistent stories point very strongly toward the environmental hazards as the cause or causes of these unexplained illnesses. Unless the science addresses these environmental hazards, we will never be able to adequately explain and hopefully solve these medical problems. . . .

Chemicals . . . are the greatest masquerader in modern medicine . . . because they penetrate into all sorts of systems and organs, and those organs get dysfunctional, and those dysfunctions bypass symptoms, and symptoms can mimic so-called quantifiable disease, including arthritis, even *PTSD* [post-traumatic stress disorder; italics added in report].

(Shays, 40)

In contrast to the views of the preceding researchers, the head of the VA's Environmental Agents Service, Frances Murphy, M.D., echoed Dr. Joseph's words when she testified to the Shays subcommittee: "Current body of research proves that low level exposures cannot cause health effects" (Shays, 41). Dr. Murphy's use of the emphatic word "proves" seems particularly inappropriate coming right after the word "current," which seems to leave open the possibility of new research indicating otherwise. It is commonly accepted in the world of science that you cannot prove a negative—in this case you cannot prove that low level exposures do not cause health effects—and only the rashest of scientists or the most loyal of bureaucrats would assert that you can. Although Dr. Murphy is not popular with the suffering veterans, she has recently been promoted to a higher position at the DOD. Her attitude toward Gulf War syndrome has been clear from the outset. In a 1999 interview in the Alabama PBS documentary on Gulf War syndrome produced by Eddie Rollins, she stated: "There is no Gulf War syndrome,

---

[6] See <<http://www.gulflink.osd.mil/library/randrep/bw_paper/>>, p. 177.

meaning that there is no single unique illness that all Gulf War veterans suffer from, and that's the major misconception."

Dr. Murphy's statement dismissing the concept of Gulf War syndrome plays into what appears to be a DOD and VA strategy that might best be called "divide and conquer." Officials in these departments admit that there are many veterans who report signs or symptoms like joint pains, extreme fatigue, gastrointestinal problems, asthma, and other respiratory problems, but they assert that these are conditions that appear throughout the general population and no one has proved that these symptoms can be tied to service in the Persian Gulf.

The controversy over the term "Gulf War syndrome" is not simply an issue of semantics. This issue lies at the heart of the ability of veterans to obtain free health care from the VA or, in the case of the large number who are no longer able to work, to obtain disability payments so that they can support themselves and their families. It is important not to let the DOD take away the term "Gulf War syndrome," which is broad enough to cover the situations of most sick Gulf veterans, who have multiple symptoms in different organ systems. The case of the term "chronic fatigue syndrome" (CFS) is parallel. In 1994 the Centers for Disease Control and Prevention defined CFS by a set of rather complex criteria stating that a person has CFS if he or she has experienced for at least six months (1) chronic fatigue and (2) four out of a list of eight other symptoms. Obviously, such a definition covers patients with different groupings of symptoms and does not fit Dr. Murphy's "single unique illness" criteria.

The syndrome commonly called multiple chemical sensitivity, or MCS, may well present the best umbrella for covering almost all cases of illness arising from exposures in the Persian Gulf. Many of the sick veterans are reporting that they developed extreme sensitivity to the chemicals in substances like diesel fuel or exhaust, cleaning products, and perfume after they participated in Desert Storm. In a 1999 article in *Archives of Environmental Health*, a group of 34 researchers and clinicians proposed the following criteria for the clinical diagnosis of MCS:

1. The symptoms are reproducible with repeated exposure.
2. The condition is chronic.
3. Low levels of exposure result in manifestations of the syndrome.
4. The symptoms improve or resolve when the incitants are removed.
5. Responses occur to multiple chemically unrelated substances.
6. Symptoms involve multiple organ systems.[7]

---

[7] "Multiple Chemical Sensitivity: A 1999 Consensus," *Archives of Environmental Health* 54, no. 3 (1999): 147-49.

Dr. Claudia Miller approaches these issues involving new-onset sensitivity to commonly encountered substances from a slightly different framework. In her October 26, 1999, testimony to the House Committee on Veterans Affairs, Dr. Miller stated:

Over the past six years, I have served as a consultant to the VA's referral center of Gulf War veterans in Houston. The vast majority of the veterans there reported multiple new intolerances since the War. Among the first 59 patients, 78% reported new-onset chemical intolerances; 40% experienced adverse reactions to medications; 78% described new food intolerances; 66% reported that even a can of beer made them feel ill; 25% became ill after drinking caffeinated beverages; and 74% of smokers felt sick if they smoked an extra cigarette or borrowed someone else's stronger brand. More than half reported new intolerances in all three categories—chemical inhalants, foods, and drugs or food/drug combinations.

One mechanic said that before the Gulf War his idea of the perfect perfume was WD-40 [a penetrating oil used to free rusty screws]. Since the war, WD-40 and a host of other chemicals make him feel ill. Many veterans no longer fill their own gas tanks because the gasoline vapors make them "spacy" or sick. Some won't drive because they become disoriented in traffic and they fear causing an accident. Or they can't find their cars, forget where they are going or get lost in once familiar areas. One VA study found excess motor vehicle deaths among Gulf veterans and interpreted this as possible increased risk-taking behavior (Kang and Bullmann, 1996). What the veterans tell me is that they get confused, go off the road, mistake the accelerator for the brake, and have trouble judging stopping distances when they are exposed to gasoline, diesel exhaust, or freshly tarred roads.

Researchers at the Robert Wood Johnson Medical School in New Jersey and at the University of Arizona have noted similar multi-system symptoms and intolerances to common chemicals, foods, and drugs among the veterans (Fiedler et al., 1996; Bell et al., 1998). And a CDC study found that ill Gulf War veterans reported more chemical intolerances than healthy veterans (Fukuda et al., 1998).

These studies are confounded by a phenomenon called "masking," which occurs when people become intolerant to many different things (Miller and Prihoda, 1999a). As they go through a day, symptoms triggered by fragrances, hair spray, vehicle exhaust, foods, and medications pile up so they feel sick most of the time. No one cause can be isolated because there's too much background noise, and patients often underestimate the number of exposures that affect them.

This problem is not altogether new. German researchers described similar intolerances in chemical weapons workers after World War II (Spiegelberg, 1961). Nearly 20% of agricultural workers on a California registry for organophosphate pesticide poisoning (Tabershaw and Cooper, 1966) reported that even a "whiff" of pesticide made them sick with symptoms like those of the Gulf War veterans, as did dozens of government workers a decade ago, after the EPA headquarters became a "sick building" following remodeling (EPA, 1989). Similar outbreaks of chemical intolerances have been reported in more than a dozen countries (Ashford et al., 1995).

These observations suggest that we may indeed be dealing with an entirely new mechanism for disease, one which has been referred to with the acronym "TILT," or "Toxicant-Induced Loss of Tolerance" (Miller, 1996, 1997, 1999). Any one toxicant appears capable of initiating this process. TILT involves two steps, initiation and triggering (Ashford and Miller, 1998): (1) First, a single acute or multiple low-level exposures to a pesticide, solvent or other chemical causes loss of tolerance in a subset of those exposed; (2) Thereafter very low levels of common substances can trigger symptoms—not only chemicals, but various foods, medications, alcoholic beverages and caffeine. Symptoms involve several organ systems. These intolerances are the hallmark of TILT, just as fever is the hallmark symptom of infectious diseases.

Over the past several years, the finger has been pointed at a number of potential causes for Gulf War syndrome—everything from the oil shroud to pesticides, vaccinations, and pyridostigmine bromide. What set off the Gulf War veterans? The answer is "all of the above." Exposure to any one or any combination of these toxicants may, in fact, be capable of causing a general breakdown in tolerance that can result in a plethora of beguiling symptoms.

We do not know exactly how this breakdown in tolerance occurs. We do know that rats with nervous systems sensitive to organophosphate pesticides are also intolerant of diverse drugs and have increased gut permeability which in humans is associated with food intolerance (Overstreet et al., 1996). This suggests the breakdown might involve the cholinergic nervous system, which regulates processes throughout the body.[8]

The personal histories from Gulf veterans in Part II illustrate Dr. Miller's theory of Toxicant-Induced Loss of Tolerance. Many of these veterans describe their sensitivity to various chemical substances and the ways in which this sensitivity, which developed after they went to Desert Storm, causes them

---

[8] Statement submitted to the Committee on Veterans Affairs, Subcommittee on Benefits, U.S. House of Representatives, October 26, 1999. The cholinergic nervous system that Dr. Miller believes may be involved in Gulf War syndrome will be discussed in more detail in Chapter 5 on PB pills.

to develop headaches, nausea, breathing difficulty, or other symptoms. This sensitivity or lack of tolerance greatly limits their ability to do something as simple as putting gasoline in their car or attending church, where exposure to perfume and aftershave may make them sick. The kind of driving problems that Dr. Miller describes are illustrated by the experience of Sfc. Terry Dillhyon, who reports:

> I've had to give up driving. . . . I was unable to determine distance. I would look and see traffic coming and pull out and then have to swing over. I could see a green light, but when it changed to red, it would still be green to me. I would drive right through it. After the last time I had a near fatal collision, nothing was said. My wife looked at me, I looked at her, we changed sides, and she drove.
>
> The next time at the VA hospital, they ran some more tests on me to check my balance and my coordination; I guess it would be sort of like giving someone a field sobriety test. I could not pass the test. My balance is affected by chemicals I smell. In 1994, I had to start using two canes, and that worked for about six months. If I happened to smell something like gasoline or perfume, however, it would affect my coordination and I would fall down.
>
> (GWS video footage)

One Gulf veteran who was extremely sensitive to diesel exhaust unfortunately had a skeptical physician who believed that he was just having psychological problems. The physician suggested that to get over his phobia about diesel exhaust, this veteran should drive right behind diesel trucks whenever he could. Given the effect that diesel exhaust has on a large number of ill veterans, most of whom report that it makes them vomit or at least feel very nauseated, this physician was offering dangerous advice that could have caused a fatal accident.

Sergeant Dillhyon reports that his extreme sensitivity to chemicals sometimes causes him to lose consciousness: "When my wife cleans the house, I have to leave the house because I can literally be knocked unconscious from some of these chemicals, household chemicals that are used for cleaning the bathrooms and things of that nature" (GWS video footage).

Sfc. Roy Twymon is also plagued by new chemical sensitivities that he never had before the war: "I notice that lots of things bother me that never bothered me before. Different perfumes, different colognes, gasoline, cigarette smoke, I just automatically get sick, and sometimes it takes me days or weeks to recover" (GWS video footage). He reports that on one occasion a perfume exposure in an elevator caused his blood pressure to shoot up so high that he was hospitalized for a few days. Sergeant Twymon's severe health problems include migraines, joint pains, lesions on his legs, urinary urgency and incontinence, and rectal incontinence. He ruefully notes, "The government's not even paying for my diapers."

Chapter 5

PB Pills

The U.S. troops called them PB pills, and the British and Australians called them NAPPs (nerve agent pretreatment packs). These tablets contained a drug called pyridostigmine bromide that was given to approximately 250,000 U.S. troops during Desert Storm in an attempt to protect them against possible Iraqi use of nerve agents. Was the treatment worse than the risk of death or extreme disability that would have resulted from an Iraqi attack with nerve gas? That is one of the lingering questions as researchers attempt to learn what has caused debilitating illness in so many who served in the Gulf War.

The following reports of adverse reactions to the PB pills come from Gulf War veterans:

About three days after I started taking the pills, my eyes were jittery, my vision was jumping, I was seeing double, and I was nauseated. By the fourth day, I was vomiting a little blood, so I went to sick-call. They told me to cut the dose in half and said there was nothing to worry about. At least I no longer vomited any blood after I reduced the dosage. Many other people in the unit reported having similar vision problems.

S.Sgt. Pat Browning (Part II, 159)

The pills made me feel really strange. And I didn't really want to take them, although I felt the necessity to protect myself in the event of direct chemical exposures, which we had been told was a real possibility. I wanted to come back home, and I believed it was in my best interest to continue taking them, even though they made me feel really strange, made my heart race. It was almost like an out-of-body experience. Although I was still able to function, things were altered around me, time, space. I was more than happy to discontinue taking the things.

S.Sgt. Bob Jones (GWS video footage)

I had suffered very much with migraine as a teenager, but I hadn't suffered for some years. And within maybe 48 hours of taking the NAPPs tablets, the PB tablets, I got my migraines back. And I felt nauseous and had more trouble with diarrhea. There was also some loss of sensation—loss of physical, sexual sensation basically. A lot of people experienced it. I thought it was just me, I thought it was just tiredness and one thing or another. Having spoken to people since and [learning] they all suffered the same thing, I can only assume it had something to do with the tablets. And it did stop when we stopped taking the tablets.

S.Sgt. Anne Selby (GWS video footage)

The day before the air war, I believe—I would need to check on those dates for sure—but sometime in that time frame we were instructed to take PB pills. We were in fact instructed to go down the line and ensure all our troops actually took the PB pills and swallowed them. Shortly after that we had a gentleman from our battalion headquarters who went into cardiac arrest, almost within a few hours of taking the first pills. Myself and a reservist who was a PA actually started CPR on this individual three times. We went with him all the way to the medevac hospital. They started CPR on him there several times and brought him back, and the interesting part is that after all of that his medical records now show that he had just a pulled muscle in his chest.

Sgt. Mike Ange (GWS video footage)

Doug Rokke, who was a nuclear/chemical/biological officer during the Gulf War, described PB pills in this way:

The simplest way to understand pyridostigmine bromide, the little white tablets that came in a blister pack, is that they are a carbamate-based pesticide. If you want to think about this, what they did is they went and got you a whole bunch of gumdrops and sprayed them with pesticide and said, "Eat them." Over 50 percent of the people who took the pyridostigmine bromide had immediate pesticide-related health effects. That was expected, that's what's in the physician's desk reference, and what's always been known. You can't eat pesticides and have a good day.

(GWS video footage)

Although PB is a highly toxic substance, it has been used for a few decades to treat myasthenia gravis patients. This prior use of PB was an important factor in the DOD's decision to give it to troops during Desert Storm and remains a key element of all arguments about the possible role of PB as a causative factor in Gulf War syndrome. This previous use of pyridostigmine bromide is discussed in a detailed report on PB compiled by the RAND Corporation, which was asked by the DOD to survey existing research on PB.[1] I am indebted to the author of this report, Beatrice Golomb, M.D., Ph.D., for her extremely helpful discussion, which I have drawn upon extensively in writing this chapter.[2]

One of the many issues that Dr. Golomb investigated in her review of the literature on pyridostigmine bromide was the use of PB to treat myasthenia gravis, a condition in which patients experience increasing weakness in their voluntary muscles. Dr. Golomb cogently notes, however, that although myasthenia gravis patients tolerate dosage levels of PB that are considerably higher than those given to our troops, PB moves these patients toward a normal state, while PB given to a healthy person will move that person away from a normal state. "One analogy is the difference between how insulin affects diabetics and those not suffering from the condition. A severe diabetic may tolerate or require 60 units of insulin or more each day to bring his or her blood sugar *toward* normal. Yet far smaller doses may induce hypoglycemic coma or even death in a nondiabetic subject" (RAND *PB*, 3:8).

There was a reason, however, why Coalition commanders turned to the toxic PB pills to protect their troops. To follow their logic, one must first understand how nerve agents work to wreak havoc in the bodies of humans and other animals and produce almost certain death if no antidote is available. They damage living organisms by interfering with some of the most basic parts of the nervous system, including the cholinergic system that enables nerve cells to send messages to muscle cells or other nerve cells.

A neurotransmitter called acetylcholine (ACh) is essential for the control of muscles, both voluntary and involuntary, and for glandular and brain function. A nerve cell uses acetylcholine to send a signal to a muscle cell to cause contraction or relaxation of the muscle. Normally, an enzyme called acetylcholinesterase (AChE) breaks down the ACh after it has served its purpose. Nerve agents act by binding to AChE and preventing it from breaking down ACh. The result is a buildup of ACh at the junction between the nerve cell and the cell to which it is sending a signal, and this buildup of ACh causes the receiving cells to become overstimulated and hyperactive. At these crucial junctions where messages are passed to other nerve cells or muscle cells that initiate a wide range of cellular activity, this excess ACh can lead to malfunction throughout the body.

As the RAND report notes, AChE inhibitors like nerve agents, organophosphate pesticides, or PB lead to an excess of ACh that first causes

---

[1] See <<http://www.rand.org/publications/MR/MR1018.2/mr1018.2>>. Section and page numbers are from the Internet version.

[2] Dr. Golomb is a physician who also has a Ph.D. in biology with a specialization in neurobiology. She is a staff physician at the San Diego VA Medical Center, an assistant professor of medicine at the University of California at San Diego, and a research associate professor in the University of Southern California's Psychology Department.

"hyperactivity of smooth and of skeletal muscles . . . and then paralysis (with high enough doses). . . . Early skeletal muscle symptoms include twitching and cramps." These reactions "coincide with axonal 'backfiring,' in which a signal travels up the 'axon,' the nerve process that relays signals, in the reverse direction to that by which signaling ordinarily occurs" (RAND *PB*, 3:2). These skeletal effects are associated with ACh receptors called "nicotinic receptors," which are found in skeletal muscle. What are known as "muscarinic receptors" are found in the smooth muscle of the internal organs. Muscarinic effects from a buildup of ACh may include gastrointestinal symptoms like cramping, nausea, diarrhea, and vomiting; excessive salivation; tearing of the eyes; runny nose; bronchospasm; frequent urination; and bladder or bowel incontinence. The RAND report also raises the question of whether the PB pills the soldiers took in the Gulf could have caused an ongoing dysregulation in their cholinergic systems.

Sfc. Roy Twymon, who has suffered from migraines, joint pains, rashes, lesions on his legs, and fatigue since the war, has described the devastating effect that incontinence problems have had upon his life:

> From the time we was given the PB pill, we was told to continue to take them. We kept on taking them, and we kept on taking them till after the war. And I started having diarrhea, my bowel was a different color. I had to run to the outdoor toilet sometimes because it was so severe.
>
> And this kept on happening, kept on happening, kept on happening while we was over there. Then when we got back, my soldiers started complaining, and they was sent to the hospital, sent to psych, told it was all in their head.
>
> I kept on dealing with it, and one day [after I got back] it really hurt me and struck me. I was coming from fishing with my son, and I wasn't even a block away from the Seven-Eleven in San Antonio, Texas, and I couldn't even make it to the Seven-Eleven, and I soiled on myself. I knew then there was something terrible wrong with me.
>
> Then as I went on with my bowel and bladder problem, I realized what was going on, and when I ran into some of the individuals that was in my unit, some of the guys, I would pull them aside and ask them if they was having some of the same problems. I said, "You can tell me if you want to, you know, but you don't have to tell me." And all of them that I spoke to said yes, they was having the same problems and some more problems. And I told them, I said, "Well, you need to get rid of your pride and go forward and tell people, go tell the doctor about what's going on because you and I is not the only one."
>
> They found nerve damage to my internal sphincter muscle. The sphincter muscle is the one that helps hold your bowel.
>
> So when you have to go to the bathroom or get the urge to go, you have to be whupped in the bathroom, or you'd best be running, or you

just go on yourself. I'm 44 years old now, and I know 44-year-old men
that haven't been to the Gulf War don't have this problem. So, you
know, it started when I came back, and I know it happened over there
because there's too many of us having the same problem. . . .
    I miss a lot of events with my kids, you know, their activities. . . .
My son plays college football. Could you imagine me going to a
college football game, eighty, ninety thousand people trying to get into
the same restroom with you? No, I'd soil on myself, so all of these
activities and things that my kids have been into since I've been back
and the things that I've missed, no one can give that back to me, no
one.

                        (GWS video footage)

As Sergeant Twymon's statement about other soldiers he served with
having similar incontinence problems indicates, incontinence among the Gulf
War veterans is probably much more widespread than is realized. Obviously,
people find it extremely embarrassing to admit that they have this problem.
Sgt. Bob Jones, a former paratrooper who served in an artillery unit in Desert
Storm, has admitted, however, that he shares this difficulty:

    Things just got to the point where I had diarrhea on myself at work a
    couple of times, and I said, enough is enough, I need to get help. It's
    real embarrassing to be standing around all your men and all of a
    sudden you can't even make it to the bathroom in time.

                        (GWS video footage)

    But despite all the problems that usage of PB may have caused, when the
alternative was the possibility of death or severe injury from nerve agents,
there were compelling reasons for the Pentagon to decide that PB was the
lesser of evils. The problem is not so much that the decision was made to
order our troops to take PB but that the DOD and VA do not seem to be
willing to admit that PB could be a large factor in the present debilitating
health problems that the Gulf veterans are experiencing and to take responsibility for their care or support in the cases of those who are unable to work.
    To understand more clearly why the decision facing the Pentagon was so
difficult, one must realize that military planners did not have the luxury of an
extended period of time in which to make a decision, perhaps even to conduct
some additional research on pyridostigmine bromide. Less than six months
after Saddam Hussein invaded Kuwait on August 2, 1990, Coalition forces
launched Desert Storm with the air attacks on January 17, 1991. By that time,
the decision had been made, for better or for worse, to order the troops to take
PB pills as soon as the air war started because it was feared that Iraq would
retaliate immediately with its terrifying chemical weapons.
    To counteract the effects of nerve agents, which by binding to AChE
prevent it from breaking down ACh, two standard anti-nerve agent treatments

are used. Atropine counteracts the muscarinic effects of nerve agents, and pralidoxime (2-PAM), if given in time, pulls off nerve agents that have bound to AChE. It thus enables the enzyme to carry out its normal function of breaking down the ACh after it has served its function at the synapses between the nerve cells and the cells being signaled. Soldiers fighting in the Gulf War carried automatic injectors containing atropine and pralidoxime that were to be used in the event of a chemical attack (RAND *PB*, 3:9).

While these two antidotes are fairly effective against the nerve agents that Iraq was known to have stockpiled—sarin and VX—they were of no value against soman. U.S. intelligence agents knew that Russia possessed soman, but they did not know if Iraq had obtained soman from Russia in order to have a chemical weapon against which traditional anti-nerve agent treatments would be powerless. As the RAND report notes, at the time of the Gulf War, the USSR had only recently broken up, and there was some fear that given the lack of governmental authority in Russia and the dire financial problems almost all Russian citizens were facing, even random individuals might try to make a lucrative sale of soman to Iraq.

The problem facing the Pentagon while the decision on PB was being considered in the fall of 1990 was that research on the use of PB to counteract the lethal effects of soman was sparse. Some tests had been done with rats, rabbits, guinea pigs, and rhesus monkeys, but for various reasons similar outcomes might or might not occur in human subjects. Although it was obviously impossible to give human subjects PB and then give them soman to see what happened, one study showed that pretreatment with PB before exposure to soman conferred significant protection in a group of rhesus monkeys.

Researcher Jim Moss, whose work will be discussed in the next chapter, has this to say about the DOD's reliance on animal studies in its decision to give PB pills to U.S. soldiers:

Another interesting thing about PB is the utter and complete hypocrisy expressed by the DOD regarding animal studies. PB was secured for use in the war based on only animal studies (and it did not perform very well at that). The result was that the DOD decided to risk the lives and health of over 250,000 U.S. soldiers based on limited animal studies.

Now, many years after the war, the DOD time after time discounts animal studies that look at the possible connections between PB and Gulf War illnesses, saying that such extrapolation between species is unreliable. So, animal data are OK to justify the use of an untested drug but not good enough to make connections between Gulf War illnesses and the same drug.[3]

---

[3] Jim Moss, personal communication to the author, January 2001.

The paucity of research studies on the use of PB was just one obstacle that DOD officials had to overcome in order to use PB in the Gulf War. While the FDA had approved pyridostigmine bromide for the treatment of myasthenia gravis and for use in a certain complication arising from anesthesia, it had not given its approval for the use of PB as a pretreatment to protect against nerve agents. After extensive negotiations with the DOD, the FDA finally gave its permission for PB to be used as what is called an investigational new drug, or IND. Moreover, the FDA in this case waived the usual IND requirement that the drug be administered under a policy of informed consent. The FDA, however, did accompany its waiver by a requirement that information about the way PB works and its potential side effects was to be given to the soldiers instructed to take the drug. Unfortunately, the Pentagon failed to make such information available to the troops in any widespread way.

FDA officials agreed to the waiver of informed consent because they were well aware of the potential danger posed by possible Iraqi use of soman. Soman is more difficult to defend against than sarin and other nerve agents because the window during which antidotes must be given is extremely tight. The term "aging" is used to describe the process by which the AChE to which a nerve agent has attached itself undergoes a chemical change that permanently inactivates the AChE. Unfortunately, aging occurs very rapidly in the case of soman. Within two minutes of exposure to this deadly nerve gas, half of the AChE will have been permanently inactivated so that pralidoxime or other oximes can no longer pull off the attached soman and free the enzyme to perform its essential task of breaking down ACh that is no longer required to serve as a neurotransmitter. In the case of other nerve agents like sarin and VX, however, there is a period of several hours during which treatment with atropine and pralidoxime will be effective.

PB was seen as a potential defense against soman because although soman binds irreversibly to AChE within two minutes of exposure, PB binds to AChE temporarily. It eventually separates, freeing up the AChE to return to its normal function of eliminating ACh that has already served its purpose. Thus PB can be viewed as a "reversible poison" that keeps soman from carrying out its irreversible incapacitation of AChE. The trick was to give just the right amount of PB. Enough had to be given so that once the PB left the AChE to which it had bound, the amount of AChE freed from the PB would suffice to prevent serious physiological damage. On the other hand, if soldiers took too much PB, so much of their AChE would be tied up that they would be unable to function on the battlefield. Too high a level of PB could be lethal. British research had suggested that the goal should be to inhibit 20 to 40 percent of the AChE (RAND *PB*, 3:8). To achieve this level of inhibition, U.S. troops were ordered to take 30 mg of PB every eight hours.

The problem is that giving each soldier the same dose in no way guarantees similar outcomes. In her testimony before the subcommittees on Health and Oversight and Investigations of the Veterans' Affairs Committee of the

PB Pills 61

U.S. House of Representatives on November 16, 1999, Dr. Golomb spoke to this issue:

Regarding theories of possible heightened susceptibility to PB, one theory proposes that there may be widespread individual differences in processing of PB. Indeed, our review found evidence of differences at many levels. First, the desired dose of PB was not taken by all the veterans in the approved manner; some took more and many took less. However, even supposing the same oral dose of PB, there are 7-fold differences in the resulting steady-state blood level of PB in humans. Moreover, for the same blood level of PB, there are many-fold differences in the percent of enzyme inhibition induced by PB; thus depending when after PB administration one looks, there may be up to 15 to 25 fold differences in enzyme inhibition for the same oral dose. Finally, for the same measured enzyme inhibition, there are widespread differences in clinical effects, including toxic effects of PB. These widespread differences in processing of PB from one individual to another could potentially lead to substantial differences in susceptibility to effects of PB, including chronic effects if any occur.

The second theory notes that whereas ordinarily most PB is excluded from entering the brain by what is termed the "blood brain barrier," which bars access of many substances, some of the recent evidence from animal studies suggests that quite a bit of PB may access the brain under some conditions, such as stress, heat, and chemical combinations. These are conditions to which some PGW [Persian Gulf War] veterans may have been exposed, thus increasing the chance for brain effects of PB to occur. In addition, there is literature that indicates PB itself may enhance access to the brain of normally excluded substances, such as infectious viruses.

[The] third theory notes that toxic effects of PB may be greatly enhanced, in some cases in a synergistic fashion, by concomitant exposure to other factors like pesticides and nerve agent, to which some veterans may have been exposed. These three theories, which describe mechanisms by which some individuals may have increased susceptibility to effects of PB—due to differences in processing, differences in environmental exposures, or combinations of these— were all found to be viable (i.e., had enough supporting evidence that they could not be rejected).

In her testimony, Dr. Golomb also discussed possible ways that PB could lead to long-term health problems:

The most important theory regarding mechanisms by which PB may lead to chronic illness—perhaps selectively in those with heightened susceptibility—suggests that PB may change regulation of a key nerve signaling chemical called "acetylcholine" (ACh). ACh is known to be vitally involved in regulating muscle action, pain, mood, memory, and sleep, domains that figure prominently in complaints of ill PGW veterans.

PB acts by blocking the enzyme that normally breaks down excess ACh. The consequence is increased, unregulated action by this nerve-signaling chemical. The body responds to this inappropriate increase in ACh action by putting into place mechanisms to suppress the excess ACh activity. Thus, signaling cells may reduce production and release of ACh and may withdraw nerve terminals from receiving cells. Receiving cells may reduce the number of receptors to which ACh may bind and reduce the affinity of these receptors for binding to the signaling chemical. And there may be increased breakdown of ACh.

Since these mechanisms designed to suppress ACh action occur in response to the excess ACh action induced by PB, one might expect that they would go away as PB is withdrawn. But in fact, existing evidence from studies in animals suggests that the timecourses of these effects differ widely from one another. Some are short lived and are unlikely to explain chronic illness in PGW veterans. However, other effects are long lasting or permanent, lasting in some instances as long after stopping PB as anyone has looked.

Could such long lasting or permanent changes in regulation of ACh action relate to chronic symptoms reported by PGW veterans? The answer is, we don't know; much more needs to be understood about the specifics of these changes and what their relation may be to clinical effects. However, we do know that ACh is critical to regulation of muscle action, pain, memory, and sleep—domains that are disrupted in ill PGW veterans; thus it is plausible that chronic changes in regulation of ACh could produce symptoms of the types veterans report.

. . .

The issue now is the very complex one of trading off uncertain health risks—but risks now known to be biologically plausible—against uncertain gains from use of PB in the warfare setting.

More information about the risks involved in PB use has recently become available in a study published by L. Li et al. In this study, which was supported by a contract from the U.S. Army, the researchers investigated the phenomenon of apoptosis, or programmed cell death, in the brains of rats given PB at dosage levels ranging from 0.5 to 1.85 mg/kg twice daily for four days. The lower level would be less than the dosage level the Gulf War veterans received, and the upper level for the rats would be less that 50 percent higher than the level the Gulf War veterans took. To study the neurotoxicity of PB, the researchers gave the rats PB for a period of four days, sacrificed them at various intervals up to thirty days, and examined their brain tissue. Apoptotic brain cell death occurred in the cerebral cortex across the entire dosage range, and at the higher level of 1.85 mg/kg, brain cell death was also noted in the striatum and hippocampus. The researchers also found that rat brain cells exposed to PB in a culture underwent apoptosis. Their results showed that treatment of the rats with PB for only four days produced a "prolonged apopotic response, which was evident in rat cortex up to 30 days after the last dose. Active apoptosis persisted, despite recovery of serum ChE [AChE] activity. These in vivo and in vitro observations indicate that pyrido-stigmine can initiate a prolonged neurodegeneration."[4]

It is particularly gratifying to see that the U.S. Army is awarding some contracts to researchers who are investigating the various toxic exposures our troops faced in the Gulf War instead of simply supporting more and more studies designed to blame Gulf War syndrome upon stress.

---

[4] L. Li et al., "Muscarinic Receptor-Mediated Pyridostigmine-Induced Neuronal Apoptosis," *Neurotoxicology* 21, no. 4 (August 2000): 541-52.

Chapter 6

Pesticides, Diesel Fuel, and CARC Paint

Pesticide Use in Desert Storm

The warm climate of the Arabian desert is hospitable to insects, so Coalition forces had to defend themselves not only against enemy soldiers but against disease-carrying insects. Malaria was a distinct possibility because of the presence of mosquitoes that might be carrying this disease. Sand flies were not only bothersome for soldiers trying to fall asleep at night, they could also transmit sand fly fever or a serious parasitic disease called leishmaniasis. These circumstances prompted widespread pesticide use during Desert Storm.

Major Doug Rokke, Ph.D., was an officer in a U.S. Army NBC (nuclear/biological/chemical) unit during the Gulf War and witnessed the misuse of pesticides:

Although the pesticides were ordered through the U.S. Army supply chain, the majority of the pesticides that were required did not arrive in theater. Consequently, a whole group of individuals just went out and bought pesticides on the open market throughout Saudi Arabia, Kuwait, and Bahrain. What those pesticides were, nobody knows because you just went out and bought pesticides in a bag, and after all, who knew what language was marked on it. The problem is, nobody knew what the exact chemical structure was, nobody knew what the concentration was, nobody knew what the safety was, and then they just started spraying pesticides all over the place. [Some of] the pesticides that could have been purchased and used would have been totally illegal for use in our country.

(GWS video footage)

Gulf War veterans have given these accounts of their exposure to pesticides during Desert Storm:

On a nightly basis, we would spray our uniforms with pesticides. There was a chemical spray that they gave us to spray our uniforms. We had to hang them outside so that the excess spray would dissipate in the air. We weren't supposed to put them on immediately after spraying them.

The sand fleas were a problem. We used to put flea collars around the legs of our cots, or we would put flea powder on the floor around our cots to try to keep the sand fleas away from us while we were sleeping. We slept with nets over us to keep the flies off. The flies were ungodly. It wouldn't be nothing to go up to the mess hall and see a pile of flies where they had put some food out [as a bait] and let the flies land on it and then sprayed them to kill them. They would be like an inch thick, a pile of flies sitting on the ground outside the mess hall as you're going into the mess hall.
S.Sgt. Tim Smith (GWS video footage)

One of my jobs as a medic was to pass out malaria pills to the troops in our unit every day. There were lots of mosquitoes around, so malaria was a real threat. As a result, we used a lot of DEET. We had two kinds of government issue—a cream to put on our skin and spray containing what you might call industrial strength DEET. We weren't supposed to spray the stronger version in confined spaces, but lots of soldiers used it when they ran out of the cream, which was pretty often. They would spray it on their skin and uniforms while they were inside the tent. Some troops even wore flea collars around their wrists and ankles.
Sfc. Terry Dillhyon (GWS video footage)

Pesticide was sprayed around the periphery of each tent, and later on we used spray cans of pesticide inside our tents to keep away scorpions, sand vipers, fleas, sand ticks, and flies.
S.Sgt. Pat Browning (Part II, 159)

The high level of pesticide use in the Gulf War, as well as the use of some pesticides that are illegal in the United States, was a significant exposure that could have produced Gulf War syndrome in some soldiers. Many civilians have reported developing multiple chemical sensitivity, with symptoms that closely parallel Gulf War syndrome, through exposure to pesticides that were sprayed in their home, apartment building, or workplace. In the RAND report titled *Pesticides,* which was commissioned by the DOD and released on January 12, 2001, the authors summarize their view of the issue in this way:

Evidence of the biological plausibility of AChE inhibitors as a potential cause of symptoms similar to those reported by ill PGWV [Persian Gulf War veterans] suggests that these compounds could be among the potential contributing agents to some of the undiagnosed illnesses seen in PGWV.

. . . .

Given the evidence to date and the literature reviewed, it is inappropriate to rely upon exposure to pesticides . . . as the explanation for the myriad health problems reported by PGWV. However, we think it equally inappropriate at this point to completely rule out pesticides as a potential contributing factor.

(RAND *Pesticides*, 9:5)

Pesticide use may have carried an extra risk in the Gulf War because large numbers of soldiers were exposed not only to pesticides but also to the insect repellent DEET and PB pills. Researcher Mohamed Abou-Donia, Ph.D., a professor of pharmacology at Duke University Medical School, has performed several studies on the effects of exposure to a combination of chemicals.

In a study published in 1996 in the *Journal of Toxicology and Environmental Health*, a research group led by Abou-Donia investigated the effect on hens of a combination of the insect repellent DEET, the insecticide permethrin, and pyridostigmine bromide (PB).[1] The researchers hypothesize that normal detoxification mechanisms involving liver and plasma enzymes are overwhelmed by the concurrent administration of these compounds, allowing excessive amounts to reach the nervous system.

Hens were chosen for this research because their nervous system is particularly vulnerable to toxins. In the research study, one group of hens was given DEET, another group was given permethrin, and a third group was given PB. These chemicals were given to the chickens at a dosage level that would be approximately equivalent to three times the level that would have been experienced by soldiers in the Gulf.

The chickens in each group showed no signs of neurological damage when these chemicals were given separately. But when researchers gave hens a combination of any two of these three chemicals, the neurotoxic effects were clear. The hens had trouble flying, they stumbled when they walked, and some had tremors. The results were even more startling in a group of five hens that were exposed to all three chemicals concurrently: "Concurrent treatment with PB, DEET, and permethrin caused severe diarrhea, shallow rapid breathing, and moderate inactivity within 15 min of dosing starting on the first day. All animals developed a gait disturbance, and in one this progressed to paralysis. . . . All animals exhibited body tremors 22-34 d[ays] after dosing. Two animals exhibited convulsions after 22 and 34 d[ays] into the study."[2] Four of the five hens died during the experiment. Thus it was clear that there was an important synergism among these chemicals.

---

[1] Mohamed B. Abou-Donia et al., "Neurotoxicity Resulting from Coexposure to Pyridostigmine Bromide, DEET, and Permethrin: Implications of Gulf War Chemical Exposures," *Journal of Toxicology and Environmental Health* 48 (1996): 35-56.

[2] Ibid., 46.

The researchers ended their article by noting the need for further studies using dosage levels of the three chemicals that would be approximately comparable to the levels encountered by the soldiers. In June 2000, Abou-Donia announced at a conference sponsored by the DOD the results of just such a study that the DOD had funded. He described these results when we interviewed him for our video:

We hypothesized from the first studies that combined chemical exposure results in increased toxicity resulting in neurological deficits. We hypothesized that the mechanism is that combined chemical exposure impedes the body's ability to detoxify itself of these chemicals. . . .

What we demonstrated is that when giving rats the most realistic dose level that the veterans were given during the Gulf War or were exposed to during the war, we found that the animals did not look much different from the controls. Maybe they lost a little bit of weight, maybe ten percent more loss of weight, which actually made them look a little more active; they looked very normal. However, when we challenged these animals to do certain tasks, we found that there was deficiency in their behavior. There was muscle weakness, they were slower, they had problems performing the various tasks.

To find out the reason behind that, we looked at the nervous system. We found that the combined chemical exposure resulted in the breakdown of the blood brain barrier. The blood brain barrier is a mechanism by which the brain is protected from chemicals or foreign objects that are present in the bloodstream going to the brain. *We found that in combined chemical exposure, there were actually breaches of the blood brain barrier and leaks that could have resulted in the penetration of chemicals or pathogens like bacteria or viruses to the brain and also could have resulted in essential chemicals leaking from the brain to the bloodstream* [italics added].

We looked also at the pathology of the brain. We looked under the microscope at the various components of the brain and found actually there was a breakdown of many cells in the brain, including cells called microglia, which are cells of the nervous system that support the neurons. The results definitely explain the neurological deficits and the behavioral deficiency that we saw in animals that seemingly looked normal.

The results also may parallel this condition of the veterans that came from the Gulf War. They looked normal. Most of their complaints were subjective; they could not be confirmed. The only way to confirm that was actually to look into the brain, specifically under the microscope, which obviously we couldn't do with humans, but we could do it in animals. So our results show that combined chemical

exposures definitely result in increased neurological deficits and cause problems that are related to the brain.
(GWS video footage)

Researchers have in general assumed that pyridostigmine bromide does not cross the blood brain barrier to any significant extent because of its positively charged quaternary ammonium group. Hence it was thought that PB given to soldiers might affect the peripheral nervous system but would spare the brain. As Dr. Golomb notes in the RAND report on PB, however, a number of studies on the use of PB referenced in military reports going back to at least 1981 indicated that this "blood brain barrier impermeability was not absolute" (RAND *PB*, 7:1). In December 1996, researchers in Israel published the results of an experiment showing that the blood brain barrier does in fact become more permeable to PB in the presence of stress. A team led by Alon Friedman, a biochemist at Hebrew University in Jerusalem, showed that when mice were given PB and then subjected to a forced swim, a procedure that induces stress in the mice, "an increase in blood-brain barrier permeability reduced the pyridostigmine dose required to inhibit mouse brain AChE [acetylcholinesterase] activity by 50% to less than 1/100th of the usual dose."[3]

In his latest study of the effects of combined chemical exposure on rodents, Abou-Donia decided to add the element of stress to the study. Hence he used (1) a control group of mice who were exposed to neither the chemicals nor stress, (2) a group of mice subjected to stress alone, (3) a group of mice exposed only to the combination of DEET, permethrin, and PB, and (4) a group of mice exposed to both the chemical combination and stress. The stress consisted of placing the mice for five minutes in plastic tubes that did not hurt them but made them feel uncomfortable. According to Abou-Donia, the group of mice exposed to stress alone looked a "little bit worse than controls," and those exposed to the chemical combination alone looked worse than those exposed to stress alone. As the researchers had suspected, "we found in every case that the severest changes in the brain were seen in the animals that were exposed to both chemicals as well as stress. Chemicals and stress were really bad, so our conclusion was that not only chemical exposures produced the problems, but obviously stress was a factor" (GWS video footage).

Abou-Donia's research is highly relevant to the issue of Gulf War syndrome because the penetration of toxic chemicals to the brain would mean that the crucial functions throughout the body that are controlled by the brain and the central nervous system would be in jeopardy. Sfc. Sherrie McGahee,

---

[3] Alon Friedman et al., "Pyridostigmine Brain Penetration Under Stress Enhances Neuronal Excitability and Induces Early Immediate Transcriptional Response," *Nature Medicine* 2, no. 12 (December 1996):1382-85.

whose case was discussed in the Introduction, would appear to have brain damage that affects her ability to talk and to walk.

The use of the term "Gulf War syndrome" for the varied health problems afflicting the Gulf veterans makes sense to Abou-Donia. Referring to the various chemicals to which so many Gulf veterans were exposed, he has stated:

This cocktail of chemicals seems to impede the body's ability to detoxify and neutralize these chemicals. When we think about Gulf War syndrome, what do we really mean by syndrome? Syndrome means that we have people with many signs and symptoms that do not fit a single disease or a single illness, so they are called a syndrome. And it makes sense that it is called a syndrome because the veterans were not exposed to one ... mixture of chemicals. They were exposed to many chemicals. Not everyone was exposed to the same cocktail; there were several cocktails. That's why we have several different symptoms. However, we should keep in mind that most of the symptoms ... are related to the central nervous system and problems with the nervous system. The other fact that also would contribute to the multiple symptoms and the variety of symptoms is the fact that individuals differed genetically and in every aspect. There are people who have genetically low enzymatic activity of the enzyme that normally protects the body against chemical exposure. Those people would be at most risk following exposure to a mixture of chemicals.

When we talk about the Gulf War syndrome, which resulted from exposures to a cocktail of chemicals, it is very similar to what we have known for many years as multiple chemical sensitivity.

(GWS video footage)

Abou-Donia sees the controversy surrounding Gulf War syndrome as part of a larger problem—a widespread failure to recognize or emphasize the potential for chemical exposures to cause disease, a failure that he sees even in the medical community:

One of the problems we have, [one] that most medical schools are guilty of, is that we don't really teach enough toxicology. At Duke University [Medical School], our students stay here for four years, and they get only two hours in four years of toxicology, and that really is one of the problems. We don't teach our physicians that chemicals can cause diseases. When I teach my two hours in four years, I use as the first and last slide a slide saying "Chemicals can cause diseases." ... I want ... these medical students ... to always keep in mind that exposure to chemicals can lead to diseases that are very similar to what we know of nervous system diseases. One of the problems that we are facing today is that we are exposed to many chemicals. Some

of them are good, some are bad, but the major problem is the combination, the cocktail of chemicals. Many chemicals that we're exposed to
are harmless when they are used as a single component, but when we
use them together, that's when we have a problem.

(GWS video footage)

A Florida researcher by the name of Jim Moss preceded Abou-Donia in
studying the effect of a combination of pyridostigmine bromide and DEET,
and his pioneering research and activities as a whistle-blower cost him his
job. Dr. Moss is a Ph.D. entomologist who was hired as a research associate
for the U.S. Department of Agriculture (USDA) in Gainesville, Florida, in
1990. His job was to study insecticides and learn how to make them more
effective. In January 1993, Moss was investigating how boric acid kills
insects, and when he happened to mix boric acid with an organophosphate
pesticide, he found that the two had a synergistic effect. Then in November
1993, he found that when he combined the insect repellent DEET with an
organophosphate pesticide, there was also a synergistic effect. Having heard
press reports about ill Gulf War veterans who thought they might have been
exposed to organophosphate nerve agents, Moss decided to notify the DOD,
USDA, and a company that produced a DEET repellent about his research.

Dr. Moss also heard that troops in Desert Storm had been given PB pills,
which themselves have an anticholinergic action similar to that of nerve
agents. This knowledge led him to begin research looking for synergism in
combinations of PB, DEET, the insecticide permethrin (which was widely
used in the Gulf), and the organochlorine compounds lindane and DDT. His
studies demonstrated, as the research of Abou-Donia would show a few years
later, that there was indeed a dangerous synergism among these toxic
chemicals. That work was the beginning of the end of Dr. Moss's career, as
an article in the *St. Petersburg Times* on January 11, 1997, reports:

In 1993, when Moss first suspected DEET might be a factor in Gulf
War ailments, a top USDA official called Gainesville to stop him from
spreading his suspicions outside the lab, records show. The lab
director told Moss to cease his "unauthorized" DEET research and
warned that his career was at stake.

According to this article, the lab director pointed out to Moss that DEET
was sold around the world and "studies on its potential toxicity would
obviously be of a sensitive nature" and would not be welcomed by either the
DOD or the major corporation that markets a DEET repellent.

Moss believed in the integrity of his research, however, and he believed
that it was important to try to understand what was causing the health
problems of sick Gulf War veterans. Hence he agreed to testify on May 6,
1994, before the Senate Veterans' Affairs Committee, chaired at that time by
Senator Jay Rockefeller.

Blowing the whistle comes at a high price when your opponents are the DOD, the USDA, and a major corporation. When his contract at the Gainesville research center ran out, it was not renewed, even though Dr. Moss had worked there for four years. He has not been able to find a job in his field of entomological research. A major source of job opportunities for an insect specialist would normally be government agencies. They would hardly be likely, however, to hire a researcher who has incurred the wrath of the USDA and raised questions about the safety of the DEET that the DOD distributed to our troops in the Persian Gulf, some of it in an extremely concentrated form. Another major source of job possibilities would be with corporations who market pesticides, but they are obviously eager to show that their pesticides are safe. They would be unlikely to hire an entomologist who places the common good above the financial interests of his employer.

Jim Moss may have lost his career, but there is an occasional reward for the courageous whistle-blower. On September 13, 1998, he was awarded the Florida Distinguished Service Medal by the Governor of the State of Florida for Meritorious Service to Florida National Guard Persian Gulf War veterans. The press release from Colonel Bruce Pettyjohn, M.D., of the Florida Army National Guard Medical Corps, contained these passages:

[James Moss] originated some of the concepts linking pyridostigmine bromide . . . to a mixture of other chemicals also used during the war, which together may be one of the causes of the often debilitating Gulf War syndrome.

At great personal sacrifice (it cost him his job with the Department of Agriculture), Dr. Moss persisted in his research efforts, communicating with the Presidential Commission on Gulf War Illness as well as testifying before the Senate Veterans' Affairs Committee.

For many years, Dr. Moss has been assisting . . . in preparing affected National Guard soldiers for medical reviews for consideration of their illnesses as service connected.

In 1997, Moss was a coauthor of two papers related to the synergistic effects between PB and adrenaline or caffeine.[4] This is an important contribution because during Desert Storm there would have been no shortage of either adrenaline or caffeine.

---

[4] Leslie Chaney et al., "Toxic Interactions Between Pyridostigmine Bromide (PB), N,N-Diethyl-m-toluamide (DEET), Adrenergic Agents and Caffeine," *Toxicologist* 36, no. 1 (March 1997):21; and "Potentiation of Pyridostigmine Bromide Toxicity in Mice by Selected Adrenergic Agents and Caffeine," *Veterinary and Human Toxicology* 39, no. 9 (August 1997): 214-19.

Diesel Fuel Use

Varied uses of diesel fuel in the Persian Gulf theater provided another set of toxic exposures in the Gulf War. Trucks driving through the tent compounds would stir up the omnipresent sand, and the whirlwinds caused by helicopters as they took off and landed on the desert floor were a very troublesome problem that jeopardized the motors of expensive aircraft. Hence military planners decided to lay down diesel fuel in major traffic areas as a sand suppressant.

> On many occasions there would be trucks that would lay diesel down where we slept, where we ate, and where we played. We walked on it all the time. The reason they were pouring diesel fuel on the ground was to keep the sand from blowing. Looking back on it now, I wonder why they would expose us to all this fuel when they must have known it would be bad for our health.
>   Sp4c. Bobby Lawson (GWS video footage)

The use of diesel fuel as a sand suppressant was not the only major diesel exposure for the troops, however. At night, temperatures in the desert drop rapidly, so kerosene heaters were used in the tents. Diesel fuel, which is closely related to kerosene, was burned in most of these heaters, and reports from veterans suggest they were not adequately ventilated:

> There were six men to a tent, and each tent had a kerosene heater in it. You would put it in the middle, and in the morning you would get up and light it and everyone would lie there until the tent got hot. But after a while, your eyes would start burning; there was an odor in the air constantly when you used that stuff.
>   S.Sgt. Tim Smith (GWS video footage)

> We also heated our tents in Tent City with pot belly stoves. The smell was awful and made us sick.
>   Sp4c. Bobby Lawson (GWS video footage)

Another exposure to diesel fuel occurred because in many instances trucks were used to transport diesel fuel on some occasions and water on others without being adequately cleaned:

> The water we bathed in and washed our clothes in was oily, so after a shower we would have an oily film on our skin that smelled like diesel fuel. We later realized that the same trucks were often used to carry water and diesel fuel.
>   S.Sgt. Pat Browning (Part II, 159)

CARC Paint

The use of CARC (chemical agent resistant coating) paint for vehicles and other machinery is another toxic exposure that has been suggested as a possible cause of Gulf War syndrome. As part of the Desert Storm operation, thousands of vehicles were sent to Saudi Arabia. Most of them arrived in theater painted with a three-color pattern known as "woodland camouflage" that was inappropriate for action in the desert. All these vehicles as well as other machinery such as generators had to be repainted immediately with a desert camouflage pattern. The paint used during this hasty operation was CARC, a special polyurethane paint that will not absorb nerve agents during a chemical attack. Thus tanks or trucks could be decontaminated after a nerve-agent attack by washing them off with an appropriate decontamination fluid.

The DOD report on CARC paint that is available on the DOD website <<http://www.gulflink.osd.mil>> explains some of the hazards associated with this paint:

> Several compounds in CARC formulations, if taken into the body in sufficiently high concentrations, may cause short- and long-term health effects. The most notable of these compounds is hexamethylene diisocyanate (HDI). . . . Exposure to high concentrations of aerosolized HDI during spray painting leads to immediate respiratory irritation and watery eyes. Long-term exposure can cause or aggravate respiratory problems, in particular, asthma. The use of personal protective equipment, such as respirators, coveralls, eye protection, gloves, and head coverings, can prevent or minimize exposures to HDI.
>
> (DOD *CARC,* 1:1)

In December 1990, military planners set up two large CARC spray-painting operations near the Saudi ports of Ad Dammam and Al Jubayl that were staffed by members of the 325th Maintenance Company of the Florida Army National Guard. The soldiers in this unit had no experience in spray painting, and they did not have proper protective equipment. Nevertheless, by February of 1991, they had painted over 8,500 vehicles and other equipment.

Painting operations took place in large tents that were shaped like Quonset huts. The tent flaps at each end were usually kept open, but when the wind was high, the flaps would be closed, adding to the buildup of paint mist inside the tent. There were no fans or blowers available. According to the DOD report, "There was typically a noticeable cloud of paint overspray outside the maintenance tents" (DOD *CARC,* 4:3). When members of the Guard unit soon began to report health problems, inspectors arrived on the scene. They recommended many changes in the training given the soldiers and said that protective equipment like air-supplied respirators and the necessary air hoses and air compressors to support these respirators should be in use. Unfortunately, much of this safety equipment did not arrive in time to help the painters. The available air compressors often broke down, and even when they were functioning, the DOD report notes: "Due to a shortage of air hoses, the air compressors (which carry the air from a source to the painter's respirator) were placed in close proximity to the paint tents. As a result, air contaminated with some amount of overspray could have been pumped into the respirators" (DOD *CARC*, 4:4). The report refers to the "persistent problem of unsafe working conditions" and states in its discussion of the health concerns:

> While it is well known that the isocyanates found in polyurethane paints pose the most significant health risks, solvents in the paints, thinners, and cleaning products are also known to pose a secondary health risk, if absorbed in sufficient quantity. . . . Inhalation of airborne droplets containing HDI released during spray paint applications is a well-documented hazard. Direct skin contact to wet CARC is another avenue of exposure that causes irritation of the skin and mucus membranes, and possible absorption of solvents.
>   (DOD *CARC*, 3:1-2)

The symptoms that the soldiers in this company reported while they were working with the paint included not only respiratory problems but also headaches, nausea, vomiting, and dizziness. Unfortunately, the soldiers assigned to the painting station near Al Jubayl slept in tents that were located only 50-200 yards from the tents in which the CARC paint was sprayed. Since the site was located in a depression, a haze of paint often hung over the camp.

The exposures to CARC were thus inescapable for the soldiers of the 325th, who worked in paint spray during the day and often slept in a haze of paint at night. One particularly relevant comment occurs in the DOD report: "Once a person is sensitized to isocyanates, an exposure to levels as low as the parts-per-billion range can cause the onset of episodes of wheezing, shortness of breath, chest tightness, and coughing. Sensitized persons may suffer progressive worsening of respiratory symptoms with recurrent exposures" (DOD *CARC*, 3:2).

Sfc. Terry Dillhyon's unit used CARC paint to paint their vehicles and equipment just before they deployed to the Gulf. He came back from the war with severe asthma, demyelination of his nerves, and many other health problems. He is now highly sensitive to a wide variety of chemicals, and those associated with painting operations in particular are a great problem for him:

> While I was in the hospital [he spent six weeks in a VA hospital for evaluation], they were taking me to have an MRI, and they were

rolling me down the hallway and they went by a room where the floor was being stripped and they were using a paint stripper. I actually went unconscious, and they had to take me to the emergency room and give me oxygen and everything, just over a floor stripper.

(GWS video footage)

So many members of the 325th Maintenance Company were having health problems after the war that they contacted their U.S. representative, Charles Canady, who helped them get attention from the DOD and the VA. The latter eventually sent representatives to Florida to evaluate the situation. By October 1999, a total of 163 soldiers from this one company had registered with either the DOD (active duty) or VA (retired) with regard to their health problems. Since only 200 members of the unit were involved in the painting operations, this is a very high percentage of ill veterans. Seventy of the 200 have respiratory problems; 10 now have asthma.

A few members of the 325th Company have received disability compensation, but Sergeant Dillhyon has not been so lucky. He has been sending off applications for disability and medical care for eight long years, waiting for help that never comes. The VA has, however, provided him with a motorized scooter-chair and a lift to put it into the back of his pickup truck. When we filmed him for our video, he demonstrated this equipment for us and said proudly, "This is freedom." And he didn't seem to notice the irony of his statement.

Chapter 7

Robert Haley's Research Team

For years the Department of Defense and the Department of Veterans Affairs argued that Gulf War syndrome either didn't exist or if there were sick veterans, their illnesses were simply related to stress. This attitude meant that these departments concentrated their research efforts on studies tied to the stress theory. One of the two clinical trials now being carried out by the DOD and the VA is a study of the effects of exercise and counseling in a group of ill Gulf War veterans. For this study, the DOD and VA are spending $4 million on exercise equipment and $8 million on psychiatrists, psychologists, and other counselors. Only someone who has not heard the stories of sick veterans would think that their desperate situations could be fixed by exercise and counseling. Exercise and counseling won't keep veterans' teeth from rotting and falling out, it won't reverse demyelination of nerves, and it won't cure sleep apnea or chronic diarrhea or the host of other health problems that the veterans are experiencing.

Fortunately for the 100,000 veterans suffering from Gulf War syndrome, Ross Perot has been passionately interested in their plight and has been infuriated by the bureaucrats who have shown so little real interest in getting to the bottom of the problem. Perot had watched as the DOD and VA took almost twenty years to acknowledge that exposure to Agent Orange in the Vietnam War had ruined the health of large numbers of Vietnam veterans. He was determined to do what he could to prevent history from repeating itself, so he provided a crucial $2 million to a research team at the University of Texas Southwestern Medical Center at Dallas headed by Robert Haley, M.D. Other members of this team who worked on the initial research or later studies include Thomas L. Kurt, W. Wesley Marshall, George G. McDonald, M.A. Daugherty, Frederick Petty, and Gerald L. Kramer. This initial Perot grant also supported Abou-Donia's research into the effects of combined chemicals on chickens, the results of which were important for Haley's team.

Dr. Haley and his colleagues started their research by conducting a survey of a group of veterans who had been part of the Twenty-fourth Reserve Naval Mobile Construction Battalion. (Members of these battalions are called "Seabees.") It is worth noting that it was primarily members of this battalion whose testimony about possible SCUD attacks is quoted in Chapter 2; stories from two of these men appear in Part II. A total of 249 veterans were assembled in five cities for supervised surveys. Participants included sick and well veterans and active duty and retired veterans. The survey results yielded two articles that were published in the January 15, 1997, issue of the *Journal of the American Medical Association* (*JAMA*). In "Is There a Gulf War Syndrome?" the Haley team described the results of factor analysis performed on the information obtained through the survey. They concluded that the broad range of symptoms that this group of veterans reported could be grouped into three syndromes, to which they gave descriptive terms. Syndrome 1 was called "impaired cognition," syndrome 2 was called "confusion-ataxia," and syndrome 3 was called "arthro-myo-neuropathy." (Ataxia is a lack of ability to coordinate muscle movements that is associated with some nervous disorders.) The terms used to describe syndrome 3 refer to pain in the joints and muscles; in later articles, Haley simply calls syndrome 3 "central pain." The similarity of the terms "impaired cognition" and "confusion" warrants a comment. In a later article, the Haley team states that veterans suffering from syndrome 2 have the most severe cognitive symptoms. A January 8, 1997, press release from the team gives further information about these syndromes:

> The UT Southwestern researchers identified a [first] syndrome characterized by thought, memory and sleep difficulties; a second syndrome that involves more severe thought problems as well as confusion and imbalance; and a third syndrome of sore joints and muscles and tingling or numbness in the hands and feet.

The same issue of *JAMA* contained another article from Drs. Robert Haley and Thomas Kurt based on the same survey. This article was titled "Self-reported Exposure to Neurotoxic Chemical Combinations in the Gulf War." Haley and Kurt asked the Seabees about their exposures during Desert Storm to six kinds of cholinesterase-inhibitors and also queried them about other exposures that have been suggested as possible causes of Gulf War syndrome. The cholinesterase-inhibitors were chemical warfare agents, environmental pesticides, pesticides in uniforms, pesticides in flea collars, DEET (*N,N*-diethyl-*m*-toluamide), and pyridostigmine bromide (PB). The other exposures surveyed were ciprofloxacin, chloroquine, multiple immunizations, smoke from oil well fires, fumes from jet fuel in the environment, fumes from burning jet fuel in tents, petroleum in drinking water, depleted uranium in munitions, CARC (chemical agent resistant coating) paint on vehicles, combat stress, smoking, and alcohol or cocaine use.

In the group surveyed, 236, or 95 percent, reported that they had taken PB pills during the war. Veterans were asked whether they had worn a flea collar during the war, even though these collars are not intended for human use and were not recommended by the military. The Haley team found that syndrome 1 (impaired cognition) was eight times more common among the veterans who said they had worn these pet flea collars to repel insects during Desert

Storm. The researchers also found that syndrome 1 was six times more common in a group of veterans who had worked in security. The authors speculate that security personnel may have been at increased risk because they were often on guard outside the tents or buildings where others slept and thus had a greater exposure to pesticide fogging that occurred at night.

Syndrome 2 (confusion-ataxia) was found to be eight times more common among veterans who thought they had been exposed to a chemical weapons attack, and it was four times more common in veterans who were located in an area in northeastern Saudi Arabia that was very close to the Kuwaiti border on January 20, 1991, a few days into the air war. This is the date of several of the possible SCUD missile explosions that are described in Chapter 2. The prevalence of this syndrome also "increase[d] with the scale of advanced adverse effects from pyridostigmine."

Syndrome 3 (arthro-myo-neuropathy or central pain) showed a prevalence that "increased with the index of the amount of insect repellent veterans typically applied to the skin . . . and with the scale of advanced adverse effects from pyridostigmine." Soldiers used two different concentrations of DEET during Desert Storm. Although most were given standard formulations containing 33 percent DEET, some troops were given a very strong military repellent that contained 75 percent DEET. Haley and Kurt note that New York State banned insect repellents containing DEET in a concentration higher than 31percent, a ban that was being appealed at the time they pub-lished their study. In any case, it was the use of the strong government issue DEET that was particularly correlated with the risk of developing syndrome 3 in Haley and Kurt's study.

In the *JAMA* article "Self-reported Exposure ," Haley and Kurt discuss the relationship of their syndromes to a condition known as OPIDP, or organophosphate-induced delayed polyneuropathy. They note that even if exposure to organophosphates or similar substances does not produce immediate symptoms, it can produce "chronic neurologic impairment from variants of OPIDP that are often permanent." The damage to the nervous system in this case can take from one to six weeks to appear. Haley and Kurt believe that the "generally mild impairment of brainstem, spinal cord, and peripheral nerve function" that they found was "consistent with the spectrum of the OPIDP syndrome." They note that the body protects itself from choli-nergic agents such as nerve agents or organophosphate pesticides through an enzyme called butyrylcholinesterase (BuChE) as well as through a group of enzymes called paraoxonases. PB tied up much of the available BuChE, leaving the body vulnerable to pesticides and insect repellents. Later research by the Haley team would show a deficiency in a critical paraoxonase enzyme, PON-Q, among the sick veterans.

In the conclusion to their "Self-reported Exposure" paper, Haley and Kurt note that because of a synergistic effect in certain combinations "possibly aided by preexposure saturation of BuChE . . . , these chemicals may have produced the syndromes at concentrations that would not have caused problems if each agent had been acting alone." Thus their results are consistent with Abou-Donia's findings in his chicken research, which Haley and Kurt cited in their article.

Having completed the research indicating that there were three main syndromes that were associated with certain combinations of chemical exposures in Gulf War veterans, Haley and his colleagues moved quickly to conduct brain scans on some of the veterans in their original group. They chose a technique called magnetic resonance spectroscopy (MRS) to investigate the levels of certain important chemicals in the veterans' brains. Standard MRI tests usually have not revealed any structural changes in the brains of the sick veterans, but Haley's team knew that many brain abnormalities do not show up on MRI scans. Several factors directed their attention to those areas of the brain known as the brainstem and the basal ganglia. The first factor was an association between Parkinson's disease and the genetic problem that produces a low level of PON-Q. Studies had also indicated that exposure to low levels of some organophosphates affected the basal ganglia. Moreover, Haley's team noted that the veterans' symptoms were quite similar to those of patients suffering from certain degenerative diseases affecting the basal ganglia.

In a study that was reported in the *Journal of Toxicology and Applied Pharmacology* on June 15, 1999, the Haley team showed through the use of MR spectroscopy that because of a genetic polymorphism the ill Gulf War veterans studied by the team are significantly low in PON-Q. A June 16, 1999, press release from the research team states:

"One of the biggest questions about Gulf War syndrome has been why one person got sick when the person next to him didn't," Haley said. "That is one of the major puzzles that made many people think the symptoms were just due to stress. But now we know that there appears to be a genetic reason why some people got sick and others didn't, and this genetic difference links the illness to damage from certain chemicals."

Haley's study showed that people with a gene that causes them to produce high amounts of a particular enzyme did not get sick after exposure to certain chemicals in Operation Desert Storm, while others who produce low amounts of the same enzyme did get sick. The culprit gene is the one that controls production of type Q paraoxonase, or PON-Q, an enzyme that allows that body to fight off chemical toxins by destroying them. This particular enzyme is highly specific for the chemical nerve agents sarin and soman as well as for the common pesticide diazinon.

In some people, the gene causes the body to produce high levels of PON-Q, allowing their bodies to fight off toxins like nerve gas. But in others the gene directs the production of low levels of PON-Q, meaning a person cannot fight off even low levels of these toxic chemicals well.

"In our earlier studies when we found strong statistical links between Gulf War syndrome and veterans' reports of exposure to combinations of chemicals like pesticides and low-level chemical nerve agents, we predicted it might be due to a PON-Q deficiency, and now that's what we have found," Haley said. "The sick veterans in our study have low PON-Q levels in their blood, and the well ones have high PON-Q levels. We have found a genetic marker that appears to explain what made many of these veterans sick."

The veterans having Haley syndrome 2 were most deficient in this critical enzyme, a result that was consistent with their more debilitating level of illness.

At the annual meeting of the Radiological Society of North America held in late November 1999, Haley and his colleagues released the results of a study in which they used MR spectroscopy to show that a group of 22 veterans from their Seabees group had concentrations of a brain chemical called N-acetyl-aspartate that ranged from 10 to 25 percent lower than in a group of healthy veterans. Dr. James Fleckenstein, one of the researchers, was quoted in the *San Francisco Chronicle* of December 1, 1999, as saying that even a 10 percent loss of this chemical would amount to a "pretty severe hit" to brain function. The article also quotes Fleckenstein as stating: "This validates that these are sick people, not people who are crazy, or depressed or trying to get money."

In their next study, which is described in a November 27, 2000, press release for the annual meeting of the Radiological Society of America, the Haley researchers demonstrated the validity of their hypothesis that brain scans of the sick veterans would show damage in the brainstem and basal ganglia. This time they measured the ratio of N-acetyl-aspartate to creatine (NAA/CR), a ratio that would indicate functional neuronal mass. Magnetic resonance spectroscopy (MRS) brain scans of 22 veterans from the original Seabees survey group were compared with those of 18 healthy veterans and also with the brain scans of a group of 6 ill veterans who fit the pattern for Haley syndrome 2 but had been obtained from a different group of Gulf War veterans. The Haley team found that compared to the controls, "Veterans with syndrome 2 (the most severe clinically) had evidence of decreased NAA/CR in both the basal ganglia and the brainstem; those with syndrome 1, in the basal ganglia only; and those with syndrome 3, in the brainstem only."

This research establishing evidence in the veterans' brains for the damage associated with exposure to organophosphate compounds and similar substances was particularly interesting to the Haley researchers because they knew that many studies had previously shown that pesticide poisoning among agricultural workers could lead to symptoms that included fatigue, inability to think clearly, dizziness, and central pain, symptoms familiar to the sick veterans. No studies had ever been performed, however, on these agricultural workers to tie their symptoms to physiological and chemical changes in their brains.

The November 2000 press release offered this description of the results of the studies:

"This year we show that brain cell losses from specific areas of the brain correlate with different symptoms and abnormalities on specific tests," said Robert Haley, M.D., professor of internal medicine and principal investigator of the study. "This helps explain why not all patients have the same exact symptoms. Depending on which brain regions were damaged by chemicals in the war, veterans may have more or different types of symptoms."

Specifically, the new findings show that damage on the right side of the brain appears to cause certain symptoms such as impaired sense of direction, memory lapses and depression. Damage on the left side appears to cause more global confusion, including difficulties in understanding instructions, reading, solving problems and making decisions. Left-sided damage also appears to cause production of high levels of dopamine, an important brain hormone involved in movement and emotions. Damage to the brain stem appears to account, in part, for loss of balance and dizzy spells and correlates with objective tests of brain stem reflexes important in balance.

"MRS scanning continues to validate an organic basis for Gulf War patients' complaints and disabilities and in a more specific way than older tests in past research," said James Fleckenstein, M.D., professor of radiology, University of Texas Southwestern Medical Center at Dallas. "The fact that findings on MRS mirror patients' signs and symptoms underscores the power of this tool in evaluating patients with these kinds of problems."

The Haley team research published in the September 1999 issue of *Archives of Neurology* showed that veterans with syndrome 2 have an unusually high production of dopamine. The Haley team hypothesizes that injury to the cells that would ordinarily regulate the production of dopamine enables the cells to become overactive and produce too much dopamine, which may in turn lead to further cell damage.

Haley and his colleagues note that contrary to what happens in certain diseases affecting the basal ganglia, ill veterans may have been exposed to neurotoxic chemicals for a short enough time span that their disease will not affect the brain in a progressive way. It remains to be seen what the future holds for these veterans with brain damage. Haley, however, theorized in an interview with the *Dallas Morning News* that appeared on September 15,

2000: "There could be an epidemic of Parkinson's disease coming out of an epidemic of Gulf War syndrome."

Although the original research of the Haley team was supported by Ross Perot, the DOD eventually provided $3 million to the Texas researchers, albeit rather grudgingly. At the October 12, 2000, meeting of the Senate Veterans' Affairs committee chaired by Senator Arlen Specter (D-PA), testimony was taken from Dr. Haley, Ross Perot, and Dr. Bernard Rostker, Special Assistant to the Deputy Secretary of Defense for Gulf War Illnesses. It was clear from the outset that no love is lost between Rostker on the one side and Perot and Haley on the other. Perot decried the DOD's fixation on Gulf War syndrome as a manifestation of stress and said that the problem was that Bernard Rostker was "the captain of the stress ship." Rostker in turn accused Haley of going outside the normal grant-awarding procedure to lobby Congress. As a member of the audience that day, I found this accusation rather amusing because of an interchange I had had with Haley when I tried to persuade him to be interviewed for my video *Gulf War Syndrome: Aftermath of a Toxic Battlefield*. When I mentioned that a copy of the video would be given to each member of Congress, he declined to be interviewed, saying he did not want to be seen as attempting to lobby Congress.

What was even more disturbing was Rostker's suggestion that Haley had accepted government funds but had not done the research he had committed to do. There even seemed to be the hint of a threat that the DOD would hold Haley responsible for misuse of government funds. Two weeks later the DOD's contracting office sent a five-person team to Dallas to audit the scientific productivity, the accomplishment of the required scope of work of the grant, all expenditures, human rights protection, and accuracy of the data. Their report gave the Haley team a clean bill of health, entirely refuting the Rostker charges. Rostker's accusation seems particularly inappropriate under the circumstances. The DOD has to date spent over $150 million on research into the issue of Gulf War syndrome, most of it poured down the proverbial rat hole. On the other hand, almost any objective observer would agree that the $3 million that went to Haley's team was money well spent. Haley and his colleagues have been rapidly publishing the results of their studies in major peer-reviewed scientific journals, and their work has gone a long way toward demonstrating the reality of Gulf War syndrome. For the veterans who have been waiting ten long years for the world to recognize that they are ill, Haley's results have come none too soon.

The acrimonious interaction between Rostker and Haley is symptomatic of a larger problem concerning Bernard Rostker's position as the person in charge of the DOD's investigation of Gulf War syndrome. Rostker never enjoyed the confidence and trust of the sick veterans, the people he was supposedly placed in office to help. These veterans were outraged that the DOD would appoint to the job of unraveling the mystery of the illnesses plaguing them a man who was not even a physician. Rostker, who always uses the title Dr. Bernard Rostker, has a Ph.D. in economics, and many observers view his appointment as a cynical move from a government that realizes the huge cost that would arise from any admission of responsibility for the destroyed health and resulting unemployability of so many Gulf War veterans.

The public relations people working under Rostker say that he was chosen because of his ability to compile, study, and compare a large amount of data. They state that it was important to find out which soldiers were located where, who took PB pills, who had the anthrax and botulinum shots, and who was stationed near the oil well fires. But much of this information is virtually irretrievable. There are no records of who took the PB pills and who got the anthrax and botulinum shots. And during the Gulf War, the practice of producing morning reports that would indicate what units were located where on any given day had been discontinued. Therefore Rostker's expertise in organizing data was superfluous because there was very little hard data to organize. His presence in this position only reinforced the ill veterans' feeling that they have been abandoned by the DOD or VA.

One of Rostker's first projects when he assumed the responsibility for the investigation into Gulf War syndrome was to travel around the country to talk to groups of veterans. These appearances were doomed from the moment he started to speak because he offers a dry presentation devoid of any natural sympathy for the plight of the ill veterans. Rostker has also been a master at manipulating the press. For example, he has often stated that there are only 10,000 or fewer Gulf War veterans with undiagnosed illnesses. There are by even a conservative estimate over 100,000 sick Gulf War veterans, but Rostker places most of these in a different category because their medical problems have been given labels like asthma, chronic fatigue syndrome, or lupus. Rostker's misleading statements are, however, picked up by members of the press and used to minimize the problem of Gulf War syndrome. In an October 9, 2000, article in the *Washington Post,* reporter William M. Arkin chastised Congressnan Dan Burton (R-IN), chairman of the House Committee on Government Reform, for stating that "1 out of every 7 of those who served in the military during Desert Storm have Gulf War Syndrome." Arkin asserted: "Yet in this world of lies, damn lies, and statistics, these numbers are a gross deception. Of the 696,530 service members who served in the Gulf War, 3,039 are recognized to have 'undiagnosed' illnesses. The truth is that if there is a Gulf War 'Syndrome' at all, it affects less than half of one percent of those who served."

It is beyond the scope of this book to document the way in which Bernard Rostker has manipulated the information available about the illnesses of Gulf War veterans to minimize the reality of these health problems and protect the DOD from responsibility for the devastating situation in which over 100,000 Gulf War veterans find themselves. If the latter was in fact the goal of the DOD, they chose the right man for the job, and he performed his assignment well.

Paul Sullivan, former executive director of the National Gulf War Resource Center, a Washington, D.C., group that serves as an umbrella organization for Gulf War veterans' groups around the country, does not mince words: "Bernie Rostker is a liar. Bernie Rostker is a paid professional propaganda artist for the Pentagon."[1] But the depth of the antipathy that so many Gulf veterans and their families feel toward Bernard Rostker is best expressed by the statement sent to me by Tom Donnelly, the father of a Gulf War veteran:

> In the years since my son, Michael, was medically retired by the U.S. Air Force diagnosed with ALS, it has become clear to me that Mike's terminal neurological disease is but one of many maladies comprehended by the rubric "Gulf War syndrome." It is also clear that the federal official charged with continuing and perfecting the official campaign of dissembling, denial and deception is that evil gnome, "Doctor" Bernard Rostker. I hold this individual, together with a small group of identifiable others, personally responsible for the betrayal of my son and so many others and for the unspeakable horrors inflicted upon more than 100,000 Gulf War veterans and their families.
>
> You had expressed to me the thought that Rostker might bring a libel suit for being called the liar that he is. That's too much to hope for. I know lawyers who drool at the prospect of deposing Rostker.

It was welcome news to the ill Gulf War veterans when Dr. Bernard Rostker resigned from his post on January 20, 2001. The most important first step that Secretary of Defense Donald Rumsfeld can take to show good faith to these veterans is to place someone in charge of the DOD's investigation into Gulf War illnesses who is highly qualified to understand the complex medical issues involved and takes the plight of the ill veterans seriously.

---

[1] Alabama PBS Gulf War syndrome documentary, 1999. The National Gulf War Resource Center maintains a website that contains a wealth of useful information. See <<http://www.ngwrc.org>>.

Chapter 8

The Oil Well Fires

As the Iraqi forces retreated from Kuwait at the end of the war, they set hundreds of oil wells on fire in what can only be viewed as the ultimate in a scorched earth tactic. This action did not, however, catch Coalition forces by surprise. According to a DOD report titled *Oil Well Fires*, "intelligence sources knew Iraq's soldiers had wired oil wells and rigs in the Minagish oilfield with plastic explosives in the first days of the occupation." The chronology provided by the DOD report states that as Coalition bombing began on January 16-17, Iraq started to burn some of Kuwait's oil fields. In addition, some oil wells were ignited by Coalition bombing of nearby targets. By late February, over 600 oil wells were ablaze, and 85 percent of Kuwait's oil production facilities had been damaged. The DOD report notes:

The damaged well heads released approximately 4-6 million barrels of crude oil and 70-100 million cubic meters of natural gas per day.
. . .
The burning wells created a huge, widely dispersed smoke plume that degraded the region's air quality and released various potentially hazardous gases, including sulfur dioxide (SO_2), carbon monoxide (CO), hydrogen sulfide (H_2S), carbon dioxide (CO_2) and nitrogen oxides (NO_x), and particulate matter (soot) that potentially contained partially burned hydrocarbons and metals. If sufficiently concentrated, both gases and particulate matter potentially can impair health in exposed populations.

(DOD *Oil*, 3:1)

In the RAND report titled *Oil Well Fires*, which was commissioned by the DOD, author Dalia M. Spektor notes that "SO_2 is an upper-airway irritant that can stimulate bronchoconstriction and mucus secretion. Animal studies indicate that relatively low concentration exposures of SO_2 (0.1 to 20 ppm) for long periods have marked effects consistent with bronchitis" (RAND *Oil*, 3:11).

In an article published in *Science* magazine, researchers Peter Hobbs and Lawrence Radke state: "Close to the fires the smoke rained oil drops. . . . This oil, together with soot fallout, coated large areas of the desert with a black, tar-like covering. Oil spewing out from uncapped wells formed large pools of oil on the desert, some of which were alight."[1] This immense conflagration resembled a scene from hell, and those caught in it retain indelible memories of the event:

> Once the cease-fire was called and we were ordered to move south into Kuwait, we ended up in the midst of the Rhumali oil fields that were ablaze. The whole environment was just incredible to be in because we saw no sunlight for almost 45 days. The sun was completely blackened out by this thick film of smoke and soot and the vapors of burning fuel. I likened it to diesel exhaust, and it became so bad that at times I put on my protective mask to try to filter out some clean air because I had severe headaches and was nauseous from the fumes. We actually had black film and soot on our skin. You could see particles falling out of the sky on top of us.
>
> S.Sgt. Bob Jones (GWS video footage)

> I was in Kuwait, and we had 60 oil wells burning where I was. We had to move after a few weeks because the oil wells were burning. A lot of people got sick; they had asthma attacks. People that had never had asthma before had asthma during Kuwait. We were coughing up until we got back to Germany. I still coughed up, and it was black. For six months afterwards, I was still coughing up black.
>
> S.Sgt. Sherrie McGahee (GWS video footage)

> I was also found to have obstructive pulmonary disease, which I attributed to the smoke in Kuwait City. Where I was stationed, close to Camp Freedom in Kuwait City, you couldn't tell night from day. If you saw a globe in the sky, you didn't know whether it was the moon or the sun. My skin was so black you couldn't identify my skin from my watch band, a black watch band. When you spit, it looked like oil; when you blew your nose, it looked like axle grease. I mean, that's the kind of pollution I'm talking about. And the guy got after me and said, "Well, you've got this obstructive pulmonary disease because you smoke cigarettes." And I said, "No, a cigarette has never touched my lips in my entire life, unless you want to count what happened to me in Kuwait, which is probably the equivalent to a thousand packs of cigarettes a day."
>
> It was 17 days before we had enough water that any of us could take a shower. We took the shower, in a tent of course, closed in. We got

---

[1] Peter V. Hobbs and Lawrence F. Radke, "Airborne Studies of the Smoke from the Kuwait Oil Fires," *Science* 256 (May 1992): 987.

clean until we opened the tent door and put on our dirty, oil-soaked clothing because we didn't have enough water for laundry.

Col. Herbert Smith (GWS video footage)

At one point during the war, we were staying near the oil wells, and your uniform would be completely covered with black, like soot all over you. Your arms were exposed, your food, everything, your water where you took showers. It was constantly dark; there was no such thing as daylight.

Sp4c. Bobby Lawson (GWS video footage)

My breathing was not good; my breathing felt very much as though I was trying to take in glue instead of air. It was, you know, not pleasant. That continued until after we came back to the UK [United Kingdom]. I became very ill in September, and it progressed into pneumonia.

They gave me all of these antibiotics. They just tried me on one after another. Nothing worked, and then finally it seemed to settle down for a little while. And then by Christmas of that year I became ill again, and this time I got pneumonia very badly. It was what my doctor called atypical pneumonia. And because I'd had pneumonia twice within the space of three months, they decided that they were going to put me in [the] hospital and find out what was going on. And when they actually looked at my lungs and everything, they said that there was a lot of oily debris in my lungs. I didn't connect for some reason the oily debris bit and the oil well fires bit. I didn't connect it immediately. And they said, "Have you been in a house fire?" and I said no. And they said, "Well, we can't understand why your lungs are in such bad shape."

And I had a review appointment in two weeks after going in [the] hospital, and I went back and in the time that I had had, I had actually made the connection. I went back to the doctor, and I said, "Look, would oil wells have done it, burning oil wells?" And he looked at me and he said yes. He said, "When were you with burning oil? You don't work in the oil industry, do you?" I said no, but I was a soldier out in the Gulf. And he went, "Ah, yes." He said, "The fumes from burning oil wells are both toxic and carcinogenic because it sets fire to something they call the signature, which is highly toxic." And he said, "Yes, it would have, it would have done that."

And the official diagnosis for my lungs, my breathing difficulties is bronchiectasis, which is scarring of the tissue of the surface of the lung. And they just put me on inhalers and various things, and really I've been that way ever since because there's really nothing they can do, you know. The lungs will only heal themselves to a certain extent. They won't completely heal, so I'm stuck with it basically until I die.

I can't walk for long distances without my lungs filling up with fluid because your lungs try to protect you by producing more fluid. So basically what happens is that I start choking, coughing on the fluid after I've walked for a little while.

S.Sgt. Anne Selby (GWS video footage)

Ground forces were not the only troops affected when Saddam Hussein decided to destroy Kuwait's oil industry. At the beginning of the air war, Iraq began pumping Kuwaiti oil into the Persian Gulf, where many Coalition ships were stationed. Fortunately, Coalition bombing succeeded in stopping the oil flow within a week by destroying Iraq's pumping capabilities (DOD *Oil*, 3:7). But by that time the oil slick on the Gulf covered thousands of square miles and was large enough to be visible by satellite. Two witnesses before the Shays subcommittee testified about what it was like to serve on a ship in the oil-contaminated Persian Gulf:

For seven months, my husband's ship chartered through burning oil derricks in the water. They were on the oil spill. They ingested oil-infested water. They cooked with it. They showered in it. He has chemical sensitivity. He has asthma. He got it in the service.

Betty Zuspan (Shays, 31)

We suffered chemical ingestion when our drinking, cooking, washing, and bathing water became heavily contaminated with some sort of chemical that burned our mouth, throat, esophagus, and stomach. When we took our showers, we smelled of petrochemicals as well as the freshly washed clothes we put on. The food tasted of kerosene. We were in a 100 percent contaminated environment. I became very sick with digestive problems that same day that the contamination came aboard ship in our drinking water. The Navy ships' distilling plants . . . cannot filter out chemicals.

Antonio Melchor (Shays, 31)

A reporter for *National Geographic* gave a particularly vivid account of the oil well fires:

It was 11:00 a.m., yet the darkness caused by the burning oil wells was like a moonless night. The photos I brought back show the black, hellish landscape—yet they cannot convey the fine mist of oil particles that hangs in the air, nor the deafening roar of the wildly burning wells.[2]

---

[2] Thomas Y. Canby, "After the Storm," *National Geographic,* August 1991, p. 35.

Given the reports from those forced to spend weeks by the burning oil wells, it seems hard to believe that the risk to health from this exposure would not have been great. Nevertheless, the RAND report dismisses the possibility of any health risks from exposure to these fires. The summary states: "The level of pollutants measured in the Gulf were much lower than those that are known to cause short- or long-term health effects." The hundreds of thousands of soldiers who were caught for weeks near this immense conflagration would react in total disbelief to one remarkable statement the author makes: "The exposure concentrations of the pollutants measured in the Gulf, except for PM_{10} [particulate matter less that 10 micrometers in diameter], were lower than those in U.S. urban areas" (RAND *Oil*, 3:15).

The problem is that the RAND Corporation and other groups evaluating the relationship of Gulf War syndrome to the oil well fires all relied upon data that was collected starting in May 1991, after the very strong Shamal winds had started to blow in the Persian Gulf. Hundreds of thousands of soldiers were exposed to far higher levels of toxic substances during the winter months before the Shamal winds began to blow the pollution away. By the time the Army started measuring the pollution, a large percentage of our forces had already left the Gulf, undoubtedly carrying away with them soot particles in their lungs and toxic petroleum chemicals in their fatty tissue. Swc. Fred Willoughby reports: "For several months after I got home, I would have heavy sweating, and the bed sheets and pillow cases on my side of the bed were black from all the stuff coming out of my skin" (Part II, 213).

A very different view from that expressed in the RAND report is found in a paper titled *Oil Fires, Petroleum and Gulf War Illness*, which was written by Craig Stead, a chemical engineer and expert on health effects related to exposure to petroleum. Stead submitted his paper to the CDC Conference on the Health Impact of Chemical Exposures During the Gulf War, held February 28 through March 2, 1999. He has also submitted written testimony on this subject to the Shays subcommittee. In his report to the CDC, Stead states: "The fires have been dismissed as a cause of Gulf War illness by all government agencies, including the IOM (Institute of Medicine), PAC (Presidential Advisory Committee), DOD (Department of Defense; Office of the Special Assistant, Defense Science Board), and the VA (Veterans Administration, VA Persian Gulf Scientific Panel)" (Stead, 4). In testimony to the Shays subcommittee, Stead stated:

In 1994, the Army issued the final Kuwait Oil Fire Health Risk Assessment. The Assessment used Gulf air pollution data gathered in May through November 1991. Air pollution from the oil field fires during this time was much less than during the Gulf War for the following reasons: The months of May through November [when the study was done] have the Shamal winds blowing from the northwest causing the smoke plume from the oil field fires to disperse widely and ascend to great heights. During the Gulf War (February and March)

low wind speeds and air inversions were common. Under these
conditions the smoke plume was on the ground, creating high localized
levels of air pollution to which the troops were exposed.
(Shays, 32)

The Shays report provides the following additional information:

An Institute of Medicine [IOM] document confirms Mr. Stead's
statement: "The Army Health Risk Assessment could not launch a
successful air-sampling effort until the beginning of May, after the
more stagnant air conditions of the winter months had passed. Those
who undertook the sampling efforts did so with this knowledge."
Principal author of the Army report, Dr. Jack Heller, also confirmed
the Stead statement: "What we measured at the time we were there
starting in May when the Shamal winds were strongly blowing and
there was a lot of thermal lofting of the pollution [sic]. We didn't have
those ground level impacts [present during the war]. In fact the whole
time I was there I had [only] one ground level impact.
(Shays, 32)

According to Stead, during this single "plume touchdown" or ground level
impact that the Army measured on May 12, 1991, "smoke and particulate
levels ranged from 924 micrograms per cubic meter to 1824 micrograms per
cubic meter compared to a USEPA significant harm level of 600 micrograms
per cubic meter. The World Health Organization found smoke and particulate
levels of 5400 micrograms per cubic meter immediately after the liberation
of Kuwait [late February]" (Stead, 2). What the data for the May 12, 1991,
plume touchdown or inversion indicates is that during inversions—and there
were many during February and March—there were indeed levels of toxins
that were as much as nine times the level that the EPA has established for
significant harm. Exposures of this magnitude would in all likelihood be a
strong contributing factor to Gulf War syndrome.

Stead focuses, however, not only on the inversion episodes but also on the
soldiers' exposure to soot and oil rain. The oil rain resulted because in many
cases a jet of unburned oil shot up through the flames, and the oil that was
thus dispersed throughout the atmosphere eventually fell to earth as an oil
rain, coating the uniforms and any exposed skin of the soldiers in the area.
In their article in *Science,* Peter Hobbs and Lawrence Radke, note: "Close to
the fires, the largest oil drops approached millimeter size and rained out
quickly; smaller oil drops fell out within a distance of ~50 km [30 miles]
from the fires."[3] Unfortunately, no study was done to analyze the content of

---

[3] Hobbs and Radke, "After the Storm," 988.

the oil rain, but Stead quotes from an early version of the DOD oil well fire report an especially horrific account of this toxic rain:

There were . . . days when the smoke [plumes] "hugged" the ground and turned the sunlit, bright day into a dark of night. [We] traveled the "coastal highway," from Kuwait City down to Saudi Arabia . . . and the petroleum-thickened air was so impregnated that we choked on oil while breathing through our doubled-up scarves. . . . We were forced to stop and clear the raw petroleum off vehicle windshields and our goggles constantly. At [times] on the highway the . . . air was so thick our vehicle headlights could not penetrate the air further than 10-15 feet, and Marine escorts were needed to walk . . . ahead of the vehicles to keep us on the highway.

(Stead, 35)

In his report, Stead notes that the oil rain was not only a temporary inconvenience but also a serious health threat:

The oil rain was Kuwait crude oil with volatile components removed. The oil rain would correspond to a light lubricating oil fraction contaminated with soot. The heat of the oil well fires could cause thermal cracking of higher boiling compounds. Thermal cracking creates higher boiling aromatic compounds and lighter boiling compounds by breaking large petroleum molecules. Higher boiling aromatic compounds have consistently been linked with carcinogenicity and toxicity. Thus, the oil rain may have become more toxic from thermal cracking of the Kuwait crude in the oil fire heat.

(Stead, 14)

The DOD report on the oil well fires refers only obliquely to the oil rain:

The most severe exposures to U.S. troops from the oil well fires occurred when they were in proximity to the damaged or burning wells. During these incidences, troops were subjected to short-term exposures where they were literally drenched in unburned oil and/or covered with fall-out (i.e., soot, smoke, and other by-products of combustion) from the oil well fires.

(DOD *Oil*, 5:3)

Stead draws upon 1990 research about fog oil conducted by W. G. Palmer of the U.S. Army Biomedical Research and Development Laboratory to show how dangerous it was for soldiers to inhale the fine oil mist that sometimes surrounded them:

Petroleum inhalation can lead to two forms of lipoid pneumonia. One form causes a circumscribed lesion similar to a tumor within the lung and is called a granuloma or paraffinoma. Extensive loss of pulmonary function can occur with this type of lesion. A second form of lipoid pneumonia is diffuse pneumonitis in which oil droplets are spread throughout the lung. This type of lipoid pneumonia can be accompanied by bacterial infection.

Lipoid pneumonia symptoms can range from occasional cough to severe, debilitating breathlessness and pulmonary illness. Commonly chest X-rays will not detect any lung changes to indicate the presence of lipoid pneumonia. Accurate diagnosis can only be made through lung biopsy or other invasive procedures. Advanced lipoid pneumonia can lead to permanent loss of lung capacity from fibrosis. Lung damage from lipoid pneumonia can vary from slight to severe with necrosis and hemorrhage.

Inhaled petroleum with an aromatic content would be expected to partition in the lung. The aromatic portion of the oil is fat-soluble and would pass through the lung wall to be deposited in the adipose [fatty] tissue. It also is possible some of the non-aromatic portion of inhaled petroleum would pass through the lung wall and be deposited from the blood in the spleen, lymph nodes, liver and kidneys. The aromatic and other petroleum fractions distributed throughout the body would cause systemic toxicity which expresses through many symptoms. . . . An extensive literature review by the author has found petroleum exposure associated with the following symptoms: cancer, fatigue, breathlessness, cough, skin rash, headache, diarrhea, weight loss, memory loss, immune suppression, chemical sensitivity.

Skin exposure to petroleum has been known for many years to cause skin cancer, rashes, eczema, acne, and dermatitis. . . . Aromatic content is a key toxicity parameter for petroleum; the higher the aromatic content, the greater is the toxicity. Aromatic compounds boiling between 500 and 1000° F. have been found highly carcinogenic. . . . Reports of the oil rain forming a sticky coating on surfaces suggest it was similar to a lubricating oil in viscosity and boiling range. This is effectively a weathered crude, similar to that found in an environmental spill, and would contain a high level of aromatic compounds and asphaltic and resinous compounds.

(Stead, 16-17)

It is worth noting that the symptoms Stead lists as being associated with petroleum exposure are very similar to those experienced by veterans suffering from Gulf War syndrome.

Animals in the Persian Gulf were adversely affected by the oil well fires. Stead quotes an EPA report stating: "Sheep, goats and camels grazing in the areas impacted by the burning wells have turned black from the falling drops of oil and have started to lose their fur and die" (Stead, 18). He also notes: "Inspection of sheep in a Kuwait slaughter house after the war found the sheep had lipoid pneumonia; there were massive clots in the lungs. Also observed were dark granulated livers and blood clots in the hearts" (Stead, 18).

It is particularly unfortunate that government agencies such as the IOM and the Army's Environmental Hygiene Agency and its successor agency, the Center for Health Promotion and Preventive Medicine, did not consider the issue of oil rain. This glaring oversight, combined with their admission that the data upon which they relied was obtained under conditions that did not match those experienced by the soldiers in Desert Storm, casts serious doubt on the validity of their conclusion that the oil well fires posed no risk to the soldiers' health.

These agencies minimized the risk of exposure to burning oil wells despite the existence of a clear warning about the danger that had been issued on January 9, 1991, just before the air war began, by the U.S. Army Intelligence Agency:

> Owing to Iraq's defensive "scorched earth" plan for Kuwait, the overall Kuwait oil infrastructure presents a serious hazard to advancing ally ground forces. There is overwhelming evidence that once ordered, the Iraqi forces will initiate demolition of oil wells, oil-gathering centers, oil-storage depots, pumping stations, large tank farms, refineries, and oil/product loading terminals. Demolition of these facilities and complexes will result in massive fires—"burning Kuwait."
>
> The danger of oil fires, toxic gas, and smoke in the Kuwaiti Theater of Operations [KTO] is *very serious*. These dangers . . . are as follows: 1) Associated toxic and highly flammable gas from spilled raw sour crude oil from nonburning oil wells; 2) Intense heat of oil-well fires, possible natural-gas wells, and fire trenches; 3) Dense smoke and superheated gases from these fires. By far the greatest danger is from dissociated hydrogen sulfide gas and highly volatile light ends [gases] released from wellhead blowouts. *In the KTO, the prevailing winds generally blow from the north-northwest southward toward Saudi Arabia.* Smoke and gases from Kuwaiti fires and blowouts most likely will be blown in the face of northerly advancing [United States] forces along the southern front of the KTO [italics added in Shays report].
>
> (Shays, 32-33)

Large numbers of soldiers now suffering from Gulf War syndrome have reported that they had a significant exposure to the oil well fires. In testimony before the Shays subcommittee, Debby Judd, an Air Force nurse during Desert Storm, testified on the results of a survey completed in 1995. This survey, which was carried out by the Operation Desert Storm Association, obtained information from 10,051 sick Gulf veterans. Judd reported:

Specific to the oil in the environment there, those breathing or enveloped in oil fire smoke was 96 percent; within clear visual area of the oil fires was 90 percent; worked in, lived in, or made travel through the burning oil fields was 72 percent; washed in water with an oily sheen was 68 percent. Those having oily taste to their food was 66 percent, and those with oily taste to the drinking water was 65 percent.

(Shays, 31)

The DOD report states:

One of the greatest dangers from non-burning oil wells was from dissociated hydrogen sulfide (H_2S) and highly volatile light ends (e.g., methane, ethane, butane, benzene, and toluene). . . . Under cool, calm atmospheric conditions these toxic gases are found in pockets of very high concentrations (10,000 to 20,000 parts per million [ppm] of H_2S)—concentrations that would quickly saturate standard-issue protective masks' activated carbon filters. A Foreign Service and Technology Center (FSTC) Scientific and Technical Analysis Bulletin . . . warned not only of fire and smoke hazards, but also of the likely threat of hydrogen sulfide, a gas that can cause dizziness, disorientation, vomiting, and death.

(DOD *Oil*, 3:4-5)

Another issue discussed in the DOD report was the oil lakes formed during Iraq's scorched earth campaign:

An additional concern was the large crude oil pools or lakes formed as a result of the damage sustained to the well heads and the subsequent release of free-flowing oil to the surrounding terrain. Damaged, unignited oil wells freely spewed thousands of barrels of oil a day onto the Kuwaiti landscape, creating more that 100 oil lakes covering an area of 19 square kilometers. . . . These massive pools of standing crude oil released large amounts of organic vapors into the atmosphere.

(DOD *Oil*, 3:8)

Despite these concerns about the release of toxic substances caused by the destruction of the oil wells, the DOD report nevertheless concluded: "The potential dangers of H_2S notwithstanding, medical examinations and health screening studies uncovered no evidence of any adverse health effects from exposure to H_2S" (DOD *Oil*, 3:5).

In fact, most veterans report that the physical examination they got when they returned to the States was quite perfunctory. And as Stead notes above, problems like lipoid pneumonia would not have shown up on a chest X-ray even had such X-rays been routinely performed on returning troops.

The health screening studies to which the DOD report refers undoubtedly include those performed on a group of soldiers from the 11th Armored Cavalry Regiment, which was based at Fulda, Germany, but was deployed to the Persian Gulf between June 10 and September 20, 1991. This was a particularly poor group to choose for a study if one was interested in determining whether proximity to the oil well fires, oil lakes, and oil rain had caused health problems. First of all, firefighters had started extinguishing the blazes and capping the oil wells on March 16, so by the summer and fall months when the 11th Armored was in the Gulf region, large numbers of the blazes had already been extinguished. Second, as noted above, during the summer months the strong Shamal winds were blowing most of the pollution away. Third, soldiers of the 11th Armored were stationed at two locations, one 30 miles from the oil well fires, the other 80 miles (Stead, 23). By contrast, veteran Ronald Matthews testified to the Presidential Advisory Commission on February 7, 1996, "I lived six city blocks from the fires for almost two weeks. I flew in the stuff every day (Shays, 31)."

According to the RAND report, several weeks after they returned to their base in Germany, 1599 soldiers from the 11th Armored filled out a survey concerning symptoms they had experienced before, during, and after their deployment to the Gulf. The report notes: "The symptoms that appeared once or a few times during the first eight weeks in Kuwait but were not experienced before going to Kuwait were headache (55 percent), lightheadedness (48 percent), fatigue or weakness (45 percent), skin rashes (41 percent), and diarrhea (42 percent)" (RAND *Oil*, 3:13). Despite these symptoms, the author of the report seems to suggest that the reduction of symptoms that occurred upon the troops' return to Germany indicates that there have been no long-term health effects. There is no indication, however, that the DOD has ever done a follow-up study on these soldiers of the 11th Armored to see how many of them continue to experience serious health problems or have developed such problems since returning from the Persian Gulf.

One often-quoted study was done on a group of American firefighters sent to the Gulf to extinguish the blazes. According to the DOD report, medical screening studies performed by the University of Texas on about 110 firefighters (who used no respiratory equipment) showed: "1) no objective evidence exists of any significant illness; 2) firefighters reported no symptoms similar to those Gulf War veterans reported; and 3) firefighters reported no delayed-onset of illnesses" (DOD *Oil*, 5:4). It is worth noting, however, that these firefighters received neither PB pills nor anthrax vaccine and arrived in the Persian Gulf long after any low levels of nerve agents had dissipated from the atmosphere. Thus they did not experience the same combination of exposures that large numbers of U.S. soldiers did.

Another study measured blood levels of volatile organic compounds (VOCs) in the blood of U.S. personnel living in Kuwait City, a group of the firefighters, and a control group of people living in the United States. The results showed that VOC levels were no higher in the U.S. personnel living in Kuwait City than in the U.S. controls, but it must be noted that the blood samples for the U.S. personnel group were drawn in May 1991, when many of the oil well fires had been extinguished and the Shamal winds were clearing out most of the toxic fumes. The firefighters' blood was drawn in October 1991, when almost all the fires had been put out. Two problems with the study, in addition to the fact that samples were taken well past the peak of pollution, are that the study used only a small group of subjects and the half life of this group of VOCs in the blood is less than four hours. Thus the amount of VOCs in the firefighters' blood would vary greatly depending on whether samples were drawn after they finished a work day or after they woke up in the morning. Nevertheless, the RAND report notes that for this group of firefighters: "Median levels of ethyl-benzene were 10 times higher than in the Control Group, while benzene, toluene, and xylene levels were more than double those of the Control Group" (RAND *Oil*, 3:12)

The DOD report states that department staff members contacted several firefighters to check on their health status several years later and found that "Generally, the firefighters are in good health and have not exhibited any of the symptoms that veterans commonly report." Of course, the word "Generally" is quite vague. Would it cover a situation in which 10 percent of the firefighters contacted were in fact having health problems? More important, as the authors of the DOD report note, firefighters are a self-selected group in that anyone who had a tendency to respiratory problems or sensitivity to chemicals would almost certainly quickly leave that line of work. Hence their ability to undergo exposure to the oil well fires without major health consequences does not necessarily mean the same is true for the average soldier.

Both the DOD report and the RAND report consider the main danger from air pollution in the Gulf to be associated with very fine particulate matter, what is called PM_{10} to indicate that the particles are less than 10 micrometers in diameter. When the air samples were taken, the Shamal winds were blowing, putting a tremendous amount of very fine sand into the air. Although the air samples also contained soot from the fires, the researchers consider the sand to be the primary health risk. The finer particles, those less than 2.5 micrometers, are particularly dangerous because they can be inhaled deep into the lungs. According to the DOD report, "The carcinogen potency of air pollution resides usually in the particulate fraction. Polycyclic organic chemicals and semivolatiles are associated with the particulate fraction and could have a prolonged residence time at sensitive sites in the respiratory tract when inhaled" (RAND *Oil*, 3:11).

One important health consequence that government researchers may be missing is the sensitization to chemicals that seems to have occurred with so many Gulf soldiers. In my interviews with ill veterans, almost all of them have mentioned an extreme sensitivity to petroleum products, a sensitivity that they had not had before the war. And this sensitivity seems to have spread over the years to other chemical substances.

I spent eight years in the 82nd Airborne Division as a paratrooper [before Desert Storm], and I had extensive exposure to jet fuel and jet fumes, and it never bothered me. But after coming back from the Gulf War, and having been in the oil fields for that length of time, breathing in the noxious fumes on a daily basis, now just the smell of diesel fuel makes me severely nauseated, dizzy, and very sick. And I try to avoid getting behind school buses. In particular, fuel products bother me extensively, as do other odors and smells. Perfumes—I don't wear any type of cologne because it makes me nauseous.

S.Sgt. Bob Jones (GWS video footage)

Gasoline—that makes me sick at my stomach.

Sfc. Sherrie McGahee (GWS video footage)

I couldn't pump my own gas . . . the gas fumes would make me vomit. . . . If I breathed automobile fumes, truck fumes, again I'm nauseous, trying to not vomit.

Col. Herbert Smith (GWS video footage)

I have problems breathing on buses because of the diesel fumes and to some extent with cars because of the petrol fumes. I have problems using household disinfectants and chemicals because it causes my airways to close, and it causes me to start choking.

S.Sgt. Anne Selby (GWS video footage)

When my husband first came back from Saudi, to even put gas in his vehicle, he would throw up. To change oil, his hands, it looked like little worms would come out on his hands. And they told him he had an allergic reaction to petroleum products. . . . Whenever I would use a pine-scented cleaner, when he'd get out of the truck, he would have to get right back in, he couldn't even come in the house. He would just start throwing up.

Margaret Wilcoxen (GWS video footage)

The biggest thing is the sensitivity to stuff. You used to go out all the time and paint your house and use the thinners and stuff, and now you've got to avoid the use of the thinners. When you pump your own gas, like myself, I've got to turn away so I don't breathe the fumes. The chemical sensitivity is becoming just unreal, and you notice it now. Before, when you would pump gas, you used to stand there and

smell the fumes, you know, great, this stuff don't bother me. And now
you've got to try to hide and pump at the same time.
                                    S.Sgt. Tim Smith (GWS video footage)

I couldn't pump gas after the war. My wife had to pump it while I sat
in the car or truck with the windows rolled up. The automatic air
freshener dispenser in our office was also making me sick.
                                    Sfc. Terry Dillhyon (GWS video footage)

I was in a transportation company that went to the Gulf War. . . . For
the previous six years, I had driven a tractor-trailer truck and had been
around diesel fuel and exhaust every day without it causing any
problems. . . . I was a reservist for a number of years after the Gulf
War, but . . . I couldn't drive a truck because every time they would
crank up the trucks, I would get deathly ill from the diesel exhaust.
                                    S.Sgt. Pat Browning (Part II, 159-60)

For Pat Browning and so many of her fellow veterans with Gulf War
syndrome, the chemical sensitivity that they developed in the war is a burden
that affects every aspect of their lives. One of the most devastating consequences of chemical sensitivity is the huge impact it has on one's ability to
work. Pat is a truck driver, but she can no longer work in that occupation.
Mechanics who have become sensitive to petroleum products can no longer
repair cars or other machinery. In our GWS video, Sfc.Terry Dillhyon and
Sfc. Roy Twymon both describe perfume exposures that put them in the
hospital for a couple of days. Trying to find a job where one can avoid
exposure to substances like petroleum, cleaning products, paint, new carpet,
or perfume and aftershave lotion quickly becomes an exercise in frustration,
as is indicated by the stories in my earlier book, *Casualties of Progress:
Personal Histories from the Chemically Sensitive.* One particularly sad story
of a chemically sensitive civilian comes from testimony that a former
chemical engineer named Abner Fisch gave in June 1996 before the New
Mexico Governor's Committee on the Needs of the Handicapped. Abner
could no longer work in the chemical industry, and he stated in his testimony
that since 1984 he had tried twenty different jobs. One excerpt will indicate
the kind of frustration he faced as he tried to earn a living:

In other cases, there have been jobs I had to quit because new carpet
was installed. I had a job as a counselor in a halfway house and had to
quit the job when carpeting was put in. I was a personal care atten-
dant, and when the family remodeled the house and put in new carpet,
I had to quit. I was flipping burgers and running a cash register, and
I got a very good performance evaluation after two months and after
four months, but when they hired new employees who wore perfume
and kept scheduling me with them, I had to resign. I do substitute

teaching, and when I substitute teach, every day when I come home I have to wash my clothing to get the perfume off.

Six weeks after he testified, Abner Fisch gave up the long struggle and took his own life.

Chapter 9

Depleted Uranium

During the ten years following the Gulf War, there was hardly a mention in the media about the use of depleted uranium, or DU, in the war. Few people even knew what the initials DU stood for. It seems quite remarkable that without the vast majority of Americans even noticing, the United States could have put into widespread military usage a weapon that is deadly efficient, yet arguably immoral to use. At last, in January 2001 the DU issue has become front-page news as countries like Italy and Portugal are raising questions about cancers developing in their troops who served in areas of Kosovo where the United States was using DU munitions.

Uranium is a heavy metal that occurs in nature as a mixture of three isotopes: ^{234}U, ^{235}U, and ^{238}U. Enriched uranium, used in nuclear weapons and nuclear power plants, consists of the relatively more radioactive isotopes, ^{234}U and ^{235}U, which have been removed from the original uranium. This leaves a residue consisting primarily of ^{238}U that is known as depleted uranium.

Depleted uranium has a spectacular capability to enhance military operations from both an offensive and defensive perspective. It is an extremely dense metal used to coat artillery rounds; an artillery round hardened with DU has an amazing ability to penetrate a tank. In fact, there have been instances of rounds that entered one side of a tank and went right out the other side because of the self-sharpening capability of a DU round. DU has another feature that is described in a report titled *Depleted Uranium* that was released July 31, 1998, by the Office of the Special Assistant for Gulf War Illnesses, OSAGWI, under Bernard Rostker: "DU is pyrophoric—upon striking armor, small particles break off and combust spontaneously in air, often touching off explosions of fuel and munitions" (DOD *DU*, 1:1).

DU is not only a dream weapon offensively, it also has extremely important defensive aspects. Because it is very dense, it can be used to reinforce armor plates for tanks, making them highly resistant to ordinary artillery rounds. The DOD report describes one case in which an M1A1 Abrams tank reinforced with DU armor plates was under attack by three Iraqi T-72 tanks. Three rounds fired by the Iraqi tanks bounced off the American tank, which destroyed each of the Iraqi tanks with a single DU round. Given that kind of stellar performance, it's not hard to see why the Pentagon wants desperately to deflect any suggestion that depleted uranium weapons should not be used.

During the Gulf War, over 1400 Iraqi tanks were destroyed by DU munitions. One reason why Coalition forces rolled right over the Iraqis in a ground war that lasted only four days is the use of DU. American casualties in the war were only 148 killed and 467 wounded, casualty figures that seemed too good to be true and indeed are too good to be true if critics of DU are right in their assertions that Gulf veterans are already dying or suffering from exposure to DU. In retrospect, it seems odd that few Americans questioned the statistics: 100,000 Iraqis dead versus 148 Americans dead. It was almost as if the waters of the Red Sea had miraculously parted, allowing Coalition forces to pass to safety unharmed. Did our pride as Americans in the efficiency of our high-tech missile attacks that we all watched on TV during the air war make us unable to look at the incredible statistics from the ground war and think that something was strange about this picture?

Perhaps the main reason more questions weren't asked about DU and its role in this overwhelmingly lopsided victory is that members of the press were kept away from the battlefield. This was a new U.S. policy that enabled the Pentagon to control the flow of news, and it obviously worked incredibly well from the Pentagon's point of view.

This miracle weapon does, however, have its downside. Radioactivity is obviously a concern, even if depleted uranium is "drained of 40 percent of its original radioactivity" (DOD *DU,* 1:1), a fact that is hardly reassuring. Unfortunately, many people hearing the term "depleted uranium" assume that all the radioactive part of the uranium has been removed. DU also presents serious health concerns because it is a heavy metal, and like other heavy metals such as lead and mercury, it has a chemical toxicity. The DOD report describes how exposure to DU may arise when DU rounds hit a target:

Fragments and uranium oxides are generated when DU rounds strike an armored target. The size of the particles varies greatly; larger fragments can be easily observed, while very fine particles are smaller than dust and can be inhaled and taken into the lungs. Whether large enough to see, or too small to be observed, DU particles and oxides contained in the body are all subject to various degrees of solubilization—they dissolve in bodily fluids.

. . .

The three uranium oxides of primary concern (UO_3, UO_2, and U_3O_8) all tend to dissolve slowly (days for UO_3 to years for UO_2 and U_3O_8) in bodily fluids. Once dissolved, uranium may react with biological molecules and, in the form of the uranyl ion, may exert its toxic effects. Those toxic effects are: cellular necrosis (death of cells) in the kidney and atrophy in the tubular walls of the kidney resulting in a decreased ability to filter impurities from the blood.

Once dissolved in the blood, about 90% of the uranium present will be excreted by the kidney in urine within 24-48 hours. The 10% of DU in blood that is not excreted is retained by the body, and can deposit in bones, lungs, liver, kidney, fat and muscle. Insoluble uranium oxides, if inhaled, can remain in the lungs for years, where they are slowly taken into the blood and then excreted in urine. Although heavy metals are not attracted to single biological compounds, they are known to have toxic effects on specific organs in the body. Previous research has demonstrated that the organ that is most susceptible to damage from high doses of uranium is the kidney. The uranyl-carbonate complexes decompose in the acidic urine in the kidney. This reaction forms the basis for the primary health effects of concern from uranium. The effects on the kidney from uranium resemble the toxic effects caused by other heavy metals, such as lead or cadmium.

(DOD *DU*, 2:1)

Exposure of Coalition forces to DU occurred in various ways. The most serious exposure was to crewmembers of American vehicles hit by DU rounds in friendly fire accidents. There are approximately 113 soldiers in this category. According to the DOD report, "Occupants of the vehicles were subjected to wounds from flying fragments, inhalation of airborne soluble and insoluble DU, ingestion of soluble and insoluble DU residues by hand-to-mouth transfer, and contamination of wounds by contact with contaminated clothing and vehicle interiors" (DOD *DU*, 3:3) In addition to these crew members of damaged vehicles, another 30-60 soldiers entered such vehicles to try to rescue their wounded comrades. The DOD refers to the level of exposure experienced by soldiers in these two groups as Level I, which is the highest. The term "Level II" refers to the level of exposure encountered by soldiers who were exposed to DU in various ways like cleaning up tanks that had been damaged by DU rounds or removing DU munitions from damaged American tanks. Swc. Fred Willoughby was part of a group of soldiers who worked with Iraqi vehicles that had been hit by DU rounds, and he now worries about his exposure to DU:

I was also assigned along with several of the personnel in our detachment to load the ships for the trip home with equipment brought back from Iraq and other places. We were told that the equipment was clean and we had nothing to worry about. So we climbed in, over, under, and through the equipment brought in. I remember one day I was trying to chain down an Iraqi vehicle that was hit with shells. I put the chain in an opening and tried to fasten it down. When I pulled my hand back out of the hole, a human finger came with it and it wasn't mine. So how much of the equipment was really cleaned trying to remove all the DU that was in the shells? We spent approximately three weeks on this detail. But we were assured by the DOD that we couldn't get any DU. That sure didn't make me feel any better either.

(Part II, 213)

Despite this exposure to DU in the Gulf theater, Swc. Willoughby reports that he did not undergo a proper medical examination before he headed home. He recalls that "all it consisted of was two things. Question 1 —How do you feel? Question 2—Do you have any problems right now? No. OK, you can go home. Some exam, huh?" (Part II, 213).

The DOD report admits that soldiers like Swc. Willoughby were not warned about DU contamination of the equipment they were working on. In discussing soldiers from the 144th Service and Supply Company who worked in a storage area for damaged equipment, the report states: "Twenty-seven members of this unit were exposed to DU for a period of several weeks before being informed that some of the equipment in the yard had DU contamination" (DOD *DU*, 4:3).

Level III exposures included cases of lower level contact with DU. Because our troops had not been warned about the potential toxicity of DU weapons, many curious soldiers looking for souvenirs climbed onto or even inside Iraqi tanks that had been damaged by depleted uranium rounds and thus contained pulverized DU dust. Other troops passing by enemy vehicles that had just been hit by DU rounds may have breathed in the depleted uranium aerosolized by the extreme heat generated when the rounds penetrated a tank's armor or caused its fuel supply to explode.

> Our commanders never warned us about the radioactive vehicles, that we could not go around them or touch them, so basically, it was like a free-for-all, everybody just wanting to explore, to get things out of the tanks and take pictures.
> Sp4c. Bobby Lawson (GWS video footage)

> As we engaged the Iraqis multiple times on the battlefield, DU rounds were used extensively, and there were several occasions we rode right through the middle of the battle as it was ongoing and Iraqi tanks were blowing up all around us. The air was full of radioactive dust. There's no other way to describe it—pulverized uranium, depleted uranium dust from the targets that were hit. It was a free-for-all kill zone. There were destroyed Iraqi tanks and vehicles that completely littered the battlefields, and they were ablaze as we rode through them.
> S.Sgt. Bob Jones (GWS video footage)

It is clear that large numbers of American soldiers were exposed to DU, and the question of a possible relationship of this DU exposure to Gulf War syndrome is an important one. It would appear, however, that illness arising from DU exposure may be a separate issue. The other toxic exposures discussed in this book seem to have led to chemical sensitivity in a high percentage of veterans suffering from Gulf War syndrome, and many civilians have during the last few decades developed multisymptom illnesses that closely resemble Gulf War syndrome after they were exposed to toxic chemicals. Even anthrax inoculation seems to be producing illnesses that very closely resemble Gulf War syndrome, as we shall see in Chapter 10, and many of these people have developed chemical sensitivity.

Experience with radiation sickness or heavy metal toxicity would suggest, however, that the health problems produced by exposure to DU would more likely involve damage to the lungs or kidneys or the development of various forms of cancer. Because of the long latency period for most cancers, it is possible that there will be cases of cancer developing in Gulf War veterans as the result of exposure to DU in the Persian Gulf.

It should be noted that those soldiers who were most heavily exposed to DU were in general on the front lines. They were thus for the most part also exposed to the oil well fires, PB pills, possible nerve agents, pesticide, diesel fuel, and anthrax inoculation. Unfortunately, there is no way of sorting out these various exposures and deciding which ones produced what symptoms in a given veteran. Dr. Abou-Donia wants to extend his experiment in which he exposed rodents to a combination of PB, permetrin, DEET, and stress by adding DU to the combination to see if there is any synergistic effect. In the meantime, it would seem ill advised to think that DU is the sole cause of Gulf War syndrome because in any future military actions, exposure to toxic chemicals on the battlefield will almost certainly again produce illness.

The issue of DU exposure remains an important one whether or not it is linked to the multisymptom illness known as Gulf War syndrome. With concern currently mounting across Europe about the use of DU munitions in Kosovo, the *New York Times* referred on January 9, 2001, to a document released by the Joint Chiefs of Staff on July 1, 1999, warning both soldiers and civilians in Kosovo that they should not touch spent DU munitions that had been left on the battlefield. The document also said: "Personnel handling the heads of anti-tank shells or entering wrecked vehicles should wear protective masks and cover exposed skin." It is most unfortunate that such warnings were not given to our troops serving in the Gulf War.

The Shays subcommittee interviewed several scientists with expertise in the field of DU, and its report addresses the issue of aerosolized DU:

According to Leonard Dietz, a retired General Electric physicist and DU expert, at least 300 tons of DU munitions were fired over a period of four days of ground fighting. He says that if only two percent of the uranium became aerosolized upon impacting the tanks, it would generate at least six tons of depleted uranium aerosol particles. [Dietz states:] "This is a huge amount, much of which would have become airborne over the battlefields. This amount in four days is more than 10,000 times greater than the maximum airborne emissions of depleted uranium allowed in the air over Albany [New York] in one month."

(Shays, 84)

The DOD report discusses at length the estimated amount of radiation that soldiers at any of the three DU exposure levels would have received and states that even for Level I exposure, the amount is lower than the level allowed for workers in the nuclear industry. Minimizing the potential for health effects from radiation, the report sees a greater problem with DU's heavy metal toxicity: "A comparison of the estimated health risks from radiation with the possible chemical toxicity effects of soluble uranium oxides demonstrates that DU's heavy metal toxicity effects may be the primary concern" (DOD *DU*, 3:4). Although veterans like Jones, Lawson, and Willoughby are concerned about their exposure to DU, the DOD report states: "DU exposures for the Level II and Level III exposure categories are believed to be well below levels expected to produce either temporary or permanent kidney damage" (DOD *DU*, 2:2). (The kidneys and lungs are the organs most vulnerable to damage from DU.)

Some of the soldiers who underwent a Level 1 exposure when their tank was hit by a DU round actually have depleted uranium fragments embedded in their bodies. Jerry Wheat is one such Gulf War veteran. He reports that he was never told that he had been exposed to DU, but his father, who worked at a lab, tested some shrapnel fragments that worked themselves to the surface of Jerry's skin and found they were radioactive.[1]

Thirty-three soldiers who were crews of vehicles damaged by DU rounds were evaluated at the VA Medical Center in Baltimore in 1993 and 1994. According to the DOD report, these soldiers have medical problems related to the injuries they sustained in friendly fire incidents, but "they are not sick from the heavy metal or radiological toxicity of DU." Even so, the report states:

> Some veterans have multiple tiny fragments of DU scattered in their muscles and soft tissues. These fragments cannot be surgically removed without causing extensive damage to the surrounding tissues. Individuals who demonstrated increased excretion of uranium in the urine had evidence of retained DU fragments on X-rays. No detectable adverse effects on the kidneys were observed. *No cases of cancer have been diagnosed in these participants; nor would one expect any at this point since the latency period for the onset of cancers possibly related to environmental exposure is at least twenty years* [italics added].
>
> (DOD *DU*, 4:2)

Such statements can hardly be reassuring to veterans exposed to DU and other toxic substances in the Gulf. And while in this war there were only a

---

[1] "Desert Storm's Deadly Weapon," *Investigative Reports*, Arts and Entertainment documentary on DU, 1999.

few soldiers who have ended up with DU shrapnel in their bodies, that is unlikely to be the case in future wars, when our enemies will also have DU munitions.

In late 1991, twenty-four soldiers from the 144th company, whose members cleaned up damaged Iraqi vehicles but were not warned about exposure to DU, were sent to the VA Medical Center in Wilmington, Delaware, to be evaluated by Asaf Durakovic, M.D., Chief of Nuclear Medicine at the hospital. According to the Shays report:

> These soldiers had worked on battle damaged tanks and vehicles in the Gulf from January to March 1991 without protective equipment or clothing. In March, a Battle Damage Assessment Team arrived in full radioprotective clothing, inspected the vehicles, declared them "hot" and off-limits.
>
> Preliminary testing showed 14 of 24 veterans "contained decay products of radioactive uranium." According to Dr. Durakovic, urine samples sent to the Army Radiochemistry Lab in Aberdeen, MD, disappeared. Dr. Durakovic recommended additional, more compre-hensive testing—including tests to determine if the 24 veterans had also inhaled DU particles—but further tests and treatments were denied by the VA. Of the 14 veterans, 2 have since died, and the remaining members of the 144th Company have scattered around the country making medical follow-up unlikely.
>
> "None of my recommendations was ever followed. Every con-ceivable road block was put in my line of management of those patients. I was ridiculed. There were obstacles throughout my attempt to properly analyze the problems of those patients. My plan failed because of total lack of interest on the part of the VA to do anything for those unfortunate patients. I [even] received phone calls from DOD suggesting that this work is not going to yield meaningful information and should be discontinued."
>
> Dr. Durakovic was later terminated by the Wilmington VA hospital, he alleges for his outspoken views of the VA concerning the diagnosis and treatment of sick Gulf War veterans.

(Shays, 29)

In an article appearing in the *Nation* on May 26, 1997, the Director of Nuclear Medicine at Georgetown University Hospital, Dr. Harvey Ziessman, stated that Durakovic is "someone I respect and has a lot of experience in this area [internal exposure to radiation]. I certainly would listen to him."[2]

---

[2] Bill Mesler, "Pentagon Poison: The Great Radioactive Ammo Cover-Up," *Nation*, May 26, 1997, 20.

Despite its reassuring words that Gulf War veterans are not at risk from exposure to DU, the Armed Forces Radiobiology Research Institute (AFRRI) in Bethesda, Maryland, is conducting research to look at toxicity of DU fragments that have been embedded in rats. According to the DOD report:

The uranium pellets appear to be dissolving very slowly over time, leading to high levels of uranium in the kidney, urine, and bone. Despite the high DU levels in the kidney, there is no evidence of kidney toxicity, based on several assays.
. . .
These experiments demonstrate that uranium can cross the blood-brain barrier, similar to other heavy metals. Despite this, there is no evidence for behavioral neurotoxicity in male rats.
. . .
The female rats with the DU implants did not show any effects on ability to become pregnant or to carry the litter to term. . . . There were no effects of DU on the litters. . . . There was a correlation between DU levels in the maternal kidney, placental tissue, and fetal tissue. The possible effects of DU on the development of the offspring are now being investigated.

In another study, the Lovelace Respiratory Research Institute (formerly Inhalation Toxicology Research Institute), Albuquerque, NM, is conducting similar studies on rats implanted with three dose levels of DU munitions alloys. The studies will attempt to assess potential carcinogenicity of the implanted materials as well as to assess various cellular and biophysical/biochemical effects.
(DOD *DU,* 4:4-5)

On January 23, 2001, the *New York Times* website carried an article from Reuters describing the results of this Lovelace research that had just been released: "The investigators found that the soft-tissue sarcomas, a form of cancer, were significantly more likely to occur in the muscles of animals that received the DU-containing implants than in control animals." Researcher Fletcher F. Hahn commented: "It's a warning flag that says we shouldn't ignore this. It doesn't mean that (DU) is carcinogenic to humans."

Another group of Gulf War veterans underwent a heavy exposure to DU at Camp Doha near Kuwait City when a fire broke out in the motor pool area. Ammunition stored in the area blew up in a chain reaction that lasted for hours, and the fire burned for two days. According to the Shays report, "DU armor on vehicles and 9,000 pounds of DU rounds were oxidized to powder, exposing 3,500 soldiers in the vicinity to radiation and DU aerosol particles that were widely distributed by high winds. Soldiers involved in the cleanup several days after the fire were not warned of DU contamination and, therefore, wore no protective gear" (Shays, 28). The report quotes from a booklet titled *DU: The Stone Unturned,* which was written by Dan Fahey, who served as a Navy officer in Desert Storm: "Soldiers swept the compound with brooms, picked up debris with their bare hands, and were never issued respiratory masks or other protective clothing" (Shays, 28). The Shays report also quotes Leonard Dietz as saying, "This is something that would make a qualified radiological worker shudder" (Shays , 85). One soldier who helped clean up the mess at Doha was Michael Florez. After he returned to the States, he and his wife had twins. Unfortunately, one of the boys was born missing a hand; his left arm stops just below his elbow.

Gulf War veteran Chris Kornkven, former president of the National Gulf War Resource Center, used the Freedom of Information Act in 1999 to obtain a copy of the log entries involving the Doha fire. Like the crucial logs involving the sounding of the chemical alarms during the first days of the air war, these logs were missing a large number of pages, entries that would have been recorded at the height of the fire. Among the remaining items, item 31 notes: "Burning depleted uranium puts off alpha radiation. Uranium particles when breathed can be hazardous. 11ACR has been notified to treat the area as though it were a chemical hazard area, i.e., stay upwind and wear protective mask in the vicinity." One of the most interesting items, entry 56, states: "Bill Shirley (Supcom Safety Officer) came into LOC wanted to know who is conducting Safety Investigation. Wanted to keep news of 'Radiation' out of press."[3]

Major Doug Rokke, Ph.D., is a whistle-blower who is eager to get information to the press about the dangers of DU's radioactivity and heavy metal toxicity. Major Rokke was part of the NBC (nuclear/biological/chemical) team whose responsibilities in the war included handling incidents involving exposure to DU. After the war, he remained active in issues involving DU and served as the Army's Depleted Uranium Project Director from August 1994 to November 1995. Major Rokke reports that he and many of the men and women he worked with personally in the Gulf War have developed significant health problems since the war and some of his colleagues have died. He himself has frequent kidney stones and has undergone kidney surgery 15 times since Desert Storm. Breathing problems are a concern, and although he used to be a top skier and scuba diver, he can no longer engage in those activities. Major Rokke takes issue with the DOD's assessment of what happened during the war:

Since 1991, numerous Department of Defense reports have stated that medical and tactical commanders were unaware of the probable nuclear, biological, chemical, and environmental (NBC-E) exposures and never told about the medical and environmental consequences of these exposures. That is a lie. They were told. They were warned.

---

[3] These logs from the Doha fire incident can be accessed on the website <<http://www.homepage.jefnet.com/gwvrl/du-link.htm>>.

We identified the threats, health and environmental consequences in written messages and during courses.[4]

Major Rokke reports that he has lost academic positions because of his challenges to DOD policy, including his most recent job as a member of the Department of Environmental Sciences at Jacksonville State University in Alabama. The DOD is most unhappy with his frequent appearances on TV and radio condemning the use of depleted uranium, as Major Rokke notes:

> On December 2, 2000, I was told again by an Army colonel in uniform that I should cease my activities to obtain medical care for all Operation Desert Storm casualties and to force completion of environmental remediation [cleaning up DU]. Of course I said no. Well, as before, "no" is unacceptable. On December 14, 2000, I found out that of my military pay due me—$1763.19—officials from the Army pay roll office at Fort McCoy, Wisconsin, decided to recover $2725.83 of previous pay from me because all of a sudden the paperwork records of my duty have disappeared. Funny, but I had delivered the paperwork to the Fort McCoy payroll office myself, so I knew it was there. So Army officials took away $1300.32 of this month's pay, leaving me a total income of $462.87. Merry Christmas from the Army! This new method of intimidation is neat. If they can't force me to stop my work by telling me to stop, then they will starve me into submission while DOD officials continue to ignore sick warriors and all of the sick citizens of the world.[5]

One of Major Rokke's greatest concerns now is the huge quantity of depleted uranium that we have left on the desert battlefields of southern Iraq, and he is on a personal crusade to alert the world to this problem:

> During the Gulf War, they fired over 900,000 rounds of these [DU], which are now left all over the desert. . . . What we're doing is just basically disposing of our radioactive waste in somebody else's backyard, and that's a crime against God and humanity. There's no place in this country that you can take solid uranium waste and spread it in anybody's backyard. It wouldn't be allowed. . . . Unless uranium contamination is removed from all terrain, soil, vehicles, and equipment, it will remain a hazard for 4.5 billion years for any individual that inhales it, ingests it, or gets it into a wound. And consequently

---

[4] Major Doug Rokke, e-mail to author, December 8, 2000.

[5] Major Doug Rokke, e-mail to author, December 18, 1000.

any contamination that has been deliberately left there by military operations must be physically removed and properly disposed of.
(GWS video footage)

Major Rokke is haunted by the photos of Iraqi children born with extreme birth defects and thinks that someone must clean up the depleted uranium waste now contaminating large areas of southern Iraq. Not surprisingly, Saddam Hussein is using the statistics about great increases in cancer rates and birth defect rates in Iraq to attack the United States. It is important, however, to note when considering this issue that Iraqi civilians and soldiers have been exposed not only to DU left on the battlefield but also to their own nerve agents that would have contaminated areas near the chemical facilities bombed during the air war. The debate continues regarding whether the low levels of nerve agents that might have drifted over Coalition forces almost a hundred miles from such sites could have harmed our troops, but large numbers of Iraqis must have been far closer to these explosions that spread nerve agents throughout the region.

DU was an extremely effective weapon for the United States in the Gulf War, and large numbers of our soldiers might have died had it not been used, but that is not the only consideration. Mustard gas was a highly effective weapon during World War I, and the atomic bomb was the ultimate in an effective weapon, but almost everyone believes that these weapons are too horrific to be used again. All across Europe, concerns are being raised about the use of DU munitions in Kosovo and the potential risk to the health of those coming in contact with the depleted uranium. Italy, Germany, Norway, and Greece have asked that DU munitions be eliminated from NATO arsenals until the related health issues are settled.[6]

It is important to remember that DU worked so well for U.S. forces during Desert Storm only because the Iraqis didn't yet have DU. If Saddam Hussein had had DU munitions to use against Coalition forces, the score would not have been 100,000 Iraqi dead to 148 American dead. In the decade since the Gulf War, however, the list of countries possessing DU armaments has steadily grown and now includes the United Kingdom, Russia, Turkey, Saudi Arabia, Pakistan, Thailand, Israel, and France (RAND *DU*, 1:1). As the years pass, it will be only a matter of time until our soldiers are on the receiving end of DU munitions, and this time it will not be friendly fire.

---

[6] Marlise Simons, "Uranium-Tipped Arms Ban Rejected by NATO Majority," *New York Times*, January 11, 2001.

Chapter 10

Anthrax Vaccine

While the exposures that U.S. soldiers faced in the Gulf War to PB pills, the fallout from low level nerve agents, and oil well fires are rarely mentioned in the media today, the battle over the safety of anthrax vaccines shows no sign of abating. Hardly a week goes by without another story about a pilot who has refused to take the anthrax shot or a report of soldiers who have been given the vaccine in the last couple of years and are now suffering from chronic illnesses hardly distinguishable from Gulf War syndrome.

The Pentagon's decision to use the anthrax vaccine has much in common with its decision to use PB pills as a protection against soman nerve agent. Critics of Pentagon policy have suggested, however, that the significant risks associated with taking the anthrax vaccine or the PB pills greatly outweigh the small chance of death from anthrax or soman. In neither case was the decision to use these substances an easy one because of the paucity of scientific studies that would help military planners make a careful assessment of the efficacy and safety of the anthrax vaccine or the PB pills.

Like nerve gas, anthrax is a terrifying threat. Cutaneous anthrax can be cured by antibiotics, but inhalation anthrax is almost always fatal. Not only is anthrax deadly, it is relatively easy to use as a biological weapon. As *Newsweek* noted in its October 9, 1995, issue, "A couple of hundred pounds of anthrax can kill millions of people if it is effectively dispersed in the air above a large city." And *U.S. News & World Report* stated in a discussion of Iraq's biological warfare program appearing in its September 11, 1995, issue that "More than 1,500 gallons of anthrax toxin was loaded into 50 bombs and 10 missile warheads." Although military intelligence could only speculate about whether Saddam Hussein had soman in his arsenal, there was no doubt that he had anthrax. In fact, a U.S. company, the American Type Culture Collection, had obtained an export license from the Commerce Department to ship anthrax samples to Iraq during the war between Iraq and Iran in the 1980s.

The reason for alarm was indeed great, and top U.S. military officials decided to use what means were at hand to protect our troops from the deadly threat of anthrax. Because there would be almost no way to treat large numbers of people who contracted anthrax in a biological attack, the Pentagon decided to immunize as many troops as possible who would be serving in the Persian Gulf. There was an existing anthrax vaccine that had been tested in the 1950s and 1960s on groups of wool workers in mills in New England and Pennsylvania. But this vaccine had only been shown to be efficacious for cutaneous anthrax, which was not a significant threat anyway because it could be easily treated with antibiotics. No one knew if the vaccine would work against the deadly inhalation anthrax. In fact, when the FDA reviewed the anthrax vaccine in 1985, it stated, "Inhalation anthrax occurred too infrequently to assess the protective effect of vaccine against this form of the disease."[1]

The debate over the efficacy and safety of this anthrax vaccine continues today and is hampered by the almost complete lack of information on the subject in the published scientific literature. On the one side, the DOD, which implemented a program in 1998 called AVIP (Anthrax Vaccine Immunization Program) to inoculate all service members, has put out position papers assuring the public that there is no danger from the vaccine. On the other side is a Maine physician named Meryl Nass, one of the few scientists in the country who have studied the subject of anthrax and the anthrax vaccine. Thrust into sudden national prominence, she has testified on several occasions to Congress and is quoted in virtually every article discussing the safety of the anthrax vaccine. Her website, <<http://www.anthraxvaccine.org/>>, provides a wealth of carefully presented analysis of the political and scientific issues swirling around the DOD's anthrax vaccination program.

Perhaps Dr. Nass's most important message concerns the advisability of relying on vaccines against biological warfare agents when the vaccines themselves are not without serious potential risks:

> The military's Defense Advanced Research Projects Agency lists over 65 known biological warfare agents, which are naturally occurring. In addition, there are an infinite number of microorganisms that may be created using genetic engineering. There are less than 10 vaccines effective against these agents. It takes an estimated ten years, once one is aware of a microbial pathogen, to develop an effective and safe vaccine against it. The fact that we did not have an effective and safe anthrax vaccine at the time of the Gulf War, and now 10 years later we still do not have one, makes this perfectly clear. Furthermore, if we vaccinate against anthrax, an enemy can just pick a different microorganism to use. If an enemy genetically engineers a new virulent organism, we will not even be able to begin developing a vaccine against it until after it has presented itself—in other words, after it has been used. For

---

[1] Meryl Nass, "The Anthrax Vaccine Saga: How Not to Develop a Vaccine Program," a paper presented to the International Public Conference on Vaccination 2000, Arlington, Virginia, September 10, 2000, 2.

these simple reasons, the use of vaccines against the threat of biological warfare will never provide an effective defense.[2]

In her testimony to the Shays subcommittee on April 29, 1999, Dr. Nass supported this position by quoting, among others, William Patrick, the former head of the Biowarfare Program at Fort Dietrick, who stated in a November 3, 1998, article in the *New York Times*, "It takes 18 months to develop a weapons-grade (biological) agent, and ten more years to develop a good vaccine against it."

Dr. Nass's concern about biological weapons that can be genetically engineered is an important one. On January 23, 2001, the *New York Times* ran a story about a group of Australian scientists who were trying to create a virus that would make mice infertile but by accident produced a deadly virus. According to the article, "the Australian scientists . . . say the discovery of how easy it is to make such a viral killer should ring global alarm bells. They called on all nations to strengthen a global treaty that seeks to ban germ warfare."

Because of the active role she has played as one of the chief critics of the DOD's anthrax vaccine program, Dr. Nass has become the person whom soldiers now contact when they want to report health problems that they have developed following inoculation with the anthrax vaccine. Others who contact her are agonizing over the decision of whether they should take the vaccine or refuse to take it and risk being court-martialed. According to an article in the *Portland (Maine) Press Herald* that appeared on March 11, 2000, "Nass began getting calls about the anthrax vaccine in 1998. People told her they'd taken the shots, and now were suffering from problems such as bloody diarrhea, vomiting and wheezing. Some were coughing up blood. Could it be the shots? they asked." Dr. Nass initially told them that no vaccine would produce reactions like these, but after further investigation, she changed her mind. She estimates that she has now heard from over a thousand people reporting problems that developed after they received the anthrax vaccine.

On September 10, 2000, Dr. Nass presented to the International Public Conference on Vaccination 2000 a paper titled "The Anthrax Vaccine Saga: How Not to Develop a Vaccine Program." In this paper, she lists six major problems that she sees in the DOD's anthrax vaccination program:

First, long-term safety of the vaccine has never been established. Second, the old efficacy rate was fallacious and came from an older vaccine—no one knew how effective this newer vaccine would be. Third, the stockpile was old and many lots had expired but been re-dated, as if they were new, with only a retest of potency. Fourth, the lots were extremely heterogeneous, with variable side effects and potency. Fifth, the manufacturer was far out of compliance with good manufactur-

[2] Ibid., 7-8.

ing practices, and had never had its anthrax line properly inspected. Sixth, use of prophylaxis against biological warfare was not an FDA approved indication.[3]

In her discussion of her first point, the long-term safety of the anthrax vaccine, Dr. Nass quotes Dr. Kwai Chan's GAO (General Accounting Office) report to Congress. (The GAO is a watchdog agency that Congress uses to investigate what is going on in departments of the executive branch of the government such as the DOD or VA.) Dr. Chan stated: "In our discussion with scientists at Fort Dietrick, the estimates of [the] number of people who may have received this vaccine over a 30 years period range from somewhere between 200 to about 2,000 at the most. And we don't know who those individuals are. There has been no follow up."

When Dr. Nass testified to the Shays subcommittee on April 29, 1999, she noted that "The DOD says the vaccine has been safely and routinely administered to veterinarians, laboratory workers, and livestock handlers since 1970." But she pointed out that "(1) The veterinarians and livestock handlers cannot be found, and do not appear to exist. (2) Four hundred to 500 laboratory workers and special operations troops per year have received this vaccine. They have not been screened for adverse effects."

One advocacy group that has been campaigning against the mandatory anthrax inoculation program decided to check out the statement about prior use by veterinarians or livestock handlers. They were particularly concerned to verify this assertion because it was being widely used to reassure soldiers who were given the anthrax shots that they were perfectly safe and had been used for years with no problem. Although they checked with veterinarians and veterinary schools around the country, they were unable to turn up any of these veterinarians who supposedly have received the anthrax vaccine.[4]

In the 1960s, the CDC supervised a study on the current vaccine that had to be carried out to show that the vaccine was safe before it was licensed. Dr. Nass notes that in this study the investigators were only actively checking for reactions at the injection site such as redness or swelling. She states that they "paid only cursory attention to systemic reactions. . . . In fact, at one mill a large number of systemic reactions were reported, but this was blamed on an overzealous nurse."[5]

---

[3] Ibid., 2.

[4] See <<http://www.dallasnw.quik.com/cyberella/Anthrax/V_survey.html>>.

[5] Nass, "Anthrax Vaccine Saga," 2.

In discussing the DOD's current vaccination program, Dr. Nass has stated:

In eleven months 550,000 vaccine doses had been administered but only 39 VAERS (Vaccine Adverse Effects Reporting System) reports had been filed with the FDA. When Congressman Shays asked the Defense Department about the vaccine program, because of the large number of reports of serious illnesses that had reached Congress, he . . . was told that the total adverse reaction rate was only .007%, and that anthrax vaccine was safer than childhood vaccines. What DOD did was to take the total number of reports to FDA of adverse effects and call it the sum total of all adverse events.

However, it turned out that the military had instituted a policy to limit the reports of adverse events before the first vaccination was ever given. Although normally physicians and vaccine recipients are encouraged to report to FDA any adverse reaction they choose, military medical personnel were told that only adverse reactions which resulted in hospitalization, or more than 24 hours of lost duty time could be reported to FDA. This kept the reporting rates remarkably low.[6]

According to Dr. Nass, when the DOD changed this restrictive policy because of testimony to congressional committees, the total number of reports of adverse reactions rose to 1,500, or one in every 300 persons who received the vaccine, a higher rate than for any other vaccine used in the United States. She notes that a far higher rate of adverse reactions was found in a study done at Tripler Army Medical Center involving 603 medical personnel. This study showed that 43% of those who received the vaccine had mild systemic reactions and 5% had moderate or severe systemic reactions.[7]

One Air Force pilot who has become prominent because he has refused to take the anthrax shot is Major Sonnie Bates. Major Bates reported for duty at Dover Air Force Base in Delaware in August 1999. Within a few weeks of his arrival, he learned that many people in his squadron were reporting that they had become seriously ill after taking the anthrax vaccine. In the face of this evidence, Major Bates made an agonizing decision that he knew would jeopardize his 13-year career as a pilot. He refused to take the vaccine. As the highest-ranking field officer who had refused to take the vaccine, Major Bates faced the possibility of spending five years in prison. (Enlisted men receive much shorter jail time if they refuse the vaccine.) After Major Bates appeared on *60 Minutes* in early February 2000, the Air Force decided to cut a deal that allowed him to avoid a court-martial, and by the end of March he was out of the Air Force. On February 21, 2000, Major Bates wrote a memorandum to

---

[6] Ibid., 5-6.

[7] Ibid., p. 7.

Brigadier General Starbuck in response to the Article 15 proceedings against him. In this memorandum, Major Bates presents a list of the health problems reported by 15 members of his squadron, the 9th Airlift Squadron at Dover AFB, after they took the anthrax vaccine. Several of these accounts follow:

Michelle P. suffered from thyroid damage, an autoimmune disorder, chronic fatigue, and dizziness.

Bill L. was grounded for several months. After the vaccine, he developed cysts on numerous places on the inside and outside of his body, to include his heart. He has undergone surgery to remove some of the cysts and was hooked up to an IV for six weeks. He became incapacitated at the controls of the airplane due to this illness. He was on a basic crew, so the other pilot basically flew the airplane solo to Germany.

Jim G. suffers from severe chronic joint pain, thyroid damage, and has an autoimmune disorder. Both of his arms are in braces due to the severe joint pain.

Dave H. experienced diverse symptoms, which included chronic bone/joint pain, chronic fatigue, and a loss of ability to concentrate. He has been cross-trained into another, less physically demanding career field.

Mike M. had been grounded for eight months after receiving the vaccine. He has experienced eight seizures. Other symptoms include crippling bone/joint pain, memory lapses, ringing in the ears, dizziness, and an inability to concentrate.

Brian B. suffers from severe bone and joint pain. Subsequent bone scans reveal lesions on his spine, pelvis, and ribs.

Jim R. experienced chronic bone/joint pain. He said his arms frequently go numb.

Cindy C. started experiencing episodes of vertigo, ringing of the ears, and memory lapses. She has had five vertigo episodes, described as being so severe that she couldn't walk. The vertigo has ceased since the vaccine has stopped and she is on a waiver to not receive any more anthrax vaccine until her health improves.

Michael M. is in a military hospital hooked up to a ventilator. He is paralyzed. He speaks with his eyes. The doctors say it was from the flu vaccine [not the anthrax vaccine].[8]

Many active duty soldiers are afraid to reveal that they are having any reaction to the vaccine for fear that this admission will jeopardize their career. Thus it is likely that many more members of this squadron have experienced bad reactions to the anthrax vaccine. In an article about the anthrax vaccine appearing in the *Hartford Courant* on October 12, 2000, reporter Thomas D. Williams discusses a random survey of 1,253 service members who were pilots or flight crew. The GAO found that 49 percent "had not discussed adverse reactions to the vaccine with health care professionals because they felt either they would harm their careers, lose flight status or be ridiculed. Overall 60 percent refused to disclose adverse reactions to the vaccine with a health care personnel."

Because of the widespread national media attention that his case has received, Major Bates and his wife Roxane are now getting calls from all over the United States from soldiers who report devastating effects to their health after receiving the anthrax vaccine. The Bates's Delaware home has become a clearinghouse for assembling a file about soldiers who believe that the sharp health decline they experienced while taking the series of anthrax shots is the direct result of these vaccinations.

Through his courageous stand against the vaccination program, a stand that the DOD would undoubtedly argue is detrimental to national security, Major Bates may in fact be contributing to the viability of our fighting forces. In a statement released on October 11, 2000, by the House Committee on Government Reform, committee member Christopher Shays said: "I sincerely believe the military is being blatantly untruthful to us. And I believe this program is destroying our readiness. I believe that it must stop." Committee chairman Dan Burton stated: "Because of Secretary Cohen's decision to mandate the anthrax vaccine we have lost a substantial number of pilots and air crew members. These pilots and air crew members are essential to our military readiness. They are the backbone of every military operation. Without our Air National Guard and Reserve, the United States military would be unable to respond to any national security threat or emergency." The *Hartford Courant* article states: "Burton, who has a 94-page summary of conflicting vaccine program statements made by Pentagon officials on his website, asked one general if he knew that an officer lying to the committee could be subject to a court martial."

The reports of illnesses like Gulf War syndrome arising from the anthrax vaccine administered in the late 1990s lend support to the theory that the vaccine has played a role in the illnesses reported by Gulf War veterans. Dr. Nass notes, however, that the anthrax vaccine used during the Gulf War may not

---

[8] For the complete text of this memorandum, see Major Bates's website: <<http:www.dallasnw.quik.com/cyberella/Anthrax/Starbuck2.html>>.

have been the same as the one used today.[9] There is a difference also in the way the vaccine was administered during the two periods. During the Gulf War, there was such a shortage of anthrax vaccine that only 150,000 soldiers received it and most were only given two shots. The DOD's protocol for the vaccination program established in 1998 called, however, for a series of six shots, with an annual booster. Dr. Nass and others note that many soldiers who have been vaccinated in the last couple of years did not develop a severe reaction until the fourth shot.

One study suggesting a possible relationship between Gulf War syndrome and the anthrax vaccine was published in the January 1999 *Lancet*. The authors stated that "Vaccination against biological warfare and multiple routine vaccination were associated with this CDC multi-symptom syndrome in the Gulf War cohort."[10]

Major Doug Rokke was involved in the anthrax vaccination program in Desert Storm as an NBC (nuclear/biological/chemical) officer. He lists many problems involved in the use of the anthrax vaccine that make it difficult to sort out the relationship between the vaccine and Gulf War syndrome:

(1) The anthrax vaccines arrived in theater just in a box; there was no temperature control. So therefore you don't know what the quality control is or what the safety of the anthrax vaccine was.

(2) By command directive, we were not allowed to record the names of the individuals that received the anthrax vaccine.

(3) We were not allowed to record any adverse reactions that were observed from the administration of the anthrax vaccine.

(4) We were not allowed to record the lot numbers of the anthrax vaccine that was administered.

So in other words, nobody knows what happened, who got what, when did they get it, and what happened to them when they received the vaccine. And to top it off, we have no idea whether the vaccine was safe or not because it was shipped in a box and the temperature was up and down from say, freezing, all the way up to say 130 or 140 degrees Fahrenheit.

(GWS video footage)

Dr. Nass notes another problem with the anthrax vaccine: "some lots were 40 times as potent as other lots." She points out that this variation in the vaccine makes it extremely difficult to study its effectiveness or potential for causing

---

[9] Meryl Nass, telephone communication to author, January 2001.

[10] Catherine Unwin et al., "Health of U.K. Servicemen Who Served in Persian Gulf War," *Lancet*, vol. 353, January 16, 1999. See p. 11, note 6, of the present work for the definition the CDC has used to evaluate Gulf War illness.

side effects. Moreover, the manufacturer has repeatedly changed the dates on expired lots. Dr. Nass stated in her April 29, 1999, testimony to the Shays subcommittee: "The majority of complaints of illness have been associated with vaccination using lots 020 and 030. Each lot contains approximately 200,000 doses."

There is only one facility in the country that is licensed to manufacture the anthrax vaccine. It was formerly called the Michigan Biologic Products Institute, but has been renamed BioPort by the purchasers of MBPI. Dr. Nass describes the many problems at this plant:

> When [the] FDA finally went in and did a thorough inspection one month before the current vaccine program began, they found so many problems that they immediately quarantined 11 lots of vaccine, and the manufacturer "voluntarily" shut down for major repairs and renovations. Although those renovations have since been completed, the FDA has not allowed the manufacturer to reopen, and new lots of vaccine that have been made in the last 15 months remain under quarantine.[11]

Dr. Nass points out that the FDA policy in 1985 concerning its approval of the anthrax vaccine stated that "Immunization with this vaccine is indicated only for certain occupational groups with risk of uncontrollable or unavoidable exposure to the organism." (These groups were assumed to be people working with certain animal products or lab workers investigating anthrax.) Dr. Nass therefore argues that the use of the vaccine for prophylaxis against biological warfare was not approved by the FDA and thus the anthrax vaccine should be treated as an investigational new drug, or IND. This is a crucial point because according to FDA policy, IND drugs are supposed to be administered only to consenting individuals and adverse reactions would have to be carefully recorded. In a letter that they sent to the FDA on November 3, 1999, Congressmen Burton and Sanders, together with two other congressmen, stated: "We also urge that the FDA place the anthrax vaccine back under Investigational New Drug (IND) status."[12]

Dr. Nass finds especially disturbing the statements from blue-ribbon panels that have considered the possible relationship of the anthrax vaccine to Gulf War syndrome. In one such statement, the NIH Technology Assessment Workshop Panel said: "No long-term adverse effects have been documented." It is frustrating to Dr. Nass that no one within the government seems interested in performing studies on the long-term effects of the anthrax vaccine or releasing the results of the study on long-term effects carried out at Tripler Army Medical Center in Hawaii beginning in September 1998. As she stated before the Shays

---

[11] Nass, "Anthrax Vaccine Saga," 3.

[12] For a copy of the letter, see <<http://www.anthraxvaccine.org/henney.html>>.

subcommittee, "If you never look for something, you are sure never to find it." At least the Institute of Medicine committee investigating Gulf War syndrome said: "The Committee concludes that in the peer reviewed literature there is inadequate, insufficient evidence to determine whether an association does or does not exist between anthrax vaccination and long term adverse health outcomes."

One other issue that has been prominent in the recent anthrax controversy concerns the possible use of squalene as an adjuvant in the anthrax vaccine. (Adjuvants are substances added to a vaccine to increase its action.) This issue drew more attention when a researcher at Tulane University found antibodies to squalene in the blood of many veterans suffering from Gulf War syndrome. After denying for years that there was any squalene in the anthrax vaccine, the DOD has recently announced finding trace amounts in the parts per billion range. As researcher Dr. Jim Moss has noted, however, trace amounts like this could easily arise from the broth in which the bacteria for the vaccine are grown.[13] Since squalene occurs naturally in the human body and other organisms, the development of antibodies to it could be one of the autoimmune effects that seem to be part of the development of Gulf War syndrome in many veterans. For Dr. Nass, squalene could be a red herring that diverts attention from more productive lines of inquiry.

In the RAND report on PB, Dr. Beatrice Golomb notes that the aluminum regularly used as an adjuvant in the anthrax vaccine is known to make the blood brain barrier more permeable. Thus it is possible that the aluminum from the anthrax vaccine increases the penetration of the blood brain barrier that Dr. Mohamed Abou-Donia documented in rodents who were exposed to a combination of DEET, permethrin pesticide, and PB.

In December 2000, the DOD temporarily suspended its anthrax inoculation program for all soldiers except for those deployed to Korea or the Middle East. The reason cited was a shortage of vaccine, a shortage that conveniently enables the DOD to back off from a program that was drawing ever-increasing criticism.

It seems unlikely at this point that anyone will be able to sort out the degree to which the anthrax vaccine may have contributed to the development of Gulf War syndrome in some soldiers serving in Desert Storm, although extensive serologic tests could indicate which ill veterans received the vaccine. Soldiers faced many different exposures during the war, including anthrax vaccine, nerve agents, oil well fires, PB pills, pesticides, diesel fuel, and depleted uranium. All one can say is that it is likely that different individuals developed chronic illness as the result of different combinations of these exposures.

Relevant to the issue are the opinions of two physicians who are researchers in the fields of chemical injury and chemical sensitivity. Dr. Claudia Miller has noted: "The focus has often been to look for the single cause of Gulf War syndrome, but in fact, it may be a combination of all of these different things

---

[13] Jim Moss, e-mail communication to author, November 2000.

and different exposures in different persons, so it's important to keep this in mind" (GWS video footage). Gunnar Heuser, M.D., a toxicologist in the Los Angeles area and an assistant clinical professor of medicine at UCLA, views the issue from this perspective:

> I see patients who have a history of chemical injury. I have seen patients more recently who were involved in the Gulf War and now developed Gulf War syndrome. The patients who come to me with Gulf War syndrome have exactly the same complaints as the patients I see from chemical injury. So one statement I can make is that all their symptoms can be explained on the basis of chemical exposure alone. I am very much aware there was more than chemical exposure in the Gulf War. There were infections, there were vaccinations, there were all kinds of warfare, there was radioactivity. And these are all controversial issues, but my point is a patient with Gulf War syndrome has exactly the same complaints as patients of mine who have never been to the Gulf War but have had chemical exposure.
>
> (GWS video footage)

As Drs. Miller and Heuser indicate, there are many routes by which people can arrive at the kind of debilitating chronic illnesses that are plaguing the Gulf veterans. Long before Desert Storm began, many civilians had reported developing the condition known as multiple chemical sensitivity as the result of exposure to substances like pesticides, new carpet, paint, or solvents. Thus it should seem hardly surprising that many soldiers exposed to toxic chemicals in the Gulf War have developed a chronic illness that resembles MCS. It would be a potentially dangerous mistake to think that we could avoid having thousands of soldiers develop chronic illness in a rematch with Saddam Hussein in the Persian Gulf or in other engagements fought on toxic battlefields merely by eliminating the use of the anthrax vaccine.

Chapter 11

Theories and a Possible Treatment

We may never fully understand the mechanisms that have produced Gulf War syndrome, but the complexity of the situation has spawned many theories about the physiological basis for this condition. One comes from Howard B. Urnovitz, Ph.D., a biotechnologist who has a laboratory in Berkeley, California, and is the scientific director of the Chronic Illness Research Foundation. Dr. Urnovitz's interest in Gulf War syndrome is a natural outgrowth of a life-long commitment to helping to unravel the mystery of chronic illness, a commitment that arose from the deaths of several family members who succumbed to cancer and other chronic diseases. Jim Tuite now works with Dr. Urnovitz, serving as the Director for Interdisciplinary Sciences of the Chronic Illness Research Foundation.[1] Tuite was the second author of an important paper that Dr. Urnovitz published in May 1999 in *Clinical and Diagnostic Laboratory Immunology*.[2] Tuite describes the results of that study in this way:

We found that the [sick] veterans are showing evidence of fragments of what appear to be chromosomes in their serum, that is, in the acellular portion of their blood where there should not be any RNA. We're finding sections of RNA or nucleic acids that are consistent with sections of chromosomes that are associated with diseases that are known to be linked to the kinds of exposures reported by veterans in the Gulf. We've also linked similar damage in cases of multiple myeloma cancer, which is a cancer known to be associated with chemical exposure, MS [multiple sclerosis], lupus, chronic fatigue syndrome, and other chemical exposures. So what we have found is that there is evidence, genetic evidence, that these vets were exposed to toxic hazardous compounds.
(GWS video footage)

Dr. Urnovitz takes a broad view of disease, as he explained in testimony to the Shays subcommittee on February 2, 2000:

---

[1] The foundation's website is <<http://www.chronicillnet.org>>.

[2] Howard Urnovitz et al., "RNAs in the Sera of Persian Gulf War Veterans Have Segments Homologous to Chromosome 22q11.2," *Clinical and Diagnostic Laboratory Immunology* 6, no. 3 (May 1999): 330-35.

The GAO [General Accounting Office] report recognizes medical science's conventional approach to chronic illnesses. The paradigm continues to be a search for a *single* causative agent. The weakness in this conceptual approach is that most chronic diseases are multifactorial. This single causative agent approach was formulated long before science recognized that the human body can sustain damage at the cellular and molecular level from a variety of physical, chemical, or biological insults, and long before we determine the vast arrays of hazardous materials to which these veterans were exposed. Assigning any one entity as the causative agent will impede any progress in designing medical control of a chronic disorder.

. . .

It would appear that the human body has a mechanism for confronting toxic exposures. We all know that we are given our physical characteristics from genetic material or genes. . . . What we learned by simultaneously studying GWS, cancer, AIDS and multiple sclerosis is that the genes have the ability to "reshuffle" and create new genes. We reason that these new genes are used to adapt to the toxic environment in which we live.   It seems that there are confounding events that turn this reshuffling mechanism from a normal protective process to a disease state. . . .

Through a research blood test we recently developed, we have been able to identify material in the sera of patients suffering from chronic illnesses that likely play a critical role both as a marker of the illnesses and a mechanism for the reshuffling. This discovery of the reshuffling process resulted from the identification and analyses of a type of nucleic acid, RNA, found in the serum or plasma of GWS veterans. It took us several years to break the code on just one RNA molecule that we were able to isolate.   It has been our goal to collect RNA from as many veterans with GWS and clone, decode and catalog the reshuffled genes with respect to patient symptomology. This approach should allow us to group ailments according to the pattern of each gene sequence. . . . We plan to initiate our own program mapping the detours that the human genome takes with respect to toxic exposure and chronic disease. The ensuing catalog of reshuffled genes should assist in establishing diagnostic protocols and tailoring treatments for each patient.

The single greatest obstacle to achieving this goal with respect to the veterans has been the lack of sufficient private sector funding for research into an issue that most people believe is the responsibility of the government.

. . .

It is my professional opinion that the clues to solving significant medical problems in the world today: cancers, AIDS, heart and liver diseases, autoimmune and neurologic disorders, vaccine safety, chemical injuries, and military associated ailments,—lie in the blood of these veterans who suffer from GWS and possibly in the blood of their families. Once we break and catalog the code of the reshuffled RNA, we may finally have a clear direction in how to treat chronic illnesses. The Gulf War veterans will become heroes again for a second time.

Dr. Urnovitz's theory has found a powerful supporter in Luc Montagnier, M.D., one of the two men who shared the credit for discovering the HIV virus. Dr. Montagnier serves on the Scientific Advisory Board for Dr. Urnovitz's Chronic Illness Research Foundation. When Dr. Urnovitz presented the above testimony to the Shays subcommittee on February 2, 2000, he also gave subcommittee members a copy of a letter of support from Dr. Montagnier that contains this passage:

I have been following the interesting work of Urnovitz and his col-leagues. They have reported on the detection of RNA molecules in the blood of veterans with Gulf War Syndrome (GWS) which seems to be specific for the disease. I am aware of their ability to detect similar blood RNA molecules in several other chronic diseases. . . Since 1963, RNA has been shown to be self-replicated, spliced, edited, reverse-transcribed and to be endowed with enzymatic activity. This new observation suggests that RNA may also be involved in the process of disease. It is my opinion that the detection and identification of blood-borne RNA is an important contribution to the field of medicine that will result in our further understanding of the nature of chronic disease and chronic disease progression.

. . .
[I] strongly advise that future research on Gulf War Syndrome should include the study of the detected genetic material, i.e., novel RNA in the sera of these veterans. . . . I foresee that the study of GWS may have major consequences for other chronic diseases.

The kind of research that Dr. Urnovitz is pursuing is far more worthy of support than most of the research projects upon which the DOD has spent over $150 million; too many of these projects have been designed to explore a psychological basis for Gulf War syndrome. Unfortunately, the DOD seems reluctant to put money into research like that performed by Dr. Urnovitz or by Dr. Haley that is focused upon establishing medical tests that will show the damage done to the bodies of our soldiers during the Gulf War. Once it is possible to present convincing evidence of this damage and its relationship to toxic exposures in the Gulf, the government will have a moral obligation to provide medical care for these veterans and to support those whose chronic illness prevents them from working. As long as the DOD and VA can argue either that Gulf War syndrome does not exist or if it does exist, it is merely the product of stress and is not related to toxic exposures, they can evade assuming any major financial commitment to these ill veterans.

Dr. Haley has not only been hard at work performing research that substantiates the physical basis of Gulf War syndrome, he has also published an article titled "Is Gulf War Syndrome Due to Stress? The Evidence Reexamined" in the *American Journal of Epidemiology*. In this very technical and detailed analysis, Dr. Haley reviewed the 16 articles from peer-reviewed journals that were cited by the Presidential Advisory Commission in its final report in which it suggested that Gulf War syndrome might be due to PTSD [post-traumatic stress disorder]. In the conclusion to his paper, epidemiologist Dr. Haley states: "My reanalysis of these studies, however, shows that, when the sensitivity and specificity of the psychometric scales used to measure PTSD rates were taken into account, virtually all of the apparent PTSD actually represents falsely positive error of measurement."

The stress theory of Gulf War syndrome was given further emphasis in the report released on December 20, 2000, by the Presidential Special Oversight Board appointed by President Clinton to evaluate how the DOD was handling the issue of Gulf War syndrome. Pat Eddington, executive director of the National Gulf War Resource Center, was quick to react: "This is exactly the kind of whitewash we were expecting. Given the PSOB's well known cozy relationship with the Pentagon, the report's tone and conclusions were hardly surprising."

This Oversight Board, chaired by former Senator Warren Rudman, was comprised of one woman and six men–Rudman, Jesse Brown (then head of the VA), and four high-ranking retired officers of the Armed Forces. The executive director was a retired colonel. The sole woman on the board was Dr. Vinh Cam, who holds a Ph.D. in cellular immunology/immunotoxicology. Dr. Cam worked for 11 years at the EPA and now serves as a private consultant regarding issues of airborne toxins and environmental and occupational health. She appears to be the only member of the board in a position to make an informed, independent judgment about the issues of toxic exposures in Desert Storm and their potential contribution to Gulf War syndrome. Selecting board members from the old boy network of retired admirals and generals made sense only if the covert purpose was not to engage in any serious investigation of the DOD's handling of the issue of Gulf War syndrome but to instead whitewash the whole affair. After a considerable expenditure of taxpayers' money in an investigation lasting over two years, the board issued a final report that basically rubber-stamped the way Gulf War illness had been handled by Bernard Rostker and the DOD. Given the composition of the board, it should surprise no one that there was a lone dissenting voice championing the cause of the veterans, and this was Dr. Vinh Cam, who states in her dissenting opinion:

In my three page review . . . of the draft Final Report, I had two major concerns: 1) oversight of Dr. Roestker [*sic*] and DOD and 2) the Board's statement of stress as causality for Gulf War Illnesses. In the Final Report although my first concern was addressed by reducing the praising of Dr. Roestker [*sic*] to two references (pages 10 and 70), the Board's statement on stress has remained unchanged. I thus find it compelling to submit the following dissenting remarks. . . .

As an individual Board member, I was never asked about the causality of Gulf War Illnesses (GWI). The Board, as a group, was never asked such a question. Furthermore, the Chairman of the Board himself, more than once, stated in public hearings and at our own internal meetings that it was not the Board's charter to address the cause of GWI. He had cautioned Board members against making any statement regarding causality of GWI. Given these facts, I was surprised to see such a statement in the Final Report. Although it is acceptable to mention that the review of past research studies has indicated the impact of combat stress—that's why stress is listed among the risk factors—as indicated in Chapter 7, the Board statement of stress as causality is inconsistent with the Board's charter. This statement does not faithfully reflect all Board Members' assessment of GWI issues. . . .

Furthermore, it reflects a two tiered review process. . . . Not all Board members were given equal weight in shaping the content of the report. . . .

With regards to the implementation of the Presidential Advisory Committee's recommendation on "DoD . . . should place a higher priority on addressing pre- and post-deployment surveillance . . ." it was difficult for me to assess DoD's compliance. I was not given any opportunity to do a field visit, my exposure to this issue was merely limited to DoD presentations to the Board. What could be and couldn't be done by Board members was controlled in an ad hoc manner by the Executive Director and/or the Chairman. My requests to attend events organized by Gulf War veterans and to invite veterans to speak at our board meeting were viewed with suspicion and reluctance and generally denied. There was a deliberate attempt to curtail my contacts with Gulf War veterans. I don't understand how I can effectively assess DoD programs without talking to the very people for whom they are intended.

There is no question that the Board had given a significant technical contribution to the review of OSAGWI [Office of the Special Assistant for Gulf War Illness (Bernard Rostker)] Case Narratives. At times though, the Presidential Special Oversight Board (PSOB) acted more like an extension of OSAGWI, a higher level of technical review rather than an Oversight Board in the traditional sense of exerting strict scrutiny over OSAGWI's work. . . . The lack of full disclosure of the contacts between selected Board members and OSAGWI leadership remains an issue. There was no fire wall between the oversight party and the party being under oversight.

The tone of certain sections of the report might lead the reader to think that the past stress driven theory of GWI at DoD is being revived by PSOB. A strong and in-depth analytical tone as expected from an oversight report is missing, and instead the report is dominated by a contriving effort to advocate stress as "likely a primary cause of illnesses . . ."

In her dissenting opinion, Dr. Cam unfortunately omitted the end of the sentence that concludes the above excerpt. The relevant passage of the final report, as it appears at the beginning of Chapter 7, states: "The Board concludes that stress is likely a primary cause of illness in at least some Gulf War veterans and a likely secondary factor in potentiating other causative agents in producing undiagnosed illnesses among some Gulf War veterans." On the face of it, this is a reasonable statement; among 100,000 ill veterans there are bound to be at least some in whom stress was a primary cause of illness. The second part of the statement can also simply refer to research like that conducted by Dr. Abou-Donia, which shows that stress combined with PB, DEET, and permethrin pesticide produces a greater breakdown in the blood brain barrier in rodents than do just the three chemicals combined.

Despite Dr. Cam's unfortunate truncation of the crucial quotation, a careful reading of the whole report yields the impression that she is right on target with her objections. There is far too much emphasis in the report upon the role of stress and far too little emphasis upon the role of toxic exposures. And even though a large amount of DOD research money has already gone into investigating stress and post-traumatic stress syndrome, the Presidential Special Oversight Board actually urged that even more money be spent in researching the role of stress in Gulf War illness. It would be far more useful, for example, to spend research money on major studies involving brain scans of suffering Gulf veterans. Every ill veteran who has reported to me that he or she has had a SPECT or PET brain scan has said that it showed abnormalities.

Unfortunately, "stress" has become a code word in the debate over the reality of Gulf War syndrome, a term too readily used by officials like Bernard Rostker to stave off any questions about the role of PB pills, exposure to low levels of nerve agents, excessive pesticide use, oil well fires, anthrax vaccine, and depleted uranium. And if the covert aim is to avoid assuming a huge financial obligation toward the ill veterans, stress is the thing to emphasize. Call a veteran's illness PTSD or depression and the amount of disability payment is far less than the payment for damage to the brain or central nervous system.

The reluctance of the DOD and the VA to accept the idea that more than stress and psychological problems is involved in Gulf War syndrome has taken a huge toll on the sick veterans. Not only must they struggle with pain and illness day after day, they also have to deal with physicians or family and friends who do not take their problems seriously. The following statement from Colonel Herb Smith illustrates the extremes to which a suffering veteran can be pushed by these skeptical attitudes:

To me the worst news a person can have is to be sick and not know what it is, not know what to expect. The way I view sickness, bad news actually would have been good news because then I knew what I was dealing with, I knew what to expect and I didn't have to deal with people telling me I was out of my mind. That was so discouraging and so depressing.

(GWS video footage)

The bad news that was good news for Colonel Smith was a diagnosis of lupus. You have to be driven to your limit by physicians and others doubting the reality of your illness to reach the point where you are almost happy to find out that you have a verifiable disease, even though it is potentially fatal.

The shabby treatment of people with MCS and Gulf War syndrome arises from our society's long tradition of viewing much of unexplained illness as being psychological in origin (psychogenic). Tuberculosis was once thought to be associated with a certain personality type, and multiple sclerosis was originally considered to be psychogenic. A few decades ago many physicians claimed that children developed asthma because of domineering mothers. This erroneous belief led to a tragic consequence when many asthmatic children were uprooted from their families and sent to live in an asthmatic hospital in Denver during the 1950s and 1960s.

Col. Herbert Smith encountered these attitudes at Walter Reed and the VA hospitals he visited: "In the early days, I was seeing psychiatrists, neuropsychiatrists, psychologists, social workers because they were absolutely convinced that I had a somatoform disorder or I was a hypochondriac." Colonel Smith actually saw eight Army and VA mental health professionals, even though it is obvious from his interview on our GWS video that he is a man who is well balanced mentally and emotionally. It is unfortunate that Walter Reed and the VA did not run more tests like the PET brain scan that ultimately showed physiological problems in Colonel Smith's brain. Moreover, Colonel Smith had to consult a specialist at Johns Hopkins School of Medicine to find out that he had lupus. His friends at the Kuwaiti Embassy in Washington, D.C., offered to pay for that consultation when they learned that he had exhausted his financial resources, but it turned out that someone else paid the bill. It is indeed ironic that the Kuwaiti Embassy was more willing to help Colonel Smith than the government he had served for most of his life.

There is one research trial that the DOD and VA recently launched that involves something more than a study of stress. In this study, ill veterans who have tested positive for mycoplasma fermentans (*incognitus*) are being given the antibiotic doxycycline for a period of one year. The DOD and VA were pressured into performing this study by members of Congress and a large number of ill veterans. To understand the origin of this study, we must consider the work of an unusual pair of scientists who have promoted the theory that an infectious agent could be causing Gulf War syndrome.

Garth and Nancy Nicholson, who are both Ph.D. researchers, now operate the Institute for Molecular Medicine in Huntington Beach, California. They both formerly worked at the prestigious M.D. Anderson Cancer Center in

Houston, Texas, leaving shortly after they became involved in the mycoplasma and Gulf War syndrome controversy. Garth Nicolson has published over 400 articles in peer-reviewed journals. He held the David Bruton, Jr., Chair in Cancer Research at M.D. Anderson and was a professor of pathology and laboratory medicine at the University of Texas Medical School at Houston.

When Garth Nicolson's stepdaughter came back from serving in the Gulf War, she was sick, and Garth and Nancy themselves gradually became chronically ill with symptoms that were similar to the ones their stepdaughter and other veterans were experiencing. The Nicolsons decided that their illnesses might be caused by an infectious microorganism. Soon they were focusing their attention on a mycoplasma that they found in the blood of veterans suffering from Gulf War syndrome. (Mycoplasmas are rudimentary forms of bacteria that lack a cell wall.) Garth Nicolson described this microorganism in testimony to the Shays subcommittee on April 2, 1996:

The most common infection found in our studies thus far was an unusual microorganism, Mycoplasma fermentans (*incognitus strain*), in the blood of GWS patients. This microorganism is similar to a bacterium, and it is very rarely found in humans. Our detection of this mycoplasmal infection deep inside the blood leukocytes (a form of white blood cell) of approximately one-half of the GWS patients examined, including two out of two British Desert Storm veterans with GWS, indicated that this is not a benign infection. . . .

In our studies a large portion of the GWS patients that we have tested have an unusual mycoplasmal infection in their blood, but we have found that this infection can be successfully treated with multiple courses of specific antibiotics. . . . Multiple treatment cycles are required, and patients relapse often after the first few cycles, but subsequent relapses are milder and they eventually recover their health. In our published study approximately one-half of a small random group of GWS patients were mycoplasma-positive (14/30) and most (11/14) recovered after multiple cycles of antibiotics, and a few (3/14) are continuing antibiotic therapy. None of 21 healthy controls were mycoplasma-positive.

One of the more controversial aspects of the Nicolsons' involvement in the issue of Gulf War syndrome is their oft-repeated assertion that they have discovered one gene from the HIV virus in the mycoplasma fermentans (*incognitus*) that they have found in the blood of ill veterans. They suggest that the presence of this gene, which they call the HIV-1 envelope gene, indicates that this is a strain of mycoplasma that has been engineered for biological warfare. To complicate matters still further, they have implied that powerful forces in Texas were experimenting with this microorganism. In a pamplet titled "Summary of Persian Gulf War Illness Pilot Study on Mycoplasmal Infections in Veterans and Family Members," they state: "We strongly suspect that TDCJ [Texas Department of Criminal Justice] prisoners were illegally used in Biological Weapons testing. Thus the modified mycoplasmas detected in Gulf War Veterans may have their origin in the U.S."

The Nicolsons' assertion about finding an envelope gene from the HIV virus in mycoplasma fermentans (*incognitus*) samples is emphatically disputed by Aristo Vojdani, Ph.D., director of the Immunosciences Laboratory in Beverly Hills, California, one of the few labs in the country offering a test for mycoplasma fermentans (*incognitus*). Dr. Vojdani has issued a statement titled "Scientific Facts Versus Fiction About Mycoplasma" in which he says:

> In one study, it was suggested that pathogenic mycoplasma genomes were genetically manipulated, and part of the HIV genome was inserted into M. fermentans and that this organism (M. fermentans containing HIV genome) is responsible for a large number of disease cases among veterans. To prove or disprove this claim, we attempted to amplify various regions of the HIV genome by using primers specific for different regions of the HIV genome in the PCR [polymerase chain reaction] assay. We also utilized the extremely sensitive method of Southern Blot analysis with probes specific for the HIV genome. Using both methodologies we found no portion of the HIV genome among DNA samples of Gulf War veterans who were infected with mycoplasma. . . . The results of this experiment are clearly indicative that the above claim about insertion of the HIV genome into M. fermentans is scientifically unfounded.

Dr. Vojdani has found mycoplasma fermentans (*incognitus*) in the blood of a sizable percentage of patients with chronic fatigue syndrome or multiple chemical sensitivity who have had nothing to do with the Gulf War and have no relatives who served there. This fact would argue against the Nicolsons' theory that mycoplasma fermentans (*incognitus*) was genetically engineered as a biological warfare agent. It should also be noted that a biological weapon that is as slow-acting as mycoplasma fermentans (*incognitus*) would not have been particularly useful to Saddam Hussein.

But the most questionable aspect of the Nicolsons' work in the field of Gulf War syndrome is the flamboyant quality of many of Nancy's public statements (and even some of Garth's statements). These excerpts come from an article that appeared in the *Orange County Register* on January 23, 1997:

> "I don't care what people think about me anymore," said Nancy Nicolson, who said she is heiress to an ancient European dynasty. "I've been branded crazy my entire life. I've never been like anybody else."
> . . . .
> "I can't even keep track," she says of what she terms frequent attempts on her life by U.S. operatives intent on keeping her quiet, attempts she hasn't reported to the police.

The situation becomes even more bizarre. In November 1996, Nancy Nicolson appeared on *Geraldo Rivera* in a show called "Real-Life Mob Dolls: Wives and Daughters of the Mob." In introducing Nancy, Rivera explained that she claims she is the daughter of mobster Lucky Luciano but was sent to live with adoptive parents: "She learned, however, that she was—through genetic testing, she learned that she is the daughter of none other than Lucky Luciano . . . the man who practically invented the Mafia." Rivera questioned Nancy about an episode in which she stated that $3 million suddenly appeared in her bank account one day but later disappeared. When another woman on the show asked Nancy if the FBI or another law enforcement agency had ever followed her during her student years, Nancy replied: "Well, when I was growing up, my mother kept telling me those people were trying to kill me." She eventually ties her past life to her present life by saying, "Well, many of the soldiers who were actually, I guess, assigned to eliminate me were people we eventually helped get over that terrible illness from Desert Storm."

Nancy Nicolson's flamboyant public statements, and Garth Nicolson's apparent acquiescence in the public persona she is presenting must be considered when judging the Nicolsons' various assertions about mycoplasma fermentans (*incognitus*), its possible use as a biological weapon, and its possible contamination by a gene of the HIV-1 virus. (The Nicolsons say this gene cannot infect someone with AIDS.) Needless to say, the possible role of mycoplasma fermentans (*incognitus*) in Gulf War syndrome is a scientific issue that stands or falls on its own, regardless of the Nicolsons' involvement in the controversy.

The results of a large clinical study in which doxycycline is being given to veterans who have tested positive for mycoplasma fermentans (*incognitus*) will be announced in the fall of 2001. Even if substantial numbers of veterans show improvement with this treatment, several important questions will remain. It is possible that mycoplasma fermentans (*incognitus*) is only an opportunistic infection that attacks people whose immune systems have been suppressed by other factors such as toxic exposures. If this is the case, ill veterans may find that the antibiotic treatment helps only part of their symptoms. At any rate, phone conversations with Garth Nicolson and various people who have worked with the Nicolsons give me the strong impression that veterans and others who have tried long-term antibiotic treatment at their suggestion have usually taken the antibiotics for at least a couple of years, with only brief periods of cessation. People with whom I have spoken report that their symptoms begin to return after a few days or weeks off the antibiotics. Hence they start taking the antibiotics again, and it is not clear if these patients will ever be able to stop taking antibiotics without their symptoms recurring.

Long-term use of antibiotics raises many issues, including the development of resistant strains of bacteria. Another issue involves the chemical sensitivity that a large percentage of ill Gulf veterans are now exhibiting. Physicians in the field known as "environmental medicine," who treat patients with multiple chemical sensitivity, are concerned that long courses of antibiotics destroy good bacteria in the gut along with the bad ones, leading to a proliferation of a yeast known as *candida albicans*. These yeast give off chemical substances that are particularly problematic for the chemically sensitive. For this reason, environmental medicine physicians treating MCS patients with antibiotics almost always instruct them to take some form of acidophillus to replace the bacteria that have been killed by the antibiotics. In his pamphlet titled "Antibiotics Recommended When Indicated for Treatment of Gulf War Illness/CFIDS," Dr. Garth Nicolson states: "Doxycycline therapy may result in overgrowth of fungi or yeast and nonsensitive microorganisms. . . . To replace bacteria in the gastrointestinal system, yogurt, *Acidophillus* or *Lactobacillus* tablets are recommended."

Paul Cheney, M.D., Ph.D., a leading physician in the field of chronic fatigue syndrome, also has serious reservations about the prolonged use of antibiotics because of their adverse effect on gut flora. In a lecture in February 1999, Dr. Cheney stated that 18 months of antibiotic therapy could leave patients "gut ecology cripple[s] for the rest of their lives." Because many Gulf veterans have been diagnosed with chronic fatigue syndrome, Dr. Cheney's caution on the use of antibiotics should be taken very seriously.

The doxycycline trial illustrates how important it is for physicians who are trying out various treatments on ill veterans to know the track record for these treatments in chronic fatigue syndrome and multiple chemical sensitivity patients. Given the reservations that physicians treating these patients have about long-term antibiotic treatment, it is important that the veterans who are participating in the doxycycline study be evaluated for a possible overgrowth of *candida albicans* to be sure that they are not trading a mycoplasma problem for a candida problem.

When Dr. Urnovitz testified to the Shays subcommittee on February 2, 2000, he attempted to address the role of both toxic exposures and infectious agents in the development of Gulf War syndrome:

One of my research efforts is focused on how chemical and infectious agents interact to initiate and maintain a chronic disorder. The symptoms [of Gulf War Syndrome] are similar to those of over a dozen unexplained epidemics over the last 60 years . . . including headache, muscle pain, slight paralysis, damage to the brain, spinal cord or peripheral nerves, mental disorders . . .

. . .

It is known that the Gulf War was one of the most toxic battlefields in the history of modern warfare. Syndromes associated with organophosphate-induced delayed neuropathy [OPIDN] could explain many of the observed and unexplained illnesses. However, it may not be mutually exclusive to have tissue damage resulting from toxic exposures, which leads to inflammatory responses in critical tissues with ensuing opportunistic bacteriological, viral, and fungal infections. The continued presence of these pathogens may greatly impair a possible healing process. All of these risk factors need to be considered in trying to understand the underlying pathology of Gulf War Syndrome.

The mycoplasma issue is particularly relevant to the large number of reports of illnesses like Gulf War syndrome that have developed in the family members of sick Gulf veterans. The Nicolsons argue that ill family members have picked up the mycoplasma fermentans (*incognitus*) infection from the returning veteran. But it should be noted that this mycoplasma can be found in the saliva and mucosal linings of many healthy people in the general population. Problems only seem to develop when it enters the bloodstream.

Theories abound about what could be causing family members to become ill, but none seem particularly satisfactory. In addition to the mycoplasma theory, some people believe that something toxic or radioactive in the desert sand was mixed in with the souvenirs veterans brought home. Bob Jones's wife became chronically ill about six weeks after he got back from the Gulf War, and she is now 100% disabled. They suspect that her illness arose from her contact with sand in the box of clothing and souvenirs that Bob brought home from the Gulf. A laboratory analysis has shown that the sand contained a fungus that is quite toxic (Part II, 194).

Another theory about why families of veterans are getting sick involves the similarity, if not identity, between Gulf War syndrome and multiple chemical sensitivity. There are many cases of civilian families with no military connections in which individuals report that several people in their family developed MCS after they remodeled their house or put in new carpet or treated their house with pesticides. In my book *Casualties of Progress: Personal Histories from the Chemically Sensitive*, there are two stories about families who reported that they all became sick from a common exposure, a pesticide application in one case and a leaking oil tank in the other. Thus it is possible that some cases of family members getting sick after a soldier returned from Desert Storm may be coincidence.

An example of illnesses that are probably coincidental involves Gulf veteran Jim Davis, whose story appears in Part II, and his sister Kelly, her husband, and their two daughters, whose story appears in *Casualties of Progress*. Kelly and her family all gradually developed multiple chemical sensitivity in the mid-1990s because a leaking oil storage tank had produced a pool of heating oil in the crawl space under their house. Kelly, her husband, and their daughters suffered from a variety of symptoms very similar to those involved in Gulf War syndrome. In fact, once when Jim was home for a visit, he joked and said, "I think you people have what I have." Kelly's family had not seen much of Jim after the war, however, because he was in California, so their similar health problems were probably just a coincidence. Kelly and her family recovered their health by moving away from their polluted house. An infectious process seems less likely in this case because they all recovered without taking antibiotics.

The question of whether family members could have gotten sick through close contact with an ill Gulf War veteran is a very complex one, however, and infection remains a possibility. Another possibility, perhaps a remote one, is suggested by the story of Swc. Fred Willoughby, who reports that when he came back from the war he would often get night sweats and the sheets on his side of the bed would be black. Many veterans who spent weeks breathing the smoke from the oil well fires report that they coughed up black stuff for months after the war or sweated a black substance. One wonders if a spouse or a young child could have been exposed sufficiently to the toxins from the oil that it affected their health. That's unlikely, but it's important to consider even marginal possibilities in seeking an answer to this puzzle. Yet another possibility involves the burning semen phenomenon that so many wives reported after their husbands returned from Desert Storm. A study to analyze samples of this burning semen to see if they contain toxic substances has apparently never been completed, although a physician in Ohio reportedly began such a study.

There is clearly a need for extensive studies comparing chronic illness rates in the families of ill Gulf War veterans to the rates in families of Gulf War veterans who are not ill as well as to the rates in families of veterans who were in the service at that time but did not go to the Persian Gulf. If studies show a substantially higher rate of illness in family members of ill Gulf War veterans, then the government will have a clear responsibility to help these family members.

At any rate, it is important to note that the resemblance between Gulf War syndrome and multiple chemical sensitivity must be taken into account in any study of Gulf War syndrome. In the CDC study of four Air National Guard units, the authors noted: "Our finding that 15% of nondeployed [veterans] also met illness criteria was equally important and suggests that the multisymptom illness we observed in this population is not unique to GW service."[3]

If Gulf War syndrome is chemical sensitivity that developed as a result of the overwhelming level of toxic exposures that the veterans faced in Desert Storm, then it is not surprising that there are many cases of similar illnesses in the civilian population. To say that Gulf War syndrome is not unique to veterans who served in the Gulf War is not to say that their service in the Persian Gulf did not make them ill. For the DOD and the VA to deny responsibility for illness produced by toxic exposures in the Gulf War makes no more sense than to refuse care and compensation to the victims of gunshot wounds received in a war on the grounds that many civilians are also wounded or killed by guns.

---

[3] Keiji Fukuda et al., "Chronic Multisymptom Illness Affecting Air Force Veterans of the Gulf War," *Journal of the American Medical Association* 280, no. 11 (September 16, 1998): 103.

Chapter 12

ALS Cases

While many ill veterans cling to the hope that a cure will be found for their condition, the outlook is far bleaker for those suffering from amyotrophic lateral sclerosis (ALS), also known as Lou Gehrig's disease. A rare and fatal degenerative disease that usually begins in middle age, ALS affects the spinal cord and brain stem and leads to spreading muscular weakness. In reference to cases of ALS among the Gulf War veterans, Jim Tuite has noted: "It's unusual the numbers that are actually suffering from the illness in that it is not an illness that usually strikes young men or women" (GWS video footage).

Major Michael Donnelly is a victim of ALS whose case has become widely known through his testimony to the Shays subcommittee and his book *Falcon's Cry*, written with his sister Denise Donnelly. Major Donnelly was a fighter pilot who flew 44 missions during the Gulf War. During these missions, he often flew through gaseous plumes containing nerve agents, plumes generated by the bombing of Iraqi chemical weapon facilities. In testimony to the subcommittee, he described the evolution of his health problems:

> Upon return from the Gulf, I was reassigned to Florida [where] . . . I first started to experience strange health problems. I didn't feel as strong as I once had or as coordinated . . . [I was] always fighting a cold or the flu. By the summer of 1995 . . . [I was] stationed in Texas. . . . I was exposed to malathion fogging, an organophosphate pesticide used for mosquito control, while jogging in the evenings. I started to have serious health problems.
>
> [I had] scotoma, or blind spots, in front of my eyes and my heart would beat erratically. Palpitations, night sweats, sleeplessness, trouble concentrating and remembering, and trouble taking a deep breath. Extremely tired much of the time. By December, I had trouble walking and experienced weakness in my right leg. In January 1996, I explained my symptoms, and mentioned I had been in the Gulf War, to a flight surgeon who immediately talked about the effects of stress. I was referred to a neurologist.
>
> During the first visit with the neurologist, I heard the line that I would hear throughout the whole Air Force medical system: "There's no conclusive evidence that there's any link between service in the Gulf and any illness."
>
> (Shays, 13)

When members of the Shays subcommittee questioned Dr. Bernard Rostker about the incidence of ALS among Gulf veterans, he stated under oath that "for the population that served in the Gulf, we would expect to see roughly between 7 and 11 cases of ALS. And we're looking at nine cases of ALS" (Shays, 13). If Dr. Rostker were a medical doctor instead of an economist, he would have been more likely to realize the fallacy in his statement. The subcommittee heard a different story from Robert H. Brown, Jr., M.D. and Ph.D, the director of the Cecil B. Day Laboratory for Neuromuscular Research at Massachusetts General Hospital and a leading ALS expert. In a letter to the subcommittee, Dr. Brown stated:

> The incidence of new cases of ALS is about 1/100,000 individuals in our [overall] population. Thus, it is true to say that a group of 700,000 individuals [the number of Gulf War veterans] might, in the aggregate, be expected to show 7 or so new cases of ALS over a year's time. However, these statements about aggregate populations must be interpreted carefully. In particular, they assume an age-spread that reflects *an entire population*. If one looks at the age of onset of ALS, the mean onset age is 55 years. The number of cases showing onset *below the age of 40* is probably no more than 20-25 percent or so of the total. Thus, one might expect 0.20-0.25 cases/100,000 individuals [or an estimated 1.4-1.7 cases of ALS in the 18-40 age range]. As I understand it, there are now 9 or 11 cases of ALS in the Gulf War veterans population. *This seems excessive to me* [italics added in Shays report].
>
> (Shays, 13-14)

Because of the publicity surrounding Major Donnelly's case, veterans with ALS from all across the country began contacting the Donnelly family. As of December 2000, Tom Donnelly, Michael's father, has personally documented 28 cases of ALS among Gulf veterans.

When Major Donnelly testified to the Shays subcommittee, he spoke about the role he thinks pesticides may be playing in the health problems he and other Gulf War veterans have experienced, and he described in particular the malathion exposure that he thinks put him over the edge and led to his developing ALS. He had an important message for Congress:

> Why aren't the DOD and the VA warning everyone else who served in the Gulf War that they should avoid exposure to pesticides? How many more people are out there waiting for that one exposure that will put them over the top? Why is no one putting out the word? A warning

could save the lives and health of many individuals, could save them from going through what I am going through.[1]

In their book, Michael and Denise Donnelly mention another ALS victim, Major Randy Hébert, who fits this same pattern of a soldier who returned home with health problems but managed to stay on active duty until he encountered a strong exposure to pesticide and subsequently developed ALS.

In December 1996, Major Hébert testified to the Shays subcommittee. Looking thin and gaunt, he was barely able to speak and relied upon his wife Kim to repeat his testimony. Major Hébert described his exposure to sarin nerve gas that he thinks was released by a chemical land mine that exploded when he was breaching the Iraqi lines. Although Major Hébert struggled to speak that day, his words were carried on the evening news shows and his picture appeared on the front page of newspapers all across the country. His dramatic testimony did much to draw public attention to Gulf War syndrome. The Shays report contains this section based upon his testimony:

> Major Randy Lee Hébert of the Marine Corps believes he was exposed to chemical agents on February 24, 1991, or Ground Attack Day, based on what he heard, was told, and felt. Shortly after directing his vehicle to Lane Red One following a chemical alarm, Major Hébert, who was not wearing protective gear, was told a chemical mine had soiled the lane.
>
> Major Hébert stated: "I recall my right hand feeling cool and tingling" as he struggled into his protective clothing and gear. After removing his mask when told it was a false alarm, he received another radio message: "Your lane is dirty, chemical mine has gone off, go to MOPP 4." Major Hébert testified, "I now feel that [removing his mask] was a mistake." Shortly after, Major Hébert said, "he felt funny" and had trouble breathing.
>
> Returning home in May 1991, Major Hébert reported symptoms of memory loss, mood swings, vomiting, diarrhea, depression, and severe daily headaches.
>
> (Shays, 14)

In testimony before the subcommittee, Major Hébert also explained why he was convinced that he was exposed to nerve agents on that fateful day:

> I learned after the war that the chemical mine detonated in Lane Red One was confirmed for the nerve agent Sarin and also for the agent Lewisite Must Gas by a Fox vehicle in the lane. I also learned that two Marines in an AM-TRAC received chemical burns, and that the

---

[1] Denise and Michael Donnelly, *Falcon's Cry* (Westport, Conn.: Praeger, 1998), 226.

chemical mine confirmation was reported by the regimental commander of the Sixth Marines.

(Shays, 78)

When we interviewed Major Hébert for our video in June 2000, he had undergone the inevitable heartbreaking deterioration that destroys the bodies of ALS victims. He was almost totally paralyzed and was staying alive by means of a feeding tube and a tracheotomy. His limbs looked like those of a starvation victim. Pictures on the living room wall, however, showed a far different Randy before he was sent to the Gulf War, a young man so handsome, charming, and virile that he could have passed for a movie star or posed for a Marine Corps recruitment poster.

We filmed Randy with his six-year-old daughter sitting on one arm of his recliner and his four-year-old son on the other. His wife Kim spoke for him, asking him to verify what she was saying. Still able to move his eyes, Randy communicates with family members by blinking his eyes once for yes and twice for no. He also writes messages on a special computer that enables him to choose letters and words by activating a button with his knee. The remarkable thing about Randy is that although his body is inexorably wasting away, he still has a beautiful smile and his eyes light up when he reacts to someone. It was a memorable moment when, as we were filming Randy, his little son suddenly leaned over and kissed him on the cheek. A radiant smile spread across Randy's face, a sign of all that remains wonderful of the human spirit even in the face of extreme adversity.

Kim Hébert related for us what had happened to her husband:

When he came home from the Persian Gulf, he was agitated, couldn't keep a train of thought. He came down with depression and insomnia, he couldn't sleep, he had rashes all over his body. He was coughing, couldn't catch his breath. He never got a headache before the war. As soon as he came back, he had to take aspirin every single day, so that was really bizarre.

Then in 1994 we got orders to go to Missouri, and right before we left we sprayed the house with pesticides because we were renting it to someone. Randy spent two hours in the garage with those pesticides in the air, sweeping and cleaning out the garage, and that's what we think affected him in a big way.

From cleaning out the garage, within a couple of days we headed to Missouri to meet the truck. It's there that Randy started noticing a problem with his hand. He was trying to help move a box, and he dropped the box. His hand just wouldn't work. A year and a half later we got a diagnosis of ALS.

(GWS video footage)

Gulf veterans who have developed ALS were exposed to toxic cholinester-ase inhibitors during Desert Storm, an exposure that may have produced a neurotoxic injury that greatly heightened their susceptibility to cholinesterase inhibitors like pesticides. The label on one brand of pesticide states: "Repeated exposure to cholinesterase inhibitors may without warning cause prolonged susceptibility to very small doses of any cholinesterase inhibitors." The fact that both Michael Donnelly and Randy Hébert, like other ill veterans, are now sensitive to chemicals like household cleaning products, perfume, or diesel fuel or exhaust is one more indication that their ALS may be an unusual and heightened manifestation of an underlying disease process involving chemical injury. Jim Tuite has this to say about the relationship of ALS cases in Gulf War veterans to toxic exposures:

> One of the things that we know about exposure to these kinds of compounds, particularly organophosphate pesticides or organophosphate nerve agents, is that exposure over periods of time can actually cause changes in the biochemical mechanisms of the body, the ability to be able to resist future exposures. And so you see a phenomenon in which someone who has been exposed in the past is biochemically altered in a certain percentage of his ability to be able to defend against these compounds and then later gets exposed again and becomes much more susceptible to the effects of the exposure and it can actually lead to a long-term neurological damage or other kinds of chronic disease.
> (GWS video footage)

At present, the cause of ALS is unknown, but speculation about a possible connection to toxic chemicals has been reinforced by what is happening at Kelly Air Force Base in San Antonio, Texas. It was recently discovered that there is a large cluster of ALS cases among people who have been civilian employees at the base. The October 20, 2000, issue of the *San Antonio Express-News* carried an article by reporter Nicole Foy stating that there are now 16 cases of ALS among former or current workers. Five of these people have already died. The article also notes that five of the people with ALS all worked in the same building. Since the rate in the United States for new cases each year is only 1 or 2 per 100,000 people, the cluster of ALS victims at Kelly Air Force Base is highly significant. For years it has been known that Kelly has a major toxic waste problem. Toxic chemicals from the base have contaminated the ground water in the surrounding neighborhoods, and property values have plummeted as word has spread about this contamination. In an October 29, 2000, article in the *Express-News,* one former base employee was quoted as saying, "I worked in Bldg. 321 in the 1980s. I remember seeing blackbirds drinking from green puddles that were around the building. Later, I saw them dead with their feet sticking straight up in the air!" The Air Force has already spent just under $170 million on a cleanup project and estimates that the final price tag may reach $480 million.

The Shays report makes a further connection between toxic chemicals and ALS:

A new study by Dr. Will Longstreth at the University of Washington School of Medicine in Seattle once again suggests a causal link between ALS and the presence of toxic agents. According to the study, exposure to agricultural chemicals— including pesticides—may increase men's chances of developing the degenerative disease. Researchers say men whose histories showed high exposures to these chemicals are at 2.8 times more risk than those who were never exposed.

(Shays, 83)

In March 2000, the VA started conducting a survey to try to ascertain the number of cases of ALS within the population of Gulf War veterans. It seems unlikely, however, that the survey will yield meaningful data because of a catch-22 reason that could be termed "We'll ask, but don't tell." Testifying before the Senate Veterans' Affairs Committee meeting on October 12, 2000, Dr. John Feussner, chief research and development officer for the VA, discussed the ALS survey. He stated that the VA had notified veterans to whom it had sent the survey that if they responded positively to the question of whether they had ALS, they would have a diagnosis and therefore could lose any benefits they were receiving under a special program Congress had passed to give benefits to veterans suffering from undiagnosed illness. An audible ripple of indignation swept across the hearing room, and outraged senators asked Dr. Feussner to justify this bizarre policy. He replied that the VA's hands were tied—policy on the matter was determined by Congress and if Congress wanted the ALS cases treated differently, they would have to pass a law to that effect. At any rate, veterans to whom the survey has been sent may be afraid to report their ALS for fear of losing financial support. Thus the data collected will almost certainly significantly underestimate the prevalence of ALS among Gulf War veterans.

As life is slowing slipping away from these young Gulf War veterans suffering from ALS, there are important stakes involved in the issue of whether the DOD and VA recognize the condition to be connected to service in Desert Storm. One young man who served in a National Guard unit in the Gulf War ended up with ALS and couldn't even get the VA to buy him a wheelchair, so he had to crawl around his home. He was only 35 when he died. When veterans die from ALS, their families will get no survivor benefits unless they were still on active duty when they were diagnosed. It remains to be seen whether the DOD and the VA will do the right thing and call these ALS cases service connected or will once again take cover behind the mantra "no conclusive evidence."

Chapter 13

Chemical Sensitivity

Readers of this book who are not familiar with multiple chemical sensitivity, or MCS, may view it as just one more bothersome symptom that is simply a peripheral issue in the condition of Gulf War syndrome. I would like to suggest, however, that MCS may in fact be the mechanism that lies behind the health problems troubling the veterans. The decades-long experience of MCS patients has shown that in most cases the chemically sensitive can reduce or eliminate many of their symptoms by avoiding the chemicals that are triggering them. One MCS patient, for example, eliminated her migraine headaches by avoiding cigarette smoke, diesel exhaust, and caffeine and eliminated her joint pains by switching her heating system from an oil burner to an electric boiler.

By reading books about chemical sensitivity and joining support groups, most people with MCS have found ways to reduce their health problems. Learning to reduce unnecessary chemical exposures in their homes and trying various elimination diets will often help eliminate some of their symptoms. A physician who told her story in my book *Casualties of Progress: Personal Histories from the Chemically Sensitive* relates how her fibromyalgia (muscle pains) disappeared when she removed dairy products from her diet. (Others would not necessarily get the same effect by eliminating dairy products, however, because food sensitivities are very individual, as are chemical sensitivities.)

One young veteran who appeared on our video reports that he has had diarrhea three or four times a day for nine years; other veterans whose stories appear in Part II also report suffering from diarrhea after almost every meal. These veterans and countless others plagued by this problem might benefit from some advice about how to experiment with their diet to see if that might help control their diarrhea. There is a chance that their diarrhea is being triggered by certain foods or perhaps even pesticide residues in the foods.

It is hard for the average person to believe that multiple chemical sensitivity can be an important factor in chronic illness. It sounds too bizarre that someone could have a strong reaction to a tiny amount of perfume or to the odor of natural gas. One almost never hears about MCS from the famous medical clinics or the rest of the medical establishment, and there are a number of reasons for this neglect. One important reason is that the concept that common chemicals at levels frequently encountered in daily life could be affecting people's health is hardly a popular idea with many large corporations.

To understand why there is so much pressure against the validation of chemical sensitivity, one need only ask whether research and information on the dangers of smoking would ever have seen the light of day if virtually every U.S corporation had been selling cigarettes. Almost every corporation is at risk for losing money from falling sales revenues or from liability cases if the reality of MCS is substantiated, and corporations provide the advertising revenue that is the life blood of the media industry. A television channel or a newspaper shows real courage when it runs a story that implies that chemical sensitivity is a real problem, not just a quaint delusion, as corporations heavily involved in marketing products containing toxic chemicals would have the public believe.

When pondering the connection between chemical sensitivity and Gulf War syndrome, it is interesting to consider the role played in the issue by a physician named Ronald Gots. When Dr. Haley and his team published two articles on Gulf War syndrome in the January 15, 1997, issue of the *Journal of the American Medical Association,* their articles spawned several letters to the editor, which were printed in the August 6 issue. A letter from Dr. Victor Gordan praised their research, but a letter signed by five people was highly critical of the Haley studies. The first author of this letter was Ronald Gots, long-time spokesman for chemical interests and foe and nemesis of the MCS community. What was particularly unusual was the authors' inclusion of a line thanking DowElanco for sponsoring the research that contributed to producing the letter. At the time, DowElanco was one of the country's largest pesticide manufacturers; DowElanco gave us Dursban, now banned by the EPA for use around homes or schools. (Of course, one wonders why the journal was accepting letters to the editor sponsored by corporations with obvious vested financial interests.) The public may not be ready to believe that Gulf War syndrome is closely related to chemical sensitivity, but Ronald Gots and DowElanco seem to understand this relationship.

So who is Ronald Gots? He is a physician with a Ph.D. in pharmacology who is the founder of an organization known as the Environmental Sensitivities Research Institute. In their book titled *Chemical Exposures: Low Levels and High Stakes,* Nicholas Ashford, Ph.D., J.D., and Claudia Miller, M.D., M.S., describe the Environmental Sensitivities Research Institute as follows:

> ESRI is a corporate-supported entity with an "Enterprise Membership" fee of $10,000 per year. Board members include DowElanco; Monsanto; Procter and Gamble; the Cosmetic, Toiletry and Fragrance Association; and other companies and trade associations involved in the manufacture of pharmaceuticals, pesticides, and other chemicals.[1]

---

[1] Nicholas Ashford and Claudia Miller, *Chemical Exposures: Low Levels and High Stakes* (New York: John Wiley, 1998), 279n.

As Peter Radetsky notes in *Allergic to the Twentieth Century*, "As one of the most vocal of those who insist on the psychogenic origin of MCS, Gots provides the chemical industry just what it needs: public assurance that whatever else might be going on in MCS, chemicals have nothing to do with it."[2] When television reporter John Stossel presented an extremely negative view of MCS on *20/20*, who was the expert to whom he turned for a medical opinion about MCS? Dr. Ronald Gots of course.[3]

Dr. Gots has not fared well in the media recently, however. A front-page *Washington Post* article on July 4, 1999, titled "Cutting Claims with Fraud" described a lawsuit in which an accident victim was suing State Farm Insurance Co. In reviewing her claim, State Farm had utilized the services of Dr. Gots's Medical Claims Review Services. The *Post* quotes a 1998 opinion by Idaho District Judge D. Duff McKee in this case: "The evidence was overwhelming that the utilization review company selected by the claim examiner was a completely bogus operation. The company did not objectively review medical records but rather prepared 'cookie-cutter' reports of stock phrases, assembled on a computer, supporting the denial of claims by insurance companies."

On June 23, 2000, NBC's *Dateline* presented an hour-long program about the practices of State Farm and included a segment in which the interviewer took Dr. Gots to task for his role in supplying State Farm with reports that would allow the company to avoid paying the claims of accident victims. The *Dateline* reporter noted that they had "obtained copies of 79 MCRS reports done for State Farm," and he pointed out, "Although too small a number to draw any definitive conclusions, we were surprised to find every single medical review, 79 out of 79, favored State Farm, recommended cutting back or denying care to accident victims."

It would hardly be an exaggeration to say that Dr. Gots's fingerprints are all over anti-MCS activities and publications. He was involved in the production of a highly critical booklet titled *A Close Look at Multiple Chemical Sensitivity*, which was written by psychiatrist Stephen Barrett and published by Quackwatch, Inc. On the inside of the back cover is a statement thanking

---

[2] Peter Radetsky, *Allergic to the Twentieth Century* (Boston: Little, Brown, 1997), 180.

[3] Stossel's other "expert" who denied that MCS was a valid condition on the *20/20* program was freelance medical journalist Michael Fumento. In the 1999 Alabama PBS documentary about Gulf War syndrome, which included a discussion of illnesses among the family members of some Gulf War veterans, there is a brief but chilling comment from Fumento: "I have a prediction to make. My prediction is that eventually every single Gulf War veteran and his or her spouse and their children will die [laughs]. Why? Because everybody dies [chuckle]." Later in the Gulf War documentary, Fumento says: "If somebody tells you over and over and over, you read it in *USA Today*, you see it on the cover of *Life* magazine, 'You should be sick, you should be sick, you should be sick,' and the next thing you know, your joints really do feel like they ache."

Gots for "valuable help with this report." In Appendix C, "Reputable Consultants," Gots is one of five persons listed as scientific experts.

Of particular relevance is the Quackwatch booklet's recommendation against funding MCS research. Research funds for studies of MCS have been virtually nonexistent for decades because of a catch-22 situation. MCS opponents argue that there is no reason to fund research into a disease that has no physiological basis, and MCS advocates cannot show that chemical sensitivity is a physiologically based condition because they have no funds for studies to substantiate this position.

One of the most respected researchers in the field of chemical sensitivity is William Meggs, M.D., Ph.D., a professor at the Brady School of Medicine of East Carolina University in Greenville, North Carolina. Dr. Meggs has published many articles in peer-reviewed journals. One article, for example, presents the results of his research using biopsies to investigate damage to the nasal lining of chemically sensitive patients. In a 1998 interview, Dr. Meggs stated: "I've spent a lot of time applying for research grants to try to study these illnesses [like MCS] and the role of chemicals in these illnesses, and my grant applications come back with scathing comments [like] 'Don't spend any money on this research because everybody knows this is all psychological.'"[4]

To understand why MCS has been almost totally neglected by the medical establishment, it is important to realize that in large part medical opinion is shaped by the leading medical journals, and there are economic reasons why some of these journals might hesitate to publish articles substantiating the physiological basis of MCS. One major reason is that some of these journals are largely supported by advertising revenues from pharmaceutical companies. One such journal is the *Journal of the American Medical Association*, whose revenues help support the AMA. Unfortunately for those with chemical sensitivity, pharmaceutical companies are hardly neutral concerning MCS. In the January 2001 issue of the *Townsend Newsletter for Doctors and Patients,* Ann McCampbell, M.D., describes the problem:

The pharmaceutical industry is intimately linked to the chemical industry. That is, many companies that make medications also manufacture pesticides, the chemicals most implicated in causing MCS and triggering symptoms in people who are chemically sensitive. For example, Novartis (formerly Ciba-Geigy and Sandoz) is a pharmaceutical company that makes and sells the widely used herbicide atrazine. This helps explain why a Ciba-Geigy lobbyist submitted material to a New Mexico legislative committee in 1996 opposing all legislation related to MCS and declaring that the symptoms of people with MCS "have no physical origins." . . .

---

[4] William Meggs, videotaped interview with the author in August 1998.

The pharmaceutical company Eli Lilly used to be a part of Dow-Elanco (now Dow Agroscience), the primary manufacturer of chlorpyrifos. . . . Monsanto, known for making Roundup and other herbicides, is a wholly owned subsidiary of a pharmaceutical company called Pharmacia.[5]

Pharmaceutical companies are only part of the problem, however. Medical schools and the leading medical clinics around the country have been skeptical about chemical sensitivity, and this widespread skepticism has had devastating consequences not only for civilians who suffer from the condition but also for the more than 100,000 Gulf War veterans who now have Gulf War syndrome.

A pioneering professor from Northwestern Medical School named Theron Randolph first alerted the world to the problem of chemical sensitivity in the 1950s and soon lost his academic appointment. Decades have slipped by since Dr. Randolph raised the alarm, and very little research has yet been done on chemical sensitivity. Had there been a more open attitude toward investigating this issue, we would now be in a much stronger position to help the sick Gulf War veterans regain their health.

Although it is easy to fault the DOD and the VA for the way they have dismissed the health problems of the veterans, their attitudes are influenced by the widespread belief in the medical establishment that chemical exposures at very low levels do not have a negative impact on health. Physicians, scientists, and patients in the MCS community have argued the contrary for years, but with virtually no research money available, they have never been in a good position to prove their case.

With the ever-increasing number of chemicals being introduced into common use and the ever-increasing number of people who have developed chemical sensitivity, the time cannot be too far distant when the reality of the problem will become apparent to all. One hundred thousand ill veterans may help convince the skeptics, as they have Dr. Robert Haley, who told me: "Before I got involved in the Gulf War syndrome research, I assumed that MCS was a psychological problem. I've seen it now reported by so many veterans who clearly are not psychologically impaired that I now consider MCS and related problems a very serious medical issue in need of serious research."

---

[5] Ann McCampbell, "Multiple Chemical Sensitivities Under Siege," *Townsend Letter for Doctors & Patients* (January 2001): 20-21. <<http:.//www.tldp.com>>.

Afterword

It cannot be emphasized too much that, as Professor Mohamed Abou-Donia has noted, the soldiers sent to the Persian Gulf were exposed to a cocktail of toxic chemicals and different soldiers had different combinations of exposures. The fact remains that in the civilian population there are clearly many cases of people developing a condition almost identical to Gulf War syndrome from exposure to various toxic chemicals.

Many observers discount the possibility that a Gulf War syndrome exists because they can see no single unifying factor running throughout the spectrum of illnesses reported by Gulf War veterans. It is important, however, to consider the hypothesis that there is in fact a unifying factor in the vast majority of ill Gulf War veterans and that factor is their new sensitivity to chemicals. In testimony to the Shays subcommittee on February 2, 2000, Dr. Claudia Miller described this new sensitivity:

> During the past seven years I have served as the environmental medical consultant to the Houston VA's regional referral center. Approximately 90% of veterans interviewed described new-onset intolerances to everyday chemical exposures which set off their symptoms: 78 percent were intolerant of fragrances, tobacco smoke, gasoline vapors, etc.; 78 percent described food intolerances; 66 percent reported alcohol intolerance; 25 percent were intolerant of caffeine; and nearly 40 percent reported adverse reactions to medications—all since the Gulf War. These intolerances, resulting in flare ups of symptoms, including fatigue, headaches, gastrointestinal problems, mood changes, cognitive impairment and diffuse musculoskeletal pain, are . . . the outward manifestion of the underlying disease process.

Iris Bell, M.D., Ph.D., Associate Professor at the University of Arizona College of Medicine and a staff member at the Tucson Veterans Affairs Medical Center, found that 86 percent of the Gulf War veterans she studied in a small sample were chemically sensitive.[1]

---

[1] Iris Bell et al., "Self-Reported Chemical Sensitivity and Wartime Chemical Exposures in Gulf War Veterans With and Without Decreased Global Health Ratings," *Military Medicine* 163 (1998): 725-32.

My own sampling shows a very high percentage of chemically sensitive veterans. When I started talking to various sick Gulf War veterans on the telephone to find interesting people for my video on Gulf War syndrome or for this book, I expected that about half of them would say they were chemically sensitive. To my surprise, virtually all of them readily recounted the various ways that chemical exposures caused problems for them.

Only two veterans with whom I spoke denied having any special sensitivity to chemicals. But when I then asked the first veteran if he was ever bothered by diesel fuel or exhaust, he replied that exposure to diesel gave him asthmatic symptoms. When I asked if perfumes ever bothered him, again he said exposure to perfume gave him asthmatic symptoms. If this veteran had been filling out a questionnaire, however, he would have replied "no" to the chemical sensitivity question because that was his initial reply to me. The second veteran was quite sure that he had no chemical sensitivity, and he seemed to understand the issue because his wife has MCS. So after I talked to him, I found myself stating that every ill veteran but one with whom I had spoken had chemical sensitivity. That one exception led me to make another phone call to this veteran to ask if he was really sure that he had no special sensitivity to chemicals. This time he admitted that once when he fertilized one of his fields he had gotten sick for a week. He also told me that on one occasion when he used a pesticide for fire ants, he reacted to it.

So why would the surveys of Drs. Miller and Bell and my informal survey of dozens of Gulf War veterans be yielding much higher percentages of chemical sensitivity than did the Kansas survey by Lea Steele (17 percent) and the survey by Howard Kipen et al. (35.7 percent)?[2] Obviously, the two cases of my interviews with veterans described above indicate that for some reason veterans do not always understand questions about chemical sensitivity or do not make the connection to their personal experience. Another reason why other studies have come up with lower percentages may be that the surveys were conducted two or three years ago. With each passing year, more veterans have become aware of their chemical sensitivity. This is related in part to the phenomenon of masking, a complex concept that basically means that when a sensitive person is exposed during the course of a day to many different substances that are causing reactions, it is not always clear that a given exposure

---

[2] Lea Steele, Prevalence and Patterns of Gulf War Illness in Kansas Veterans: Association of Symptoms with Characteristics of Person, Place, and Time of Military Service," *American Journal of Epidemiology* 152, no. 10 (November 15, 2000): 991-1001.   Howard M. Kipen et al., Prevalence of Chronic Fatigue and Chemical Sensitivities in Gulf War Veterans," *Archives of Environmental Health* 54, no. 5 (September-October 1999): 313-18.

may be causing a certain symptom. Sooner or later over time, however, people with underlying, unrecognized chemical sensitivity usually run into some major exposure that puts them over the edge into obvious chemical sensitivity that begins to impact their lives in a very limiting way.

There is one government agency that is particularly well positioned to investigate Gulf War syndrome, and that is the National Institute of Environmental Health Sciences (NIEHS), an agency of the National Institutes of Health (NIH). This agency's journal, *Environmental Health Perspectives,* contains a wealth of articles on the subject of toxic exposures and frequently includes articles from the leading researchers in the field of chemical sensitivity. The time has come for Congress to take away from the DOD and the VA the responsibility for funding studies of Gulf War syndrome and give this responsibility to the NIEHS. In its November 1997 report, the Shays subcommittee stated:

> We reluctantly conclude that responsibility for Gulf War illnesses, especially the research agenda, must be placed in a more responsive agency, independent of the DOD and the VA. . . . We note with approval efforts at the National Institute of Environmental Health Sciences [NIEHS] and other public health agencies to study exposure effects and genetic susceptibility to environmental toxins. Funding for this research would be an important first step in the effort to have an independent agency, with significant expertise in environmental hazards, involved in the solution to Gulf War veterans' health problems.
>
> (Shays, 3)

The National Gulf War Resource Center has also called for the responsibility for providing research grants to be taken away from the DOD and VA and given to the NIEHS. The time has come for everyone concerned about the plight of the Gulf War veterans to urge Congress to act on this crucial issue that is devastating the lives of so many Gulf War veterans. Ten years is too long for suffering veterans to have waited for help and for justice. Cpl. Larry Perry put it very well when he testified to the Presidential Special Oversight Board on November 19, 1998:

> The DOD absolutely should be removed from this investigation of Gulf War syndrome. They got the rule book, and they got all the rules, and if they don't like them, they can change them. They can produce what they want to, and they can cover up what they want to. My war will be over when our vets get the help they need, the help they deserve, and the help they've earned.

PART II

The personal histories appearing in Part II come from a variety of sources. Some veterans sent me a written account, and I interviewed others by telephone. Several stories are adapted from the video interviews for my video, *Gulf War Syndrome: Aftermath of a Toxic Battlefield.* One story comes from testimony to a committee of Congress. In a few cases, family members have written the stories.

Col. Herbert Smith, U.S. Army (Ret.)

To the best of my knowledge, I'm the highest-ranking Army officer who served in the Gulf War who has admitted to developing serious health problems as a result of service during the war. During Operation Desert Shield, before the war began, I served with the Kuwait Task Force as a counterpart to the Minister of Health for Kuwait. I worked with Kuwaiti health officials to help them develop a readiness that would allow them to provide disaster relief and emergency medical care without the support of American health resources, which were likely to be strained. I was stationed in Kuwait following its liberation, which put me very close to the oil well fires.

I have obstructive pulmonary disease, which I attribute to the smoke in Kuwait City. Where I was stationed, close to Camp Freedom in Kuwait City, you couldn't tell night from day. If you saw a globe in the sky, you didn't know whether it was the moon or the sun. My skin was so black you couldn't tell my skin from my black watch band. When you spit, it looked like oil, when you blew your nose, it looked like axle grease. That's the kind of pollution I'm talking about. The doctor who diagnosed me said, "Well you've got this obstructive pulmonary disease because you smoke cigarettes." And I said, "No, a cigarette has never touched my lips in my entire life, unless you want to count what happened to me in Kuwait, which is probably the equivalent to a thousand packs of cigarettes a day."

It was 17 days before we had enough water that any of us could take a shower. We took the shower, in a tent of course, closed in. We got clean until we opened the tent door, but then we had to put on our dirty, oil-soaked clothing because we didn't have enough water for laundry.

As time went by, the more oil well fire smoke I breathed, the worse I got. During the last week of May 1991, I was given the option of staying in Kuwait or returning to the United States. At this time, I was suffering with flu-like symptoms (joint pain, fibromyalgia, headache, etc.), my legs were swollen, and I had enlarged lymph nodes. I did not want anyone to know I was sick, however. I did not want an illness that would end my military career. I accepted the option of returning home. By the time I arrived, I had developed a rash on my legs and my chest. My joints hurt so much that I was unable to carry my backpack or walk up a flight of stairs. My lymph nodes continued to be enlarged.

By July my feet were so swollen I could not put on my boots. I was beginning to feel slightly dizzy all the time. By this time, Walter Reed Army Medical

Center had found some unusual blood chemistry values. The rheumatologist who had been assigned to my case was sympathetic and was trying hard for a diagnosis. He was also working sympathetically with other sick Gulf War veterans. By "coincidence," he was transferred to Fort Benning, Georgia, in November 1991.

In September a bone biopsy and aspiration was conducted, and the findings put me on the multiple myeloma cancer watch list. I've had the procedure repeated from time to time. The results never change and continue to be abnormal.

I had never had headaches before the war, but now I was having them frequently and they were getting worse. My dizziness was also getting worse but wasn't bad enough yet to make me nauseous or to make me fall. By the summer of 1992, I was having violent and explosive vertigo attacks, and it was becoming more difficult to focus on anything. My concentration was so poor that I would forget how to reach my projected destination, but I just dismissed it as being an "absent-minded professor."

My anemia was also progressively increasing. My platelet count had dropped from 400,000 to less than 100,000, and my hemoglobin had dropped from 17 to 8. In the spring of 1993, I had a Walter Reed physician accuse me of faking my anemia. Needless to say, our doctor-patient relationship had collapsed. He said I was suffering from a somatoform disorder, and he accused me of bleeding myself to mimic an anemia. He ordered psychiatric evaluations from a neuropsychiatrist, a psychiatrist, and a social worker experienced in dealing with patients suffering from depression. I was depressed. I was frantic for a diagnosis that would result in a treatment that would restore me to my previous health. I even went to churches holding healing services.

At any rate, in the early days I was seeing psychiatrists, neuropsychiatrists, psychologists, and social workers because they were absolutely convinced that I had a somatoform disorder or I was a hypochondriac. They ruled out the possibility of post-traumatic stress disorder in my case. That wasn't a possibility as it turned out because they showed me the films of dead bodies and the burning tanks, and all that stuff, and they would say, "How does that make you feel?" And I would say, "Feels like we won to me," which isn't the kind of answer a PTSD person would give. So they got off of that.

But I was getting all this counseling, and they kept asking about my marriage. (They were counseling my wife too.) One day I said, "Wait a minute, do you guys know something I don't know? Are you telling me that my wife is going to leave me?" They said, "Oh, no, we don't want to imply that, but you do know that 85% of marriages will break up when somebody comes down with chronic illness." It's very, very tough on a marriage. It's very tough on my wife because in the early days, when I was really in a lot of pain and suffering from real severe headaches, needless to say, I was a very cranky, short-tempered individual. But we had been married a long time, and she knew that wasn't me.

As it turned out, the doctor's accusation that I was bleeding myself and the reports from the mental health evaluators were the best thing that could have happened to me. I wrote a letter to the Commanding General of Walter Reed requesting that I be brought before a court-martial board and prosecuted for fraud and conduct unbecoming to an officer. In response to my letter, the Commanding General assigned me to another physician.

About the same time, I started having complex partial seizures. What happens is my memory tape just stops working. I got to the point I couldn't drive myself to work, I couldn't drive myself home. I didn't know where I was. I had these blank spots. One time I set off to go to Baltimore, and when I became cognizant of my surroundings, I was on the outside of the Beltway around Washington, D.C., and I didn't have a clue how I had got there.

As a result of these seizures and my inability to find my way home from work, a battery of brain scans, including a PET (positron emission tomography) scan was ordered. It was found that I had multiple patchy areas of inadequate perfusion and metabolite transfer, or in lay language, the metabolism in parts of my brain was deficient.

I became sensitive to certain odors that had not caused me any problems in the past. Exhaust fumes from cars and trucks, gasoline vapors, the smell of cooking spinach (formerly one of my favorite vegetables), and other odors would make me vomit. I became sensitive to various disinfectants and chlorine smells like in the city water in Washington, D.C. I couldn't drink that stuff. I couldn't pump my own gas because the gas fumes would make me vomit.

I had two civilian doctors who said I had multiple chemical sensitivity disorder, but I know that particular diagnosis is held in contempt by mainline medicine. Most physicians refuse to believe that multiple chemical sensitivity is actually a disease. You can't test for it, you can't prove it, you can't demonstrate it. Therefore it couldn't possibly exist.

My vertigo attacks were becoming so frequent that it was no longer safe for me to drive a car. I was constantly nauseous and did a great deal of vomiting. I could not stand at attention with my feet together because I would fall. I could not stand at parade rest because the shoulder pain was so bad I couldn't place my hands on the small of my back. I could not even return a salute because of the pain. But I had always considered myself "super trooper," so I was absolutely certain I would make a speedy recovery. How could "Dr. Death," as those who participated in my grueling physical fitness classes called me, have a medical problem that might be serious? When I look back, I continue to be amazed that I could have been in such a state of delusion and denial.

Finally, by the summer of 1993 I could go on no longer. It even hurt to lie down in a soft bed. I ended up in the VA Medical Center in Washington, D.C., where they were investigating why so many Gulf War veterans were having so many bizarre medical problems. I had not even been aware that other Gulf War veterans were having an unusually long list of medical complaints.

Even though my neurological symptoms were dominant, I complained mostly about the pain and my overwhelming fatigue. This resulted in a delay in my diagnosis because my peripheral, central, and autonomic nervous systems were not being investigated. I can only blame this on myself, but when one is in great pain, little else matters.

It turns out that I have an autoimmune disease. My immune system was attacking me. I had bilateral destruction of my vestibular system, which explained the dizziness, the violent vertigo attacks, the vomiting, the inability to stand with my feet together, and other symptoms.

The diagnosis was SLE (systemic lupus erythematosus). Lupus is rarely found in Caucasian males over 50 years of age, and it is especially rare in the immune system focusing on the nervous system. Joint pain with osteoarthritis, fibromyalgia, and overwhelming fatigue is common in people suffering with lupus. The VA gave me a 100 percent disability rating once I was diagnosed with lupus. I was no longer a deployable asset. The Army had no use for me any more.

There was no longer any question why I was so sick with long suffering. The diagnosis of lupus settled that. To me the worst news a person can have is to be sick and not know what it is, not know what to expect. The way I view sickness, bad news actually would have been good news because then I knew what I was dealing with. I knew what to expect, and I didn't have to deal with people telling me I was out of my mind. That was so discouraging and so depressing

I've got stitches all over me where I've fallen on sharp objects, fallen into things, and my legs now are all bruised. Anytime I risk walking, I'm a high fall risk. And the pain is so bad, it's tough to walk. Sometimes I can't even get out of bed. As a matter of fact, last Wednesday I had to call my neighbor over. Wednesday morning, I couldn't get out of bed. I needed him to come pick me up and put me in my wheelchair. I could not get into the bathroom to get on the toilet. I had to have help, and fortunately, he's a real strong young man in his thirties. He's got a brother with multiple sclerosis, and he's very accustomed to picking people up, so it worked out fine because my wife still works.

I'm not, however, one of the ones most seriously affected. I think those who were most seriously affected are already dead. Even so, I'm uninsurable. Nobody will touch me with any kind of insurance. This house used to be paid for. Now I have a very large mortgage on it because in the early days I had to refinance it so that I could get the money to pay my medical bills because I didn't know what was wrong with me. In fact, the Kuwaiti Embassy finally offered to pay for me to consult physicians at Johns Hopkins School of Medicine. As it turned out, however, someone else paid for that consultation. That's how I got the diagnosis of lupus.

Sgt. Jeffrey Parquette, USANG (Ret.)

I was in the Air Force from 1984 to 1988, and then I joined the Army National Guard. I was called up with my Guard unit and went over to Desert Storm in September of 1991. We were there until June 1.

They gave us anthrax shots when we first got over there. The medics told us they were anthrax shots, but they said they were top secret so they wouldn't put them in our shot record. The next day we got a booster shot. The shots were very painful. Some guys even cried. It was just like getting a shot of hot lava—you could feel it moving up your arm into your shoulder. It was really hard to go back that second day and get another shot. It wasn't a good experience. My doctor here at home says that they might have hit a vein or artery when they vaccinated me. I still have a lump the size of a quarter in my arm where they gave me the shot.

In October, they handed out the PB pills to us, but they told us we were supposed to wait until the air war started to take them. Once the air war started, we took them for a couple of weeks, but then our commander let us stop because people were having problems with them. One guy actually passed out while he was on guard duty at the gate. We saw him collapse as we were driving out of the camp one day. Our captain jumped out to help him, and we went to get the medics. He didn't die, but we were afraid there was something wrong with his heart. When you took the PB pills, you could feel your heart racing and you would start to shake and sweat.

After the war ended, we climbed all over the Iraqi tanks that had been hit by depleted uranium rounds. There was black soot all over the tanks, so I know we must have gotten DU dust on us, but no one had warned us about DU. We were taking pictures and looking for things. We saw a lot of bodies.

When we first got back home, I had a physical at the VA hospital near my home, and they sent me a letter saying my CPK level was really high and that I had to get retested again in a couple of weeks.[1] When I went back for the second test, they said they would notify me if anything was wrong, and they never did contact me, so I thought everything was fine.

It wasn't too long after that I tried to reenlist in the National Guard and had to take a PT test. I failed the test, and that was hard to accept because I had never had any problems before doing a PT test. I always maxed them. When I was in high school, I had played varsity football and basketball, and I had

---

[1] Creatine phosphokinase (CPK) is an important muscle enzyme whose elevation is relevant for diagnosing both heart attacks and muscular dystrophy.

gone out for track. I had always been in perfect shape and was in great shape when I joined the National Guard in 1989, and I stayed in shape by doing body building.

Everything just started going downhill after I got back from Desert Storm. I used to play on three softball teams, and I had to drop back to one. I had to cut back on my weight lifting too, and my energy level was down. I started having problems at work with the strength in my hands. (My job involved grinding down metal and painting.)

Around 1994, I went to a Boston hospital to participate in a volunteer study for Desert Storm veterans, and they noticed again that the CPK in my blood was really high. They said I should have it checked out, so I went back and talked to my primary care doctor. It was still high when he had another test done, so I went to a neurologist. That neurologist had formerly worked at the VA hospital, but she told me she quit working there because of the way they hide things from their patients. When she attended a conference in Canada, she mentioned my case and told them that my CPK levels were 4,500. (The normal range is 0-200.) The doctors who heard this said they had never seen anything like this, and that's when she decided to send me to a well-known clinic. That clinic did tests on me that included a muscle biopsy and some other tests. The tests showed that something was wrong with my muscle enzymes, but they didn't know what the problem was. Then they sent me to the head neurologist at one of the best Boston hospitals. He said there was definitely something wrong with me, but he didn't know for sure what was going on. I asked him if he thought it could be Desert Storm related, and he said he didn't even want to talk about Desert Storm syndrome because there was no such thing. His attitude seemed to be that he was an officer in the Gulf War and there wasn't anything wrong with him, so there wasn't anything wrong with anyone else.

As time went on, I was missing a lot of time from work, and they put me on some medication because they thought I might have some form of muscular dystrophy, but they didn't want to say for sure. I was missing so much time from work that I finally had to quit my job and my wife and I had to declare bankruptcy. We lost our house and our car and everything. We even had to sell our furniture and my wife's jewelry to make ends meet.

In the last few months, I've been able to go back to working. I'm on light duty, but even then just walking around makes my legs get really tired and I feel worn out. When I paint, my arms get really tired and they are sore the next day. I'm always tired, and I can't do any more sports. In addition to my extreme fatigue, I have several other health problems, including some heart problems that were discovered in 1994 or 1995. I have an abnormal heart beat, and my heart sometimes stops for a while and then starts up again. They said they can't do anything about that until it gets worse. I also have intestinal problems—after almost every meal, I have diarrhea within a few minutes.

I have a real bad memory now—my wife really notices that. Some days I can't even remember my boss's name at work. I have to stand there and think for a while. It can take me five minutes to remember what his name is. And I can't remember parts of the plant where I work. When my boss tells me to go somewhere, it takes me a while to remember where that is.

Several other people from my unit are having health problems. Another friend who served with me is tired all the time now too. One young woman who served with me lost all her hair when she returned.[2] The doctors told her it had nothing to do with Desert Storm, it was stress-related.

My commander in my National Guard unit in the Gulf War was my uncle, who died suddenly a year ago at age 45. He was a lieutenant colonel by then. He was in great shape and ran every day. When he died, he was participating in Guard training, supervising PT tests. He himself had just run one of the tests and was walking away from the finish line with some friends when he said that he felt dizzy. He collapsed and died right there. Because he collapsed on military property, the military took charge of his body. They did an autopsy and reported that he had died of a heart attack. My family wanted to have some blood tests done, especially because of my health problems from Desert Storm, but we were not allowed to have those tests done. They really rushed through that case. My aunt got the money within a week. She was paid off so fast that it was just like here's the money, forget about it. Usually they wait a while to give you the survivor's benefit. This happened so fast it seemed kind of fishy.

A couple of years ago I was having lots of medical problems and my CPK was still about 2,500, so I went to the VA hospital to get my records. They asked me if I wanted my Air Force records, and I said no, I wanted my Desert Storm records. They told me it would take a couple of months to get them and had me fill out a request form asking for my Desert Storm records. Then

---

[2] Unusual hair loss is a symptom that has occurred in many ill Gulf veterans. Dr. Lea Steele's study of Kansas veterans found that 10% of the Gulf War veterans interviewed reported "unusual hair loss," while only 2% of the veterans from the same era who did not serve in the Gulf War reported this symptom (Lea Steele, "Prevalence and Patterns of Gulf War Illness in Kansas Veterans: Association of Symptoms with Characteristics of Person, Place, and Time of Military Service," *American Journal of Epidemiology* 152, no. 10 (November 15, 2000), table 4, p. 996.) Hair loss is often discounted in men, but it is hard to ignore the implications of a woman suddenly going bald. Louise Richard of Ottawa, Canada, was a nurse in Desert Storm and became bald after her return. It is worth noting that the RAND report on PB cites the case of a woman "who repeatedly experienced hair loss on institution of PB for myasthenia" (RAND *PB*, 15:1).

two months later I got my Air Force records instead. I was really mad about that, so back I went to the VA hospital. They told me they had made a mistake and it would take another two months for me to get my Desert Storm records. After waiting two more months, I finally got my records. When I went through them, I found that back in 1991 when I had had the second CPK test that I was never informed about, a doctor had written in my records that because of my extremely high CPK result, I should be asked to come to the hospital as soon as possible. And here I was reading that in my records eight years after it had been written there, and no one had ever notified me that I had a dangerously high CPK level.

So back I went to the VA hospital to show a doctor that important message that had been written in my records eight years earlier. He disappeared for about 45 minutes, and when he finally came back, he claimed they had sent me a letter about the high CPK test. Now I never got that letter, and I'm not convinced it was ever sent. They had sent it to an old address, but my former roommate was still living there, so there's no reason I shouldn't have received the letter. Anyway, you think they would follow up on something that serious. They also had my new address because that was in my records. At any rate, my local VA hospital said they would send a complaint about what had happened to the regional office. When I later called the regional office, they said they never got the complaint. So back I went once more to my local VA hospital. They claimed they had sent it, but the regional office said they never got it. Word gets around among the veterans that the VA people just drag their feet so you will give up.

S.Sgt. Pat Browning, U.S. Army (Ret.)

I was in a transportation company that went to the Gulf War. My health was good, and I had no symptoms before the war. For the previous six years, I had driven a tractor-trailer truck and had been around diesel fuel and exhaust every day without it causing any problems.

My unit arrived in the Gulf the day before the air war started. We first spent about a month in Dhahran in Saudi Arabia. Our chemical alarms went off several times during that month, and we had to go to MOPP-level four, which meant we had to put on chemical suits, masks, gloves, and boots. While we were still in Dhahran, we started taking pyridistigmine bromide pills, which were supposed to protect us against exposure to nerve gas. About three days after I started taking the pills, my eyes were jittery, my vision was jumping, I was seeing double, and I was nauseated. By the fourth day, I was vomiting a little blood, so I went to sick-call. They told me to cut the dose in half and said there was nothing to worry about. At least I no longer vomited any blood after I reduced the dosage. Many other people in the unit reported having similar vision problems.

After we left Dhahran, we moved up north. When we got to our encampment, the first thing we had to do was to set up all our tents. Pesticide was sprayed around the periphery of each tent, and later on we used spray cans of pesticide inside our tents to keep away scorpions, sand vipers, fleas, sand ticks, and flies.

About a week after we moved into this encampment, the authorities decided to spray diesel fuel on the ground all over the camp to keep the sand down because trucks would stir up the sand and dust. Sometimes they would even get mired down in it. The blowing sand was a problem everywhere we went in the desert. When we drove our trucks in convoys, we had to wear bandanas over our face to protect ourselves from the sand kicked up by the truck ahead of us. Even then we were eating sand every day.

The water we bathed in and washed our clothes in was oily, so after a shower we would have this oily film on our skin that smelled like diesel fuel. We later realized that the same trucks were often used to carry water and diesel fuel.

When I was in the Persian Gulf, I drove over a big pothole one day and hit my chin on the steering wheel. The impact broke off two crowns. By the time I got back to the States, all my teeth were beginning to deteriorate and feel loose, which couldn't have been related to the pothole incident. I ended up having to get dentures at age 35.

When I came back from the Gulf War, I was in bad shape period. The VA in North Carolina gave me a wheelchair because I could barely walk. I had to use the wheelchair for about a year, and then I used a cane for a year. At any rate, when I got back to the States after the war, I was very, very weak and I had swollen and painful lymph nodes in my legs, my groin, and my neck. I was eventually sent to the VA in Washington, D.C., for evaluation. The VA just didn't get it about the connection between MCS and Gulf War syndrome. When they were treating us in the VA hospital in Washington, they were painting the hospital wards, and it made all of us with Gulf War illness deathly sick. We told them and they wrote it down, but that was all that happened.

While I was in the VA hospital, a surgeon did a lymph node biopsy of my left cervical and accidently cut the spinal accessory nerve, so now I have spinal accessory nerve palsy. Due to this nerve damage, the muscle has wasted away on one side. My left shoulder now droops four inches below my right one. I can't shrug my left shoulder, and I can't raise my upper left arm. I also have spinal problems now because I can't stand up straight.

At first after the operation I thought I was just having pain because of the surgery. I didn't realize that the VA in Washington had botched the operation until I was back in Mississippi. I begged the VA to pay for me to travel back to Washington to have them see what was wrong, but they kept refusing to do so. It was a month before I could get permission to go back to Washington; I finally had to get my senator and congressman to pressure the VA. One of the reasons I was fighting so desperately to get back to Washington was that I was afraid that the nerve damage was going to cause me medical problems for the rest of my life. I knew I would have to pay my own bills for treatment unless I could establish that the injury was service connected because it happened in a VA hospital.

While I was back in Washington, they finally sent me over to Bethesda to see a neurologist there. He just shook his head and couldn't believe what had happened. Back at the VA hospital, one official said to me as I was crying about the damage to my shoulder: "Oh, Ms. Browning, that's not really a problem. You can wear a shoulder pad. All the ladies' clothes have shoulder pads in them." I won't tell you what I told him, but he got out of the room real fast, and I got my letter the next day saying that the injury was service connected.

I was a reservist for a number of years after the Gulf War, but even when I didn't need a cane anymore, I couldn't drive a truck because every time they would crank up the trucks, I would get deathly ill. The only thing I could do was office work. Eventually they put me on the temporary retired list. After I've been on that list another year, I'll be put on permanent retirement.

When I first came back from the war, I had a lot of problems remembering things. One day I drove my kids to school and dropped them off, but then instead of driving home I just wandered around for a couple of hours because I couldn't remember where I was going.

I had real weak muscles when I returned from the Persian Gulf, and I also had sore places on my hips, like fibromyalgia. I have migraines now, and I didn't have them before the war. After I came back, I had two duodenal ulcers, and I've developed gastric reflux. Every day I run a low-grade fever (99.8-100.3), just enough to make me always feel a little bit yucky. I have sinusitis all the time now and take antibiotics for that. I have also tested positive for mycoplasma incognitus (fermentans) like so many others with Gulf War illness.

Since I've returned from the Gulf War, I can't be around paint fumes; they make me really sick. Bleach also bothers me now, and I can no longer wear perfume. My life has been changed in so many ways by my experience in the war, and chemical sensitivity has been a big factor in those changes.

The VA says I have panic disorder. The military says I have PTSD—Post Traumatic Stress Disorder—but the VA says women can't get PTSD. I guess we can drive tractor-trailer trucks, but we can't get PTSD. After I got back to the States, I did start getting panic attacks when I drive, so I no longer drive much.[1] At any rate, there's no way you can write off everything that's gone wrong with my health by calling it panic disorder or PTSD. The VA just needs to get it together and realize that people are actually dying out there or are in misery or pain, and they need help.

I'm not well, but I am better. Maybe you just come to realize that this is the way it's going to be, and you just accept it. I don't dwell on it anymore.

---

[1] Many people with MCS report having panic attacks after exposure to certain chemicals. Pat is now extremely sensitive to diesel fuel and exhaust, so it is possible that her panic attacks while driving are related to that sensitivity.

Cpl. Larry Perry, U.S. Navy (Ret.)

When Saddam Hussein invaded Kuwait, I was the assistant officer in charge of a Navy CB detachment located in Charlotte, North Carolina. I personally called 51 of my men in November of 1990 and told them to pack their bags because we were going to the Gulf. Our CB's played a major role in the Gulf War. We were tasked with building a 200-mile road through the desert that allowed U.S. and Coalition forces to come in behind the Iraqi forces located in Kuwait, southern Iraq, and Hakoi.

The road wound up being ten lanes wide at the end and was built so fast that the Iraqis was totally surprised when they were caught in a crossfire. We came from the rear and all sides of the Iraqi troops. They never expected a road to get put through the desert in such a short period of time.

While I was there, I never fired a weapon but I sure as hell was shot at. We were hit with two direct SCUD missile attacks that Mr. Rostker's office says is now back to a sonic boom. When fireballs are in the sky, it's not a sonic boom. Our skin was on fire. We started to show immediate signs of flu-like symptoms, and the longer we stayed in Saudi Arabia, the worse some of us got.

I started having severe heartburn and diarrhea while I was in the Gulf. I also had a lot of fatigue, just plain felt bad, like I had the flu, like it hurt everywhere. They diagnosed me with bronchitis and pneumonia while I was still in the Gulf. Memory loss is also one of the things written in my medical records from the Gulf. Everyone was having trouble remembering things. It was a weird feeling.

So I came home sick, and after I got back I started having severe headaches, which I had never had before the war. They were so bad I was afraid I had a brain tumor. I also started having stinging and burning sensations, particularly in my legs. It felt like they were on fire. I also had sexual dysfunction when I returned. On top of all that, I had severe joint pain and ached all over. And when I did something just minor, I would be in bed for a couple of days, just exhausted. I slept all the time when I got home.

A lot of the men in my Reserve unit came home sick too. They just physically couldn't drill anymore. Being the assistant officer in charge, I tried to help them. But when I tried to help them, all the officers in charge and the assistant officers in charge were called to the headquarters in Huntsville, Alabama. We were told that if anyone was dissatisfied with the way things were going, they could just get the hell out.

When I kept helping my men, I was put on report and put on restriction to the chief's quarters at the reserve center. That's like being under house arrest. I was given a direct order not to talk to my men anymore. This happened two months in a row. I was given a 2.8 evaluation, which is very bad, and put out of the Reserves, ending a 22-year career. I went from being a chief petty officer with a 4.0 rating, which is a perfect rating, to being a prisoner with a 2.8 evaluation. I have never been so humiliated in all my life. The Reserve Center wanted me to file charges against the commanding officer, but I just couldn't go through it.

I've been through living hell during the ten years since the war ended. I've tried hard to work, but I just can't hold a job now because of my health problems. I had worked in construction for thirty years before I got too sick to work. I've tried eight different jobs since I've been back from the war. Some I lost because I was in and out of the hospital too much. Three jobs I was fired from because I made costly mistakes. Since the war, I can't think like I used to, can't keep numbers straight. I was shooting a grade for laying out a parking lot and instead of bringing in a foot of dirt like I should have, I took out a foot of dirt. So after they paid to haul that dirt out, they had to pay to haul it back in, plus another foot of dirt. That little deal cost the company about $20,000, so they were mad and fired me.

In another job, I put the steel in upside down in the footers of the columns. It's supposed to be laid in there a certain way for structural strength according to the blueprints, and I got it backwards, even though I had been reading blueprints for 20 years. They got rid of me too because that stuff has got to be right.

Then there was another job in which we were building a nursing home, and there was supposed to be a little "doghouse" structure on top of the roof. I built one side just fine, but when I tried to do the back side I just couldn't get the angles right. I kept sawing boards and ruining them. Finally the boss told me to get the hell off the roof.

Not being able to work was a big problem because my wife and I had gotten divorced in September of 1991. I was supposed to be paying child support for our two children, and for a couple of years I paid it by running up a $6000 debt on my credit cards. By September of 1993, I was over my credit limit, and I couldn't get any more money anywhere. To top it off, I was just feeling exhausted.

When I stopped paying the child support, my ex-wife took me to court. The judge put me in jail for five days the first time. Then my ex-wife took me to court again, and this time he put me in jail for 30 days. He did that even though I showed him a paper indicating that North Carolina had given me Medicaid because I was disabled and I had tried eight different jobs and wasn't able to work. The judge just ignored that paper and told me I could work somewhere.

That time they put me in solitary confinement for the first five days. I was in a 5' by 7' cell and couldn't even shave or shower. Then they had to take me to a hospital 125 miles away because I had an appointment there for an X-ray for a possible tumor in my thymus. When they transported me to the hospital, they put me in leg irons, a waist chain, and handcuffs. They took me through the hospital like that too. The X-ray showed a bunch of nodules in the thymus gland that were in the upper limit of normal. My doctor wanted to biopsy them, but the hospital thought they weren't big enough yet to biopsy.

When I got back from the hospital, they put me in the regular cell ward. There was a big cell that was about 10' by 40', and at night they would lock you in 5' by 7' cells that opened onto the big cell. During the day, everyone mingled in the big space. County jail is the worst thing in the world. There was some racial tension and name calling. Some people were taking other people's food. Finally, the jail officials decided to separate the groups because they were afraid someone might really get hurt. They put us six or eight white guys in a separate part of the jail that wasn't heated, and it was 8° outside. They only gave us one blanket each. Four or five of us got sick, and someone got pneumonia and had to be taken to the doctor. I managed to call out to tell a newspaper reporter what was going on, and the paper wrote a story about what was happening. After that, the sheriff himself came up with coffee, cookies, and a second blanket for each of us. They also got the heating company busy and got some heat into that part of the building the next day. Anyway, it was a terrible experience.

I had put in a disability claim to the VA seventeen months before I was thrown in jail, and if they had paid it, I wouldn't have been in this mess. And you don't think I didn't sit there and think about the VA and the DOD, me sitting in that damn jail and I didn't have the money to support my family? I was mad. I'm still mad.

The DOD absolutely should be removed from this investigation of Gulf War syndrome. They got the rule book, and they got all the rules, and if they don't like them, they can change them. They can produce what they want to, and they can cover up what they want to. My war will be over when our vets get the help they need, the help they deserve, and the help they've earned.

Editor's note: Corporal Perry's story is a combination of a telephone interview and testimony he gave to the Presidential Special Oversight Board chaired by former Senator Warren Rudman on November 19, 1998.

Sgt. William Jones, Jr., U.S. Marines (Ret.)

I was stationed at Camp Lejeune, North Carolina, serving with 2nd Battalion, 4th Marines, when Saddam Hussein invaded Kuwait. We were put on "air alert" in December 1990, which meant we could be called to go to the Gulf at any time. My mom, dad, and sister came down, and we celebrated the most memorable Christmas I have ever had.

On New Year's Eve 1990, we headed off to war. We flew into Al Jubayl and were then moved to an area known as Tent City, Camp 15. We were supposed to be at that camp about three weeks, but our equipment arrived sooner than expected, so we proceeded to move north.

My machine-gun platoon was a tight unit and worked extremely well together. The platoon was made up of six "hard back" Humvees. These vehicles were equipped with .50 caliber and MK19 40mm machine guns. I was a vehicle commander.

From the time we were told to move north toward Kuwait and Iraq until the ground war began, we were basically the eyes and ears of the battalion. At times we were so far out from the main camps that we would have to have our chow, mail, and water flown out to us. To battle boredom and loneliness, we would play cards, wrestle, and joke amongst ourselves like we had known each other for years.

To make a place to sleep, we would dig a rectangular hole in the sand and cover it with a poncho. We slept on our rubber mats and poncho liners. It wasn't the Holiday Inn, but that's the life of being a "grunt." It became second nature after a while.

When the air campaign was in progress, we were getting briefed more and more on the upcoming ground offensive. At night I would sit in my turret and observe the B52s and other Coalition aircraft flying their missions to their prospective targets. Some of the carpet bombing from the B52s was close enough to shake the desert floor you were sitting on. I can recall to this day the horizon lighting up as the "metal rain" spread throughout the desert.

We usually held church services once a week. The battalion chaplain would be flown to our positions. I will never forget the last services we had before the ground campaign. The last thing the chaplain read was the 23rd Psalm. To this day, whenever I hear this psalm, I get a chill throughout my entire body.

When the ground war was in progress, Charlie Company, 1st Battalion, 10th Marines (artillery) was in direct support of our battalion I recall this battery firing on a column of Iraqi tanks to our left front. My platoon was tasked to provide left front security for Fox Company, which was mounted in Amtracs. The "fogs of war" soon set in. One artillery round hit so close that it shook our entire vehicle. A few moments after this incident, I had a small flashback to my childhood. My dad and I have always been close to each other, and I suddenly remembered a fishing trip we had taken together when I was young.

Later on, we heard that Golf Company was in a firefight and needed our support, so we responded. I recall the smoke from the oil well fires being so thick that I couldn't see my hand in front of my face. Our night vision gear was useless in the smoke because it runs by a light source. But at last we reached the Golf Company. I recall the red and green tracers flying through the night sky. We had to call for illumination over our position. We started to receive artillery a while later. It was close enough that you could feel the ground you were sitting on shake.

While the firefight was in progress, we also had to deal with POWs. When the firefight was over, we pulled about a dozen POWs out of one bunker, where they had been for a few days. They had survived on only a few loaves of bread and very little water. On one occasion a senior Iraqi soldier had his men kneel down in front of us in a single line and asked if his soldiers could pray before we shot them. We immediately explained to him that this would not happen. We were told that Saddam Hussein was telling his solders that to become a U.S. Marine, you had to kill one of your family members. We were also told that Saddam was telling his men not to surrender because we would shoot them immediately.

Once a chemical alarm was alarmed. Through our radio communication, we were told to get into MOPP-4, which meant you put on all your chemical clothing. We already had our suits on, so to go to level 4, all we had to do was put our gloves and gas mask on. We stayed at this level for a few hours until we were told it was "all clear."

In addition to that possible exposure to nerve agents and the oil well fires, I also took the PB pills and had the anthrax shots. I didn't have any health problems during the war, however. My illnesses from Persian Gulf War syndrome began in 1993, when I started experiencing fatigue, memory loss, and difficulty concentrating. I also started having unusual hair loss and other symptoms. But when I went to my local VA hospital and took the Gulf War physical, I was told there was nothing wrong. I submitted a disability claim anyhow, but it was denied, supposedly because I didn't have any proof or documentation saying that my illnesses were connected with Desert Storm. I appealed the issue and a few months later was denied again. I gave up on the system because I was getting tired of being denied, but that was a big mistake.

A few years later I sought out a veterans' representative claims specialist through my state's veterans' services department. I would highly recommend that any veteran who is having difficulties seek a representative. I have nothing but positive and good things to say about my representative, a former marine and a combat veteran of the Vietnam War.

Last winter I participated in the Clinical Comprehensive Evaluation Program (CCEP) for Gulf Vets at the Walter Reed Army Medical Center located in Washington, D.C. I will never regret participating in the program, although I was told a few things I didn't want to hear.[1] They found that I do indeed have short-term memory loss. In a study at a VA hospital in the neighboring state, I had a picture of my brain taken, and it showed abnormalities in the left frontal lobes of my brain that explain my memory loss and concentration problems. My memory loss has gotten to the point that once when I was out on a lake fishing with my dog, I couldn't even remember how to get back to the dock. Sometimes when I'm putting away the dishes, I'll find myself trying to put a cup in the silverware drawer or a fork in the cupboard.

I also have irritable bowel syndrome. Last year I noticed blood in my stool. The doctor tried to do a colonoscopy but couldn't because he said my insides were too tensed up. He ordered a barium enema X-ray to check on my intestinal tract, but when I went to the VA hospital where they had scheduled it, the doctor started to do a colonoscopy. I told him I had received a letter scheduling a barium enema X-ray, not a colonoscopy. I never did get that X-ray, so I still have no idea why I have the bloody stools. I felt like I was being treated like a piece of meat.

I've been diagnosed with rheumatoid arthritis, and I have a lot of joint pain and muscle weakness now. My life has changed so much since the war that sometimes I feel like a candle just melting away.

---

[1] According to the DOD's website, <<http://www.gulflink.osd.mil>>, the "DOD established the Comprehensive Clinical Evaluation Program to provide an in-depth medical evaluation to all eligible beneficiaries who have health concerns following service in the Gulf." Although Sergeant Jones is enthusiastic about the program, most ill veterans have not found it very helpful, probably because the tests performed are too routine to address their health problems.

Capt. Tracy Smith, U.S. Army Reserves

Back in the summer of 1990, I was a second lieutenant with the Kentucky National Guard when Saddam Hussein invaded Kuwait. It was just another blip of information on the news, and I paid no heed as the U.S. Army dispatched the 82nd Airborne and 101st Airborne to Saudi Arabia.

As the weeks went by, however, and the buildup of troops escalated, I volunteered to be deployed. My unit had been put on alert but had been stood down. Individual members were being asked to volunteer depending on their background. Since I was a quartermaster officer with a maintenance background, I knew I would be needed and I was.

I received my call to report and was on my way to the Persian Gulf late in January 1991. I remember waking up on the flight to see the flight attendants donning gas masks. When I looked out the window of the TWA 747, I could see the oil well fires burning intensely. The sky was black from the smoke, and the flames were hundreds of feet high. I turned to my friend and said," We're not in Kansas anymore," as the hummers with the .50 cal machine guns mounted on top escorted our plane down the runway for a landing.

I reported to the replacement company and was told I would remain in the rear working at the headquarters far from the front lines. But by morning there was a change. I was called to the S-3's trailer, where he pulled out my orders from a safe. I was to report to the 18th Airborne Corp and take command of a special unit made up of 163 soldiers with training in many different areas. I would be their only officer. My mission, its people, and my orders were to be a secret. We could send mail out, but we could not give our location or a return address for our loved ones to write us back.

My transient company was formed, and I moved them out to Dragon Base, where I received further instructions, including that I was to release any females assigned to me. I remember asking the major, "What about me?" I can still remember his words, "You are an officer and don't matter."

Some time later I gathered my men to brief them on our situation. I was now responsible for 163 soldiers whose very lives depended on me and the chain of command that I established. Some had just turned 18. I said a prayer and asked God to help me lead them to get them home safely.

One of the first questions I was asked by the men I commanded was what happened to the females. I explained that they were not allowed on this mission. At this juncture I was unable to tell them what our mission was going to be, even though I knew. When they asked why I was allowed to stay on, I told them, "The Army either has great faith in my ability to lead you or I have really pissed off someone."

I also told them that the major had given me a direct order to order every soldier in my command to take PB pills to protect them from nerve agents. However, I said, "I am a woman and I trust my intuition." I told them that the Army had a history of using its people as guinea pigs without their consent or knowledge. "Everything in me and my gut says not to take these pills. I'm not going to give you a direct order that I'm not going to follow," I told them. The choice was up to them.

The war was soon over, and our special mission became obsolete with the cease-fire. My unit was deactivated, and the soldiers were reassigned throughout the theater after only a few short weeks. I was assigned back to Dhahran, where I remained until December 1991.

As I recall, only a handful of my soldiers elected to take the pills. After our mission ended, they were spread throughout the theater, so I only saw a few of them again while I was in Dhahran. But I remember that some of them who had taken the pills were medevaced out of theater within six months. They had unexplained bleeding from their colons and constant abdominal pain.

I spent almost a year in Saudi Arabia, Kuwait, and Iraq, and that period now seems a blur of moments. When I arrived, we were in a combat mode of operations: no one slept, we ate little (plenty of rations and food were available, but there was no time to stop), we did our jobs. We all worked hard.

It all took a toll on my health, as was true for everyone else. You just didn't stop for it. Everyone around me had bloody noses. We attributed that to the dry heat. We all vomited and took large doses of Maalox and Kaopectate. We had weird skin rashes and swollen lymph nodes and fevers. We were all tired and irritable, but then we never slept, ate properly, or had time for exercise. We just worked. Going to the medics or the hospital was for people who had the luxury of time to go on sick call or were bleeding profusely. It wasn't an option for most of us. We were soldiers invincible to pain and death. (A mentality that a soldier must have in order to survive both physically and mentally.) We just sucked it up and carried on the mission.

When it finally came time to go home, I couldn't wait. I heard that if you told the medical doctors that you had any symptoms or thought you had anything wrong, they would keep you another week for tests. So I lied because I couldn't stand the thought of not leaving as soon as possible. I wanted to be home and sleep in my own bed. I said I was fine despite the constant nausea, vomiting, fevers, swollen lymph nodes, and skin rashes. I was given my DD Form 214 and returned to Kentucky in December 1991. For the next month, I slept as much as possible, waking only to eat.

For the next several years, I suffered from what I refer to as "bouts." My nausea would always remain, but I would get breaks from the severity of abdominal pain and other symptoms. When I go beyond just nausea, that is what I consider a bout. When my lymph nodes swell, they usually only swell on one side of my body. Then the next time, only the other side swells. I go to my doctor and have blood tests run, but all come back normal. My mystery fevers come and go without warning or explanation. They do not respond to Tylenol or aspirin. I just wake up one day and the fever is gone. I also seem to keep bladder, kidney, and yeast infections. My menstrual cycle is unpredictable, ranging from no menses for several months to abnormally heavy flows for ten to sixty days.

Generally when I have the periods of fever, I vomit constantly and have diarrhea. I will drop ten or more pounds in about two weeks. I have periods of fatigue so severe that I can't get out of bed or am only able to go to work for eight hours (with a nap at lunch). Then poof, the fever goes away, the vomiting stops, the diarrhea stops, my lymph nodes return to normal, and the fatigue leaves. Within a few weeks, it is like nothing ever happened. The illness becomes dormant for a period of weeks or occasionally months. But it always returns, without warning or explanation. My bouts will often be triggered by chemical exposures. Once my boyfriend sprayed pesticide on my garden without asking me, and I ended up with vomiting, diarrhea, and swollen lymph nodes from that episode. Another time I tried to use some paint stripper, and that put me into a "bout" that lasted about three months.

How can I describe what it is like not to have your memory anymore? At first you tell yourself it is age or simple forgetfulness. But then you tell yourself you are only 24 or 25, too young for that. How can I describe the terror that you feel when you look at your son and can't remember his name? Or when you are driving somewhere and realize you don't have a clue where you are going or why you are in the car driving? Or the inability to remember what happened yesterday? How can you explain to a doctor that you used to have a photographic memory and could memorize everything, and then could deteriorate to the point of not remembering how to spell the word "the"?

I transferred to the Army Reserves in 1992 when I moved to California. My DA 201 File of my personnel record finally caught up with me about six months later. My medical file from Saudi never did. I met a few other Saudi Vets and we would talk about our experiences. Sometimes we would mention our health problems. I had heard that some of the vets were complaining of their health, but they were rumored to be scammers who were just looking for a free ride on the government. I wasn't like that. I wasn't going to complain. But over the next few years, I met hundreds of vets with medical problems. Many symptoms we had in common, some we did not. I wasn't sure what to think. I had heard of a Gulf War Registry where you could be examined by the Veterans Affairs hospitals. I had also heard of people being passed over for promotion and being released from active duty for complaining about their health problems from their service in the Gulf War. I had been promoted to first lieutenant while in Saudi, and I decided to wait until I was promoted to captain before I registered.

During this period, my father, Col. Herbert Smith, had also been having many health problems, and he told me about how a couple of people from his unit had died. We weren't in the same part of the country, however, so I didn't see him during this time, and I'm sorry to say that I did not believe him or at least thought he was exaggerating his medical condition. Finally, I went home for a visit with my father and stepmother. I was not prepared for what I saw. My father was pale, weak, and crippled. He was unable to carry on a normal conversation and would frequently forget what he was saying or what the conservation was about. He encouraged me to get on the Gulf War Registry, and as soon as I made captain in 1995, I went to my local VA hospital for my registry physical.

I was treated to skepticism and tons of paperwork. They also gave me statements from the government saying there was no evidence to suggest we were exposed to any dangerous toxins or harmful environmental conditions. As part of the registry, you had to be seen and evaluated by a psychiatrist for your mental fitness. That angered me, but I was confident that my medical symptoms were not psychologically manifested. I passed the psychiatric evaluation with flying colors. My physical body was probed, poked and prodded. I was sent home on antibiotics and drugs for my various symptoms. I was informed that I could use the clinics as my regular healthcare provider because I was a veteran. A few weeks later I received a letter from the Persian Gulf War Registry stating that I was physically and mentally fine.

As fate would have it, about six months later, I applied for a job that required a TB test. Now, I knew that I had had a TB test done at the VA as part of my registry, but when I contacted the VA, I discovered that part of my medical record had again disappeared. My file showed that I had gone to the VA and the tests had been ordered, but no results could be found. I remembered my father telling me that he had received a similar letter about lost test results. He also said that when he went to the VA, they would tell him that there was nothing wrong with him. Yet he would go to a civilian, independent doctor and the exact same tests would have very different results. This all made me question the integrity of the government and its efforts to assist veterans. It made me question the validity of any of the test results.

I have cultivated relationships with some of the healthcare providers at my VA hospital over the last five years. A few years ago one of the doctors let me know that they had been told not to give us diagnoses. They were told that all Persian Gulf War veterans were fine and that any symptoms that we might say that we had were psychologically manifested. And I believe the VA doctors did in fact believe that at first. But when we started pouring into the facility by the thousands, they no longer subjected us to that mentality. Their attitude towards treatment is in general much different now from what it was during the early years after the war ended. There are still a few people within the medical community who believe we aren't really sick, but I don't worry about them. There are plenty more doctors who do know something is wrong with us and want to help us.

I have said repeatedly to my mother that I wish that I had just been shot while I was over there—at least then we would know why I was in pain. I have told my doctors that I would rather have cancer than this "Gulf War syndrome." At least then I could be treated (surgery, chemotherapy, anything!) and move on with my life. (Friends, family, and doctors understand cancer. Not many people understand Gulf War syndrome.)

Three years ago my husband and I discovered that I was pregnant. My two-year-old son is a miracle in my life and a constant source of joy for me. I was not planning on having any children because of my illness and my awareness of birth defects and illnesses among veterans' children. I had a very rough pregnancy and delivery. My son was born tongue-tied—that's a birth defect in which the tongue is attached too far to the floor of the mouth. He had surgery recently to correct the problem. He receives speech, occupational, and developmental therapy twice a week, the latter because his development has been slow. He has another odd symptom—his feet constantly peel without explanation and no treatment helps. I met another Gulf War veteran about two years ago who had two sons before his deployment and one after. The first two are fine, but his third son was also born tongue-tied.

It has been ten years now since we returned from the Persian Gulf. Why are we not better or at least having fewer bouts of illness? It seems like my episodes are increasing in length, duration, and intensity. I even had new symptoms with this last bout of illness—blisters under my tongue and numbness in my body. I've been moderately to severely ill constantly for almost a year now, and this is the worst I have ever been. At the peak of this period, I was so ill that I was unable to properly care for my son or myself. (My two-year-old son should not have to hold back my hair as I lie puking on the bathroom floor.) Had it not been for my mother and the support of my friends, I would have been forced to give up custody of my son. I love my son with all my heart and soul, but I have feared for his safety and well being this past year. I have dealt with this mysterious illness for ten years now. I have learned to cope with the pain and the fatigue. I cannot say that I have learned to cope with the fear and guilt of not being able to care for my own son.

Editor's note: Gulf War syndrome has blighted the lives of three generations in this family: Col. Herbert Smith, his daughter Tracy, and her son.

Sfc. Roy Twymon, U.S. Army (Ret.)

From the time we was given the PB pills, we was told to continue to take them. We kept on taking them, and we kept on taking them until after the war. And I started having diarrhea, my bowel was a different color. I had to run to the outdoor toilet sometimes because it was so severe.

The night before we went into Iraq the wind was blowing our direction while they was bombing. And I had respiratory problems that night, and some more personnel did also. When we got up in Iraq, going down the highway we saw bodies everywhere, bodies stuck to the steering wheel, bodies lying on the floor, on the ground, vehicles burning where they had bombed the vehicle with these shells. There was all this smoke. And then we finally set up camp right next to these bunkers everybody has been talking about . They was blowing up bunkers practically every day. One day when they blew one up, it formed a big black cloud, and a lot of people had respiratory problems.

That's when I started noticing that I couldn't hold my bladder. And this kept on happening, kept on happening, while we was over there. Then when we got back to the States, my soldiers started complaining, and they was sent to the hospital, sent to psych, told it was all in their head.

I kept on dealing with it, and one day it really hurt me and struck me. I was coming from fishing with my son, and I wasn't even a block away from the Seven-Eleven in San Antonio, Texas, and I couldn't even make it to the Seven-Eleven. I soiled on myself. I knew then there was something terrible wrong with me.

Then as I went on with my bowel and bladder problem, I realized what was going on, and when I ran into some of the individuals that was in my unit, some of the guys, I would pull them aside and ask them if they was having some of the same problems. I said, "You can tell me if you want to, you know, but you don't have to tell me." And all of them that I spoke to said yes, they was having the same problems and some more problems. And I told them, "Well, you need to get rid of your pride and go forward and tell people, go tell the doctor about what's going on because you and I is not the only one."

I went to have a rectal exam, and they found nerve damage to my internal sphincter muscle. The sphincter muscle is the one that helps hold your bowel. So when you have to go to the bathroom or get the urge to go, you have to be whupped in the bathroom, or you'd best be running, or you just go on yourself. I'm 44 years old now, and I know 44-year-old men that haven't been to the Gulf

War don't have this problem. It started when I came back, and I know it happened over there because there's too many of us having the same problem. And I have to buy expensive diapers and stuff. The government's not buying diapers for me.

I miss a lot of events with my kids, you know, their activities. My son plays college football. Could you imagine me going to a college football game, eighty, ninety thousand people trying to get into the same restroom with you? No, I'd soil on myself. So all of these activities and things that my kids have been into since I've been back and the things that I've missed, no one can give that back to me, no one.

I got to where I couldn't even hardly breathe. I would get like caught up or choked, like my breath was cut off. It's just so much, you know, my migraines, my rash, my poor circulation. I had a bone marrow test. My platelets was turning over so fast, and the blood specialist didn't know why. I got anemic and had a liver biopsy. My legs swell up for no reason. I had two surgeons from Walter Reed come down, and they tell me, "Sergeant Twymon, we don't know what's going on." And I said, "Well, you the doctors, I don't know what's going on either."

I was very healthy prior to going over there. I used to run everyday. I used to lift weights—I had a weight machine in my garage. Since I've been back, they have had to go into my knees due to joint problems where my cartilage has been ate all up for some reason. I have a hole in my median condial for an unknown reason. My bone's deteriorating, and my teeth are rotting from the inside out.

I always have tried to be faithful to my country, just like President Kennedy, whom I admired, always said, "Ask not what your country can do for you, what you can do for your country." Well, that's the way I grew up, I was brought up. And, sad to say, I went and did for my country, but my country's not doing for me. They don't care. They don't care. We just a number. I guess the soonest we can die, they'll be better off, the government, because there's so many of us. And I'm tired of them trying to hide everything because the proof is there. All you have to do is look at all the soldiers that have been over there and are sick. And the sad thing about it is, you get back here and you're sick and you go to get some more insurance, and you can't even get insurance because of your illness or because you was in Desert Storm. What can a person leave back for their family to continue on to live the life that they was living if they can't get insurance?

Since I've been back from the Gulf War, I also notice that lots of things bother me that never bothered me before the war. Different perfumes, different colognes, gasoline, even the smell of smoke or cigarettes, make me get sick, and sometime it takes me days or weeks to recover.

One day I was on an elevator, and someone got in who was wearing some loud perfume. All of a sudden it hit me. I got lightheaded and I was breathing difficult, so I went to my office to sit down. And then I was still feeling lightheaded, so I went outside to see if I could get some air so I'd be all right. Then when I came back, I was still lightheaded, so I went over to a clinic in a hospital. The nurses over there took my blood pressure. They didn't say nothing at first, just put my feet up. Then they took it again. Then next thing I knew, one was on the phone, and here comes a wheelchair. They took me down to the emergency room because they thought I was having a heart attack. They started putting IVs in me, putting EKGs on me, nitroglycerin. And I was in the hospital for about four or five days because of that perfume exposure, and that wasn't the first time that had happened, with the chest pain and all that.

It's rough. A lot of people don't understand it, but it's real, and it's not in my head neither. And that's what I think a lot of people need to understand. We're not making this up. There's too many of us. I don't know what the government is going to do, but I hope they hurry up and do something soon because there's too many of us that have served our country proudly, and now we're living like we're third-class citizens.

Sgt. Jeff Tack, U.S. Army (Ret.)

During Desert Storm, I was part of the medical team that followed the tanks, so we were basically on the front lines. At times we were only a couple hundred yards behind the tanks as they were firing off their rounds, and there was a lot of smoke around us from the Iraqi tanks that were hit. We hadn't been warned about depleted uranium, so we didn't realize we were breathing DU.

One time we came under fire from some small mortar rounds that exploded in a white cloud of smoke. We got the heck out of there because we couldn't identify where they were coming from or what kind of munitions they were. They were exploding in a white cloud, low to the ground, only twenty feet up. I thought that was kind of odd.

The patients we ended up treating were almost exclusively Iraqi prisoners. We gave them first aid, cleaned their wounds, and removed shrapnel and bullets. We didn't know anything about DU, so we didn't know that we were probably getting exposed to it when we took care of the prisoners.

Once when we were on the Iraqi border, a SCUD missile was flying over us, and one of the anti-rocket teams shot it down right over our heads. We were also at Khamisiyah when they blew it up. We were downwind about a mile.

We didn't find out until later that the PB pills were actually experimental. They wanted us to stand in a circle so they could watch us take them, but nobody in our group seemed to have any serious adverse reactions. But after I got back home and got out some medical books and read what that stuff actually did, I was upset they had made us take that crap.

When I got back from the Gulf, I started noticing symptoms within a couple of weeks. I had constant muscle twitching and bad leg cramps and night sweats. I also had a couple of really bad migraines, and I had never had one before. Those symptoms lasted a month or so. The physician's assistant at the base kept telling me it must be a bug and gave me some Motrin, but I wasn't running a temperature. The night sweats and leg cramps went away in about a month, but the muscle twitching never went away. I asked several doctors about it, and they just said it was from low potassium, don't worry about it. I've had that muscle twitching ever since the Gulf War.

I had sores in my nose for three or four months, and I just figured they were from the oil well fires because I camped by the oil well fires for several weeks.

Another thing that happened after I got back was that I developed allergies to shellfish and to latex. Being a medic, I had used latex gloves for years with no problem, but now I can't touch latex. I've also developed asthma since I got back. I would have to go to the emergency room at the base for treatments when I was having trouble breathing, but they wouldn't diagnose me with asthma because they knew that diagnosis might get me kicked out of the service. I get asthma attacks from diesel exhaust and sometimes from perfume.

Even though I had these health problems after I got back, I was well enough to stay on active duty, but things got worse when I was sent to Korea in May of 1994. I was stationed in one of the camps that was real close to the demilitarized zone. There were a lot of mosquitoes and cockroaches and other insects around, so they sprayed our barracks and the rest of the base very frequently. We also used a lot of bug spray when we went out in the field and when we camped out. The mosquitoes were really horrible over there.

Looking back on it, I think that this heavy exposure to pesticides was really bad for me. I had a really big decrease in muscle strength during the time I was in Korea, and my PT [physical training] tests show that. When I got to Korea, I did a PT test in which I ran two miles in 14 minutes, but when I took another PT test eight months later, it took me 18 minutes to run two miles. The number of push-ups I could do in two minutes dropped from 70 to 37. The people running the PT tests told me that I wasn't trying hard enough and that I should put in some extra effort, so I started going to the gym. But instead of getting better, I just got worse. The harder I tried, the worse I did. They wanted to kick me out of the Army because I was failing the PT tests.

One day when I was doing push-ups my left arm just gave out. They sent me to one specialist who didn't have a clue what was going on, but another doctor with a physical therapy group saw my muscle twitching and muscle wasting and immediately sent me to a neurologist. That's when they said it looked like I might have ALS [Lou Gehrig's disease]. They sent me back to the States a few months early so I could have special tests run.

I was transferred back to Fort Sam Houston in February of 1995. In March they diagnosed me with ALS, and a couple of months later I was walking with a cane. I hadn't made any connection yet that the pesticide exposure in Korea had been so bad for my health, and I had another pesticide exposure after I got home. We had fire ants in San Antonio, so all through that first summer I was back I was constantly spraying pesticide on the lawn with a hand sprayer, wearing just shorts and a T-shirt. It never dawned on me that could be a problem. Then when I got to talking to my Dad and reading the precautions on the pesticides, I realized that spraying that crap wasn't very smart. Then that August one of my daughters got lice at school, so we all used a lindane shampoo. I used it three times because we couldn't get rid of the lice. About that time I went from using my hands well to not being able to lift them over my head.

Now my arms and legs are paralyzed. The only thing I can move is my big toes, and I still have the use of my neck and speech. Everything else is shot. I'm on a feeding tube, and I'm in a wheelchair. Before too long, I'm going to have to get a tracheotomy because I'm getting only 18% of the air I need.

I'm one of the lucky ones with ALS, however, because I was on active duty when I was diagnosed, so I get 100% disability. That means I get a disability check and all my medical bills are paid. I had to fight with them for about eight months to get those benefits, but I got them.

_____

Editor's note: This story was obtained by a phone interview with Jeff Tack.

S.Sgt. Joseph Dulka, Jr., USANG (Ret.)

On January 1, 1991, my husband Joseph Dulka, Jr., was activated for Desert Storm operations. He was a member of the 143rd National Guard Military Police Unit in Hartford, Connecticut. His unit was activated to process and guard the POWs from the war because its members were specially trained for this task.

Joe left for the Persian Gulf at the end of January 1991. When he got to the POW camps, he had many duties. One of his duties was to delouse the prisoners. In this process, the MPs would spray a powdered form of lindane on the prisoners as they walked through a tent. The lindane was in pressurized canisters. The MPs had no respiratory protection from the powder they were spraying, and they were given no instruction on its use or its dangers. The 12-hour shifts that the MPs worked meant that their exposure to lindane was prolonged.

Lindane is a known carcinogen that is used in very small amounts in special shampoos for head lice. On these shampoo bottles, there are warnings about proper use of the product and the possible side effects which may arise from its use. The MPs were using a much stronger form of lindane and using it in a different delivery system.

My husband also had other toxic exposures in the Gulf War. During Joe's tour, he wrote home daily. He was very concerned about the chemicals like lindane that he had to use and the pesticides that were heavily used around the camps. He was also worried about exposures to nerve agents that he suspected might be occurring. Years later members of his unit received letters from the Defense Department notifying them that they had been exposed to low levels of sarin because they were in the vicinity of Khamisiyah when it was blown up.

When Joe returned, there were differences in him that were apparent to the two of us. He had undergone a subtle personality change. His personality was more intense than before, sharper. His emotions were stronger. Prior to his deployment, he did not fly off the handle easily, but that changed after he got back. He would get angry quicker. His energy level was also decreasing, and he seemed to fall into a depression. Before the war, he had never been one to sit still and to my knowledge had never been depressed. Another thing that seemed unusual was that he had developed a strong sensitivity to odors. He just couldn't stand to smell things like perfume or pesticide or gasoline. Joe also had many more upper respiratory infections after he got back and had a recurring rash that didn't respond to any treatment. His eye constantly twitched, which he thought strange.

Within a month after Joe returned, I became pregnant with our son. Joe was very concerned about the baby and didn't seem to be very pleased that I was pregnant. I found this very odd since we had had problems conceiving a child for three years, and we had finally succeeded. But I soon realized that Joe was very worried about his exposures in the Gulf and what that might do to the baby. He was very careful about his clothes and anything that touched his body. He would wash his clothes separately and would only use one towel and wash it separately.

My pregnancy was not unusual, but our son was born with cleft lip and palate. I was upset by this of course, but Joe was devastated. I found his reaction odd because this problem could be repaired and handled. I did not understand Joe's devastation at the time.

I later did some follow-up investigating and found that aside from genetics, the number one cause of cleft lip and palate is pesticide exposure. Lindane is classified as a pesticide. My son was conceived one month after Joe's return from the Gulf. I am convinced that my son's deformity was caused by the lindane Joe used in the Gulf because there is no genetic history of cleft lip or palate on either side of our families.

In September of 1993, Joe began to experience intestinal problems. He had gradually been losing weight since his return from the Gulf. His energy level was very low, and he was slowly falling into a deep depression. He did not have much contact with our son. It was as though he did not want to become attached to him. In October, Joe went to see a doctor about his intestinal symptoms. His doctor ordered every test one could possibly think of, but they all came up negative. Joe got progressively worse. He was still losing weight and had constant diarrhea that would not respond to any treatment. This continued for several months, and the tests continued. Then in May of 1994, Joe came home from work and collapsed on the bathroom floor. I called his doctor and rushed him to the emergency room. He was admitted to the hospital and diagnosed with pancreatic cancer. He was given 3-6 months to live. Joe died on August 28, 1994.

Joe was 37 years old at the time of his diagnosis. Pancreatic cancer is almost unheard of in a man of this age. The disease is rare to begin with and in a 37-year-old man it is extremely rare.

I now understood Joe's devastation when our son was born. He felt he was responsible for our son's deformity. He also sensed that he was dying and didn't want to become attached to our son. He had maintained his relationship with our daughter after the war, but after he was diagnosed with cancer he pulled away from her also. It was as though he was preparing her for his demise.

Shortly before his death, Joe put a claim into the VA for benefits. He was attempting to connect his disease to his service in the Gulf War, but his claim was denied. After Joe's death, I submitted four more claims, which were also denied. When I began to investigate exactly what went on in the Gulf, I was shocked to learn about the chemical exposures there and the lack of information given to our troops. They were told what to do, but they were not told what chemicals they were using or the possible dangers that could occur from their use. I did not know the full extent of the chemical use in the Gulf until I investigated.

The lindane that the MPs used caused Joe's cancer and his ultimate death. The VA finally admitted to this. In May of 1998, I took my case to the VA Board of Appeals in Washington, D.C., and won. The VA admitted that my husband's death was the result of the improper use of lindane and granted full survivor benefits to my children and myself. It took five years of fighting the government to finally get them to admit to the service connection. It has been reported to me that the Army no longer uses lindane in the delousing process since my appeal was approved.

S.Sgt. Tim Smith, USANG

I was with one of the Army National Guard units that went to the Gulf War. I volunteered to go with this unit. I was a communications sergeant while I was there.

We arrived in Saudi in the port of Al Dammam, spent two weeks there doing different stuff, getting ready to deploy to the desert. Once we deployed to the desert, we went through little towns—Elwoddy, different towns like that. Once the ground offensive started we were in Iraq and Kuwait.

There were times during the night when I was driving an officer, taking him to meetings, that we came upon a pile of dead sheep in the middle of the desert, not knowing what had caused it or how many there were. We didn't stop, we just turned the lights on and saw the sheep piled on both sides of this dirt road. The way that it caught our sight was that we saw the eyes of the desert rats reflected in our headlights, and we said, "What are all these things?" And then when we got close enough, we could see that they were eating the sheep.

The night that we actually saw the dead sheep was the night of the first air offensive, and I was coming back from the medical facility, where I had taken somebody who had fallen, and en route back, we had gotten off the road that we usually took. Being out in the desert, all roads look the same, you know, you take a left here and a right there. That's when we came upon the dead sheep, and we didn't know if they were diseased or if there had been a chemical attack. Not being up on the front line at the time, it was like six hours that we had been gone, we didn't know what had transpired. That's one of the things that I remember vividly, seeing something that you don't normally see driving down through the desert.

On a nightly basis, we would spray our uniforms with pesticides. There was a chemical spray that they gave us to spray our uniforms. We had to hang them outside so that the excess spray would dissipate in the air, I guess. We weren't supposed to put them on immediately after spraying them. The sand fleas were a problem. We used to put flea collars around the legs of our cots or we would put flea powder on the floor around our cots to try to keep the sand fleas away from us while we were sleeping. We slept with nets over us to keep the flies off. The flies were ungodly. It wouldn't be nothing to go up to the mess hall and see a pile of flies where they had put some food out as a bait and let the flies land on it and then sprayed them to kill them. They would be like an inch thick, a pile of flies sitting on the ground outside the mess hall as you're going into the mess hall. It's the wonderful world of being in the army.

There were six men to a tent, and each tent had a kerosene heater in it. You would put it in the middle, and in the morning you would get up and light it and everyone would lie there until the tent got hot. But after a while, your eyes would start burning; there was an odor in the air constantly when you used that stuff.

The oil wells burning was a huge problem. There were times when in the middle of the day it would look like midnight. One day at 11 or noon we got a wind storm, no rain, just wind, and everything went black. But it wasn't dust, it was just like a cloud had come over you and you couldn't see anything, like nighttime at noon. It was unreal. You would look off in the distance and see the oil wells burning. You would see the smoke on the horizon, and it would just drift, whichever way the wind would blow it, you could see it drifting across the desert. You could smell it, you could constantly smell burning fuel oil and diesel fumes.

Most of the water you bathed in was unfit to put in your mouth. You couldn't brush your teeth with it. You had to use your bottled water to brush your teeth. The water was somewhat green, some of it had a tinge of diesel, a smell of diesel in it.

Well, my stomach problem, my gas reflux or whatever they want to describe it as, started while I was in Saudi. It was late, just about the time we were coming back it started, and it was diagnosed as gastric reflux. When I returned, we had a physical here, and they gave me a medication for it.

Other stuff that has come up is, I'm sensitive to the smell of gasoline. Diesel fuel, paint thinners bother me, other chemicals that I use. If I go to a party where there are a lot of women with perfume, it bothers me. Where I work I'm exposed to a lot of chemicals, and I seem to be supersensitive to them now. I can get a little smell of a paint and that will bother me. I'll fill up and my throat will get sore, whereas everybody else could just smell that, and it wouldn't bother them.

There was one instance when I first came back, I had been back maybe three weeks, and I was what they call a brazier. I would braze the pipe with silver solder and stuff. And I had developed bronchial pneumonia, and they couldn't figure out why. They cured me of it, but two or three weeks later I had pneumonia again. They did a test at the hospital, and it showed that the carbon monoxide level in my blood was three times what it was supposed to be. And from there, they determined that the job I was doing had become a risk for me and I had to change jobs, give up the job and switch into another section in the department.

Headaches, they're unreal. I take three medications for headaches. I take one before I go to bed that I can only take before I go to bed because of the strength of it, and I take one when I feel a headache coming on, and I take Tylenol. That's the three things I take for the headaches they say aren't related to my being part of Desert Storm. My doctor has tried three different medications for my headaches, which he says are cluster headaches.[1]

When I went off to Desert Storm, I left healthy, there was nothing seriously wrong with me. I had two kids I used to play with all the time, and now it's a lot different. It's work and rest and I'm not healthy now, it's cut and dried. There is something happened over there that they won't admit to.

Over half the people in the unit I was with have come down with something since they've come back that the authorities have said wasn't connected to their service in Saudi Arabia, but the normal person walking down the street in my hometown isn't going to come down with this. But what can you say, the government is either hiding something or they just don't want to let us know what's been done to us.

There were maybe 12 or 13 of us in our unit who were volunteers, who stood up and said: "Hey, we'll go. You haven't got enough people. We'll go, we'll serve with you." And there was the government saying: "Thanks a lot. You went over there, we paid you while you were there, that's good enough. We don't need to do anything else for you. You're all set." And there were Vietnam veterans over there too with us. And they're sicker now than any of us. The government, they won't admit to anything. They're slowly letting stuff out, but it's not fast enough. Too many people are really getting sick and having to put themselves in debt to take care of their own medical problems.

The biggest thing is the sensitivity to stuff that you used to, you used to go out all the time and paint your house and use the thinners and stuff, and now you've got to avoid the use of the thinners. When you pump your own gas, like myself, I've got to turn away so I don't breathe the fumes. The chemical sensitivity is becoming just unreal, and you notice it now. Before, when you would pump gas, you used to stand there and smell the fumes, you know, great, this stuff don't bother me. And now you've got to try to hide and pump at the same time. And it's not just me, it's some of the vets that were with me over there. The same thing, and they're not getting paid for their medical bills either. And it's hard to stay serving your government when they don't want to tell you the truth.

---

[1] The pain of cluster headaches is so severe that they have sometimes been called suicide headaches.

Sp4c. Bobby Lawson, U.S. Army (Ret.)

When we were engaging the enemy, the chemical alarm system went off multiple times, so many times that we were told to ignore them. That's because we kept putting on the same MOPP suit. Once you break one MOPP suit, that's it, it's no good. And we were told to use the same MOPP suit each time.

Our commanders never warned us about the radioactive vehicles, that we could not go around them or touch them, so basically, it was like a free-for-all, everybody just wanting to explore, to get things out of the tanks and take pictures on them, just to show what we did and accomplished. I have a picture of myself standing on top of an Iraqi tank.

At one point we camped near the burning oil wells. Your uniform would be completely covered with black. There was soot all over you, on your arms where they were exposed, on your food and everything. There was oil in the water where you took showers. There was so much smoke that it was constantly dark. There was no such thing as daylight.

When I took the PB pills, I was ordered to take them. I did not receive nothing about what they would do to you, and they watched you take them. Basically, what happened was, my body just heated up. I seen other personnel in my battalion throwing up, running around. Personally, I just felt like a big flame, a fire; it was unbelievable.

On many occasions, trucks lay diesel fuel down where we slept, where we ate, where we played. We walked on it all the time. They just kept pouring that diesel fuel down to keep the sand from blowing around.

When I got back from the Gulf, my parents started noticing such a change in me. I wasn't really energetic no more, I didn't play sports. I was always tired, fatigued, I wasn't the way I used to be as a young kid, always playing sports. I felt like a battery just draining, my powers leaving me, my entire body.

From the time I got home, I had chronic diarrhea, memory loss, joint pains, fatigue all the time, burning sensations in my eyes, multiple bruises. A few times I had rashes. One of my worst symptoms is the chronic diarrhea. I intake food and it just flows right out of my system, probably three or four times a day. I've been suffering with this chronic diarrhea for nine years. It hasn't gotten any better, it's just gotten worse.

I'm sensitive to a lot of chemicals now too. There's many times when I walk into a department store or a place like that, and I smell an odor and my body would just react. I have to leave right away because I start shaking and sweating. Different things will trigger my body, and I will react to different chemicals, and stuff like that.

S.Sgt. Anne Selby, British Army

Before we left, we were also given what we called NAPPs, which is nerve agent pre-treatment packs, or what the Americans call PB tablets. We were told not to take them before we were actually deployed. But when we actually arrived in Riyadh, we were all hustled into one room, where was an officer there who greeted us and said,"Welcome to Saudi Arabia," very much tongue in cheek. Then he said, "Ladies and gentlemen, you can now start taking your NAAPs tablets."And they stood over us while we took them. If you were in a static camp, it was announced every few hours that it was time to take your pyridostigmine bromide tablets. And they checked up on you to make sure that you had taken them. So we took them because, you know, being good little soldiers, we'd been told that they were there to help protect us.

I myself had noticed some slight changes when I took the NAPPs tablets. I'd suffered very much with migraine as a teenager, but I hadn't suffered for some years. And within maybe 48 hours of taking the NAPPs tablets, I got the migraines back. I felt nauseous and had more trouble with diarrhea. There was also some loss of sensation, sexual sensation basically. A lot of people had experienced it. I thought it was just me, I thought it was just tiredness and one thing or another. Having spoken to people since, however, and found out they all suffered the same thing, I can only assume it had something to do with the tablets. And it did stop when we stopped taking the tablets.

As the stay in Saudi Arabia progressed, I had noticed that along with the sickness I had been experiencing, along with the peculiar flu-like thing in my chest, my breathing was not good. My breathing felt very much as though I was trying to take in glue instead of air. It was not pleasant. That continued until after we came back to the UK. By the time we arrived back in the United Kingdom, I was feeling a little bit suspicious of everything that had gone on.

I had already applied to go to the university, and while I was waiting to go to the university, I seemed to be OK. Since it was summer, I just assumed that whatever had been wrong had passed off. And then I became very ill in the first week I started university, which would be in September of 1991. And it progressed into pneumonia, but I didn't realize it was pneumonia at first. The doctors were doing all these tests to try and find out what was wrong with me. At one stage they even suggested that I had whooping cough but since one of the vaccinations I'd been given was for whooping cough, that was not the problem.

They gave me all of these antibiotics. They just tried me on one after another. Nothing worked, and then finally it seemed to settle down for a little while.

Then at Christmas of that year I became ill again, and this time I got pneumonia very badly. It was what my doctor called atypical pneumonia. And because I'd had pneumonia twice within the space of three months, they decided to put me in the hospital to find out what was going on. And when they actually looked at my lungs, they said that there was a lot of oily debris in my lungs and had I been in a house fire?

At this point, I hadn't connected the two things—all the smoke from the oil wells and the breathing. When you're in a situation like that, you don't tend to try to separate everything out. It was just one big kind of chemical soup thing that we all seemed to be existing in. You couldn't breathe because the oil was heavy in the air, you felt ill because you'd had too many injections, plus the climate itself wasn't conducive to good health either in my opinion. So I didn't connect for some reason the oily debris bit and the oil well fires bit. I didn't connect it immediately. And they asked me, "Have you been in a house fire?" and I said no. And they said, "Well, we can't understand why your lungs are in such bad shape." And I said, "Well, I'm not quite sure what's happened." They gave me some inhalers and steroids and antibiotics that they hoped with help me breathe a bit easier.

By the time I returned for a review appointment in two weeks, I had actually made the connection. I went back to the doctor, and I said, "Look, would oil wells have done it, burning oil wells?" And he looked at me and he said yes. He said, "When were you with burning oil? You don't work in the oil industry, do you?" I said, "No, but I was a soldier out in the Gulf." And he said, "Ah, yes, because the fumes from burning oil wells are both toxic and carcinogenic. They set fire to something they call the signature, which is highly toxic." The official diagnosis for my lung problems and my breathing difficulties is bronchiactisis, which is scarring of the tissue of the surface of the lungs. And they just put me on inhalers and various things, and there's really nothing they can do. The lungs will only heal themselves to a certain extent. They won't completely heal, so I'm stuck with the problem until I die.

One of the main problems I have with regard to the breathing difficulty is that I can't walk for long distances without my lungs filling up with fluid. Your lungs try to protect you by producing more fluid, so basically what happens is that I start choking, coughing on the fluid after I've walked for a little while. Running is out of the question. Walking for long distances is out of the question. It limits what I can do workwise. Just the breathing difficulties on their own, without the chronic fatigue, without the sore joints, basically limit what I can do. I can't do any heavy lifting jobs because my lungs aren't up to it. I can't go back to doing what I originally did—I was a singer, a stage performer. Even though I can still sing, there is no way I've got the lung capacity now to carry x-amount of tunes for x-amount of hours a night, so there's no way I can go back to my former profession I had before I joined the Army.

I have problems now breathing in atmospheres where there's heavy perfume concentrate. It's hard for me to breath on buses because of the diesel fumes. I have problems using household disinfectants and chemicals because they cause my airways to close, and I start choking, very much like an asthmatic, but I'm not an asthmatic. But it's very much like asthma symptoms, which is why I use asthma inhalers, because it's the only thing they can give me. And that condition will never go away.

There is most certainly a commonality between UK veterans, some of the Australian veterans I've spoke to, and the U.S. veterans. There's a commonality of symptoms; we all seem to suffer from some sort of respiratory problems, joint problems, skin rashes, cognitive problems. I can't tell you how many conversations that I've had with both American and English vets that have been totally screwed up because either one of us have kind of forgotten where we were in the sentence, and you know, you just think, what was I talking about? And then the searching for words and stuff like that. And I've actually been face to face talking to American vets, and we've literally laughed because we both have the same problem.

A media person asked me the other day if there was any important statement that I would care to make about my experience in the Gulf, and basically I laughed and said, "Well, apart from the fact that it's absolutely destroyed my life, I'm not sure what else to say."

Sgt. Paul Perrone, U.S. Air Force (Ret.)

I joined the U.S. Air Force in September of 1986 and left for basic training in April of 1987 because I wanted to be a part of something bigger than me. My previous work experience consisted mostly of working as a security guard for several years after high school. Law enforcement work had always appealed to me. The ability to work outside and have low supervision were the main reasons, and Air Force law enforcement training was also well respected.

In August of 1990, Saddam Hussein invaded Kuwait. Having just returned from a one-year tour of duty in Korea, I knew as I watched the TV that the Middle East would be my next stop. In September of 1990, I was on my way with twelve other guys from the little-known Air Force base of Williams in Arizona to a never-heard-of base in Riyadh, Saudi Arabia. A 90-day temporary duty assignment turned into what seemed to be an eternity, but in reality, I spent only seven months in the Persian Gulf.

I never really paid attention to the loose bowel movements or minor muscle twitching that started in January of 1991. Maybe it was the long hours, the unusual climate, or the food, I thought. It would pass when I returned to a more normal activity level and a regular diet. I don't recall the exact date I got the anthrax shot, but I do recall that my symptoms started soon after I received it. Of course, I didn't make the connection until a couple of years later. When I started having symptoms in the Gulf, I thought this would pass like a case of the flu.

In July of 1991, when I was back in the States, I experienced a very bizarre incident. While I was driving down a flat stretch of road in Wichita Falls, Texas, I suddenly felt like I was on a ride at Disney World. I pulled over as the world around me spun about. Being almost three miles from the Air Force base and having no way of calling for help, I decided to drive to the base and go to the hospital. But by the time the base was in view, my symptoms had settled down, so I just went to my room and lay down. It would be months before I reported the incident.

At this point, fatigue had reared its ugly head and gradually kept getting worse. I had to make excuses for appearing tired. I was happy to be in the Air Force and did not want to make too much of my health situation. I was in the process of retraining from law enforcement to medical supply. My plan was to continue going to school now that I would be working mostly day shift and away from the extraordinary hours that are inherent in a position in law enforcement.

By September of 1991, it took about all the energy I had just to get ready for work. When I had trouble functioning in my job, my supervisors started asking questions, and they were not patient with me either. Of course, I never told them I was having health problems, so I can't really blame them. They had a mission and were depending on me. I was not pulling my share of the load and I knew it, and this only made matters worse.

In early 1992, I failed a physical fitness test for the first time in the five years I had been in the Air Force. That made me so concerned that I finally decided to seek help for my problem.

One of the most difficult things about having chronic fatigue syndrome, which I've been diagnosed with, is that it is something that nobody can see. It is not like a broken leg or a bullet wound. The sufferer is constantly struggling to be accepted by skeptical family, friends, or members of the medical community. The doctors I saw were less than sympathetic, to say the least. This only made a bad situation worse. What was to be done? Not only was I feeling ill, but just when I got up the nerve to seek help, I was put off.

Frequent trips to the Emergency Department (ED) at my base were commonplace by now. Finally, a lieutenant colonel who happened to be on duty in the ED examined me. He noticed my extreme fatigue upon minimal exertion and decided it was not a good idea to let me go back to my room, where I would be alone. He admitted me to the hospital with what he called a "mono-like illness." My white blood count was low, and my liver blood tests were elevated. Other blood tests were also abnormal.

After spending a few days in that hospital, I was flown to the medical center at Lackland Air Force Base in Texas. For eight days they performed tests that included everything from a spinal tap to an MRI. (I later learned, however, that despite the spinal tap, they did not test me for multiple sclerosis.) The best the military doctors could come up with was that I might have an ear infection. This diagnosis was supposed to describe my symptoms of loose bowel movements, frequent urination, muscle twitching, debilitating fatigue, loss of balance, blurry and double vision, and joint pain. No psychological problems were noted, even after an extensive psychological exam, but one doctor thought the whole thing was much ado about nothing.

When I returned to Williams Air Force Base in Arizona, I was sent to see a psychologist, even though the staff at Lackland had found no evidence of mental illness. The psychologist said it sounded like a panic disorder and set me to a psychiatrist. The psychiatrist disagreed with the psychologist, and on and on we went. The psychiatrist thought I had an organic illness, but he was not in a position to say what it was. Because of all the disagreement in the medical community, I was sent back to full duty with only one restriction—stay off ladders.

In July of 1992, I decided to leave the Air Force. I was told I was not entitled to any benefits, but medical documentation would be placed in my records to make it easier for me to get VA assistance. I continued to fight for my pension, and I made many trips to VA hospitals, some over 100 miles from my home. Finally, with the help of some close friends and a lot of Divine intervention, I am pleased to say I have now received what I consider to be adequate recognition from the Air Force and the VA for my illness.

My official and main diagnosis is chronic fatigue syndrome with immune dysfunction. With frequent naps, I am able to function, as long as I don't overdo it. If I push myself, even a little, I get headaches and muscle twitching. If I continue to push, I develop numbness and fatigue that can last for weeks. Asthma and chronic sinusitis are also a problem. In late August of 1997, I developed optic neuritis for the first time. I still have occasional episodes of it, but not as severe as that initial one. Because of the optic neuritis attacks, I am now under the supervision of a neurologist for possible multiple sclerosis. In addition, I am chemically sensitive, so exposure to ordinary chemicals found around the house can exacerbate my symptoms. I have tested positive for mycoplasma fermentans (*incognitus*), so I am participating in the VA's study involving long-term antibiotic treatment.

I have always been convinced that the vaccines administered during the Gulf War are a major contributor to Gulf War illness. In my case, I served in Riyadh, the capital of Saudi Arabia, some 300 miles away from the front lines, so it is less likely that I was exposed to low levels of nerve agents. While I did have some exposure to pesticides, particularly because I worked as a guard during night shifts when pesticide was being applied, I did not take the PB pills and I was not close to the oil well fires. I did, however, take the anthrax vaccine, and my symptoms started shortly thereafter.

Even though my health has been affected by the war, I will be forever grateful that I had the opportunity to serve my country in this way. I wish to express my appreciation to the many people who have over the years thanked me for my service in the Gulf War. Unlike so many veterans, I have also had the good fortune to find a few dedicated physicians who have gone far beyond their obligation to help me. Too many veterans who find themselves in a position of needing substantial medical and financial support feel torn because they feel that they love their country more than their country loves them.

S.Sgt. Bob Jones, U.S. Army

I left our base in Germany in December of 1990 and went over with a field artillery unit that was part of the First Armored Division. We went into Saudi Arabia and set up outside King Khalid Military City during the air campaign. Chemical detection alarms were continuously going off during the air war, and we would have to put on our MOPP-4 suits.

We were given the PB pills and were ordered to take them every eight hours. The pills made me feel really strange. I didn't really want to take them, but I felt the necessity to protect myself in the event of direct chemical exposures, which we had been told was a real possibility. I wanted to come back home, and I believed it was in my best interest to continue taking the PB pills, even though they made me feel really strange, made my heart race. It was almost an out-of-body experience. Although I was still able to function, things like time and space seemed altered around me. I was more than happy to discontinue taking the things.

When the ground war started, we encountered the Iraqi Republican Guard units and took incoming artillery fire. We were attached to Second Brigade, which was an armor unit, and we provided direct support for them in the heat of the battle when the armor units and the tankers were firing depleted uranium rounds. On several occasions we rode right through the middle of an ongoing battle. Iraqi tanks were blowing up all around us, and I grabbed several of my men to ensure they were not hit by flying debris and shrapnel from the exploding ordinances and vehicles. The air was full of radioactive dust, pulverized uranium from the targets that were hit. It was a free-for-all kill zone. Destroyed Iraqi tanks and vehicles completely littered the battlefields, and they were ablaze as we rode through them.

Right after the ground war ended, we were in the area near Khamisiyah. There were multiple bunkers around us, and some of these bunkers contained rounds that had chemical markings. The engineers were continually blowing up bunkers all around us as we sat in Kuwait and southern Iraq. You could feel the ground shaking under your feet as they were blowing up all these bunker complexes.

After the cease-fire, we ended up spending 45 days in the Rhumali oil fields in the midst of the burning oil wells. It was just incredible, something surreal, like being in another world. We saw no sunlight for almost all that time because the sun was completely blackened out by the smoke and soot. The vapors of burning fuel were terrible—it was like breathing diesel exhaust constantly. It became so bad at times that I put on my protective mask to try to filter out some clean air. I had severe headaches and was nauseous from the fumes. There were particles falling out of the sky on top of us, and we had a black film and soot on our skin. It was just unbelievable to be sitting in something like that. We kept wondering why they didn't move us away from this area where we were continuously breathing in all this crap.

My symptoms began in the Gulf with severe abdominal cramping and severe diarrhea. I also had terrible headaches and bouts of dizziness and tingling. Once I returned to the base in Germany, the headaches persisted, and I experienced the cramps and diarrhea on a cyclic basis. I also went through periods of night sweats. And there were periods when I would sleep a lot because I was so fatigued. My joints were stiff, and my knees would swell after I ran. It was harder for me to do things without feeling short of breath.

These symptoms became worse as time passed. And things just got to the point where I had diarrhea on myself at work a couple of times, and I said, enough is enough. I need to get help. It's real embarrassing to be standing around all your men and all of a sudden you can't even make it to the bathroom in time.

Another strange thing that happened shortly after I got back from Germany was that I had to have several spots on my body cut out. They were like precancerous growths, and they had not been present before I went to the Gulf War. Even several years after I got back, they had to cut some plugs out of my legs and my arm.

At this point, I started hearing about the connection with the Gulf War and that people were having similar problems, so I registered with the Comprehensive Clinical Evaluation Program (CCEP). They did their little evaluations and took lots of blood. They ended up sending me to all three phases of the program. Even after I left the final phase of the program, there were a lot of things that had not been explained satisfactorily and my symptoms were still there. By this point, I was also having problems with memory loss and confusion.

Ever since my return from the Gulf, I've been plagued by multiple rashes and lesions on my face, neck, arms, and back. They come and go. And I've got this deep, burning, bone pain all through my legs, and it radiates, primarily in my hips and my femur. I have multiple medications that help me tolerate the pain. They don't alleviate the constant pain, but they do make life more tolerable.

Because my white blood cell count was very high and I had severe bone pain, I had a bone marrow sample taken. But nothing could explain why I had this infection in my body and why I was having problems with my central nervous system or why I was having rashes.

I also became very sensitive to chemicals because of my exposures in Desert Storm. Earlier in my military career, I had spent eight years in the 82nd Airborne Division as a paratrooper, so I had had extensive exposure to jet fuel and jet fumes, and these things had never bothered me. But having spent 45 days in the area where the oil wells were burning, breathing the noxious fumes on a daily basis, now just the smell of diesel fuel makes me severely nauseated, dizzy, and very sick. I try to avoid getting behind school buses because diesel exhaust really bothers me, as do other odors and smells. Perfumes are also a problem; I don't wear any type of cologne because it makes me nauseous.

Before I went to Desert Storm, I was in excellent physical condition. I was a jock, a really good athlete, and I represented the 7th Corps in the Army tennis championships when I was in Europe. I was able to take my family on vacations all over Europe on the basis of my tennis ability. Now I have great difficulty walking around the block or walking up a flight or two of stairs without being totally wiped out, short of breath, and in severe pain.

To make matters worse, my wife is also chronically ill now, and we both are convinced that her illness is related to the Gulf War. At the end of the conflict, we were told to mail and ship most of our belongings back home so we would not have to bring so much gear with us on the airplane. So with the exception of my rucksack and my weapon, I boxed up all my gear and belongings—dirty uniforms and clothing from six months in the Gulf. As instructed, I mailed everything home to my family at our home in Germany. When I got home, we opened up the boxes together because I had collected a few souvenirs and mementoes to share with them. As we opened the boxes, sand and dust fell out and made little piles on the floor.

A few weeks later my wife became ill with what seemed to be a flu-like illness that persisted and seemed to progress as time went on. Prior to becoming ill, she had been a very productive teacher and had been teacher of the year. She had received her master's degree in school administration, graduating at the top of her class, but she was too ill to walk in her graduation ceremony. When she became sick, she was awaiting a position as a school administrator, but her illness became so debilitating that she could no longer continue with her profession. She required extensive treatment and hospitalizations. At one point her liver specialist was even discussing removing half of her liver. She had a large hypatic cyst on her liver that had to be drained and sclerosed.

Our children also became ill, so we began to wonder if I could have brought something strange home from the Persian Gulf in my belongings. I had the sand that covered the belongings I shipped home analyzed at a world-renowned laboratory, and they found in the samples a fungus that is quite toxic.

In 1999 the army sent my wife and me to New Orleans for an experimental antibiotic treatment. It was there that my wife went into acute renal failure after receiving massive doses of intravenous antibiotics. She also developed fluid around her heart. Her condition was so critical that the doctors were not sure whether she was going to recover and live or not. I thought that the massive IV antibiotics were killing her, so I stopped the IV pump on two different occasions. Of course, the doctor didn't like that, and the Army sent me back to North Carolina under an Army escort. We had to have my wife's parents fly to her bedside so she would have family with her. I was still very sick myself, and it was devastating to think that she might be dying in New Orleans without me by her side and I would be left to raise our three children by myself. Fortunately, she survived, but she has permanent kidney damage.

My most recent finding from the Army physical evaluation board is that I have undifferentiated somatoform disorder, which is the biggest insult that I can even begin to imagine. I have been fighting for four or five years to get medical treatment, and my medical records and evaluations are extensive. I've been hospitalized four times by both civilian and Army personnel. And after all this, they come back with one diagnosis that fits the psychiatric category in which they have placed almost all the Gulf War vets. They have left me financially destitute, on the edge of bankruptcy, watching as my wife and children wither away.

To me, undifferentiated somatoform disorder is just a catch-all phrase, an easy way to satisfy their needs and get rid of people. I can't believe that after four years of congressional hearings and people testifying to presidential committees, they are still trying to write this condition off as a psychiatric illness. That's simply disgusting.

S1c. James Davis, U.S. Navy (Ret.)

When my son Jim was twenty, he joined the U.S. Navy. Being a mother of three boys, I always knew that some day it would be their duty to serve, protect, and honor our great nation. I was proud of his years in the Navy, just as I am proud of any man or woman that wears the uniform of the Armed Services. When President Bush decided we should draw a line in the sand in Saudi and should go to war, I felt some pride, yet also fear as our son would be one of thousands who would be in harm's way.

While Jim was serving on the USS *Independence*, he received an award because his quick thinking kept a heavy piece of equipment from rolling into a helicopter. On another occasion, he was cleaning the ship when something went wrong with his protective equipment. The face masks that he and two other young soldiers were wearing were hooked up wrong, and they began to get very sick because the fuel fumes from the jets were being sucked into their lungs. Jim spent many days in sick bay after that incident. He later told me that he felt as if his eyes had popped out of his head.

Jim had another injury on the USS *Independence* when he and some of the other crew were trying to get some equipment off a loading dock and it fell on his shoulder. The object that fell on him weighed 2000 pounds, and someone who was there said he had heard the bones in Jim's shoulder snap. Again Jim was back in sick bay. Eventually he was sent back to work on light duty. Jim suffered the rest of his life because of that injury. The pain at times was unbearable as he grew older. Sometimes he would walk with his head cocked to one side. When I asked him why he didn't hold his head straight, he would reply, "I can't, Mom, it hurts too much."

After Jim got out of the service after the war, he found a job as a painter at North Island Air Base in San Diego. This was great for Jim as he had met a wonderful girl there whom he was madly in love with. But the job he was so excited about turned into a nightmare because the pain in his shoulder was increasing. Jim went to the VA for treatment, but some days he would have to wait six to seven hours just to see a doctor. He would lose pay from work, and he knew the sick time would not look good on his record. He began to take drugs; we later saw in his medical records that it said he was taking them for the pain.

In 1994 my husband Don and I went to California because of the earthquake. (He is a disaster insurance adjuster.) We were glad to be able to see Jim more now that we were only a hundred miles away from him. When we first saw him, he seemed normal, but he had lots of complaints about his health. He had a rash on his body, stomach problems, joint pains, and an ulcer on one of his eyes, and he was passing bloody stools. It was at this time that we first learned that Jim had turned to street drugs. He told us that he had been homeless because he was too sick to work and had turned to drugs to ease his pain and misery.

We took Jim to a rehab center and took his car away from him at the suggestion of what at the time we thought was a professional counselor. We were told about "tough love" and told not to send him any money or to write. After we left California, we didn't really know what was happening to him for the next year or so except for occasional phone calls to Jim and his social workers and doctors. He did complete the drug program.

In the meantime, our second son, Mike, came to live with us in Albuquerque. He had just found out he had AIDS. After seeing how much care he needed, we packed up and moved to North Carolina, where our daughter Kelly lived with her family. She is a nurse, and we knew we would need her to help us with Mike's illness. For over a year and a half, we did not work. Mike's illness took not only all our savings but our time during the next few years.

Jim, in the meantime, was being transferred from one homeless shelter to another. He wanted to come home, but we told him he couldn't because Mike was so sick. I talked to his doctors and social workers at least once a month. They all told me not to bring Jim home because we couldn't help him. They said he needed to be in their programs. One social worker told me Jim could not work because something was wrong with his brain.

We didn't expect Mike would live much past Christmas of 1995, so we asked Jim to come for a visit. He was so excited about coming home. After I paid over $500 for a plane ticket for him, his social worker told him he could not come home because he could not be away from his rehab program. After many angry phone calls from us, however, they finally allowed Jim to come home for Christmas.

I will never forget seeing Jim that first night. He was so doped up with medications, and he had gained over 100 lbs. I could hardly recognize him. He shuffled as he walked and had on some overalls that were torn and dirty and three sizes too big for him. He had no underwear on, so the gaps in his pants exposed half his body. To see him like that was such a shock because Jim had always had good taste in clothes and bought the best name brands. He was such a good-looking kid.

Jim told us that most of his clothes had been stolen. The various shelters he had stayed in had given the rest away when he had had to spend a few days in the hospital. I could not believe that this had happened to my son within one year. The next day Kelly and I took Jim on a makeover shopping trip to the local mall. We got him some pants, shirts, shoes, and a coat among other things. We had a great time, and to this day it brings tears to my eyes as I try to remember him dressed up in his new clothes.

Being a nurse, Kelly was surprised to see how many medications Jim was taking, and she was concerned that he was sleeping all the time. When he ate, he stuffed the food in his mouth as if he hadn't eaten for months. Then he would be sick and sleep again for hours. He was depressed about all the bills he was running up for medical expenses—over $6,000 and growing. His father told him not to worry about it because he got hurt while he was in the service so he should not have to pay these bills.

Jim had by this time turned in a claim because of his shoulder injury, but I told him I thought he was just wasting his time trying to get the government to do something for him. I thought he should just go to college because he could earn a lot more money that way. But Jim replied that he didn't think he could manage to go to college because of the memory problems he had developed after the war.

Jim went back to his rehab program in San Diego after Christmas, but in April 1996 we got a call from the hospital in San Diego reporting that he had tried to take his own life. I had talked to Jim a few days before, and he had wanted me to send him some money to go to a wedding to be the best man for a young man who had been a dear friend since they had been in high school together. I told him that I didn't have money to give him for a trip like that. I should have realized how strong Jim's friendship was with this young man and sent him the money, but my life was all wrapped up with caring for my other son who was dying of AIDS. I had no time to think of the needs of my other children, my husband, or myself.

In June of 1996, Jim called home and said he had been in the hospital for a week, and they said he couldn't stay any longer because he didn't have any money. To make matters worse, they had lost his shoes. He had nowhere to go because the homeless shelter wouldn't take him back since he had been away for too many days. He was crying and begging to live, but he was scared. I told him I would call him back within an hour. I talked to my family and told them I had one son who was going to die, and I did not want another son to die. Jim had to come home. At first they all disagreed with me, saying I had too much stress already in my life because Mike was so sick. We also didn't have room for Jim. But in the end, they all agreed he should come home for a few months until he could get on his feet.

When I saw Jim at the bus depot a few days later, I realized how sick he was. The next day we went to the VA because of the intestinal bleeding he was having and the pain in his guts. The doctor, however, looked at the patch on his eye and told him his ulcerated eye was more of an immediate problem than his gut problems. They admitted Jim to the hospital that day. Within the next three months, Jim had 23 visits to the VA, and they put him on a great many medications during that period. Their basic attitude was clear though from what his VA psychiatrist wrote in Jim's record: "Patient appears to be malingering for secondary gain."

Jim kept trying to get financial help from the VA because his shoulder injury had occurred in a shipboard accident while he was in the service, but he was unsuccessful. When Jim took me with him one day to talk to a VA official, that man told Jim to go get some food stamps and wait eight months. I about jumped out of my chair and asked, "Where is he supposed to live? How can he get a job with no car?" (We live 14 miles from the nearest town.)

Jim then dragged me with him to SSI to get some food stamps. I was never so ashamed in my life to be sitting in a room as my son signed up for food stamps. I refused to eat any of his food and made sure it wasn't stored in the same area as our food, but one day Jim conned me into picking up a few things with his food stamps. Not only did he get food stamps, he also had my name added to the form. As I stood in line at the grocery store that day to get Jim's food, some gal in back of me said, "My, what a big diamond you have on." Not that that wasn't bad enough, the clerk had to hold the food stamps in midair and yell to the service desk, "food stamps." I wanted to drop into a hole. I began to shake so bad I couldn't breathe. All I wanted to do was to get home and tear Jim apart limb by limb.

When I told Jim what had happened, he smiled at first, but then he got very sad and said, "Mom, I'm so sorry. I only wanted to give or share some way with the family. I know it is hard with both Mike and I living here, and I will quit getting the stamps if it causes you so much pain." Then he told me, "Mom, something happened to me in the Persian Gulf. I'm not normal anymore. I will never have a family like Kelly does. I have lost the one girl I really loved. But I served my country, and they owe me something. I was healthy when I went into the service, and I came out sick."

I never felt so ashamed in my life for the way I had behaved. I asked Jim to forgive me and promised him I would never question his reasons again. And I told him he could put his food anywhere he wanted to. To this day when I see someone with food stamps I feel so much pain for them and I ask if they are in the United States military.

A few days later Don and I had a business meeting to attend, so we had asked Jim to take care of Mike. Then at the last minute our plans changed, so I went to Jim's room to tell him that we were going to be home after all. I found him dead. When I called members of my family and told them that Jim had died, they all corrected me, saying, "No, Maureen, you mean Mike died." They couldn't believe that Jim, who was only 27 years old, had died.

After Jim's death, we talked to the coroner who did the autopsy and asked why they put "suicidal death" on his death certificate. They told me that they had called the Durham VA and asked what Jim was being treated for and had been told it was drug abuse. We then went to them and showed them the copies of the 23 office visits to the VA and told them that at the time of his death Jim was taking 15 prescription medications they had given him. After they saw that information, they changed the death certificate to accidental morphine poisoning. Even that is not quite accurate because the amount of morphine in his blood should not have been enough to kill him. The other medications that he was taking were also at a therapeutic level in his blood. The VA hadn't prescribed morphine for Jim, but he couldn't afford the medications he needed for his pain, so he took a couple of his brother Mike's morphine tablets, which were very strong.

The next few months were very hard for our family. Mike, bless his soul, took much of the blame for Jim's death, no matter how we tried to help him feel it was not his fault. We made it our mission to show him how much we loved and cared for him. He did live for two years after Jim's death.

At this point we still hadn't realized that there was a connection between Jim's illnesses and his service in the Gulf War. When we began to hear more and more about other veterans who were sick, we began to understand what had happened to Jim, and we became very angry that the Department of Defense was not admitting that their service in the Gulf War had made a lot of veterans sick. If we had only known about Gulf War syndrome before Jim died, we would have understood why he was so sick after he came home, and we would not have just blamed most of his problems on drug usage. We blame ourselves for not being more sympathetic to Jim, and that makes us all the more angry with the DOD for keeping us from realizing why he was having so many health problems. Now that we understand about Gulf War syndrome and how many veterans are suffering and dying from it, we have become very active on the Internet to find information about Gulf War syndrome and share it with others. We have joined marches, and we go to meetings of Gulf War veterans to hear them talk about their illness, pain, and fears for the future.

The Department of Defense sometimes sends out teams to hold town meetings with ill veterans. Last year they sent a colonel down to North Carolina to hold one of these town meetings. My daughter Kelly and I happened to hear that he was speaking earlier that day at a Rotary Club luncheon, so we decided to go hear him speak. He apparently didn't think that any veterans were at the Rotary luncheon, and he made fun of Gulf War illness. He said that the military should be more careful in the future to screen out people with psychological problems, and he even joked and said something like, "Would you want a wacko sitting beside you in the cockpit?" That night at a town meeting I confronted this colonel in front of 500 ill Gulf War veterans. After I had ran out of steam, my daughter Kelly stood up and questioned him about all the problems the Gulf veterans were having. When she got done, he had to stand up and apologize to that group of angry veterans.

Many people think I should not speak out about Gulf War illness because Jim took drugs. I think those people are as ignorant as those who refused to give my son help when he needed it. Jim took the responsibility for his weakness, but he did not do drugs when he was in the service.

Capt. Julia Dyckman, U.S. Navy (Ret.)

From December 1969 to December 1970, I was a Navy nurse stationed on a hospital ship in Vietnam. When we were not on the ship, we would sometimes go into areas that had been defoliated by Agent Orange. When I returned from Vietnam, I began having irritable bowel syndrome and lactose intolerance, although I had not had these problems previously.

In the Gulf War, I served as a commander in a fleet hospital, which is a tent hospital that holds 500 beds and has 1000 personnel assigned to it. Even before the rest of our group arrived in the Persian Gulf, the Navy Seabees had gone there to pour concrete pads to set up our tents for the hospital. The area where the hospital was set up was in an area of the desert that was formerly an industrial park. Five miles away was a fertilizer plant. In late January, the Seabees who were pouring the concrete heard a loud explosion near them. Some of the Seabees' shirts turned purple and many had burning sensations on their hands and face. Some wondered if a SCUD missile had hit the fertilizer plant, releasing some chemical into the air. All the Seabees were told was that the chemical was probably an industrial solvent. Many of those Seabees are really sick now, and when I first arrived at the compound, I noticed lots of dead rodents around the area. I also noticed that there were no insects around.

Once the concrete pads were ready, we came in to set up the tents and the sleeping quarters. I started having open sores on my right foot right away after I arrived—they were located near where there were some ventilation holes in my boot.

Then in February there was another explosion, and immediately after the explosion an ammonia smell came through the camp. We put on gas masks, but the hospital air conditioning and heat pump system still brought in outside air. We didn't have any chemical alarm system in our camp, but we were told that there was nothing to worry about. Soon after this explosion, however, I started having a rapid heart rate and uncontrollable blood pressure problems.

We began noticing some odd things around the hospital. Some of the synthetic fabrics on the cots were beginning to disintegrate. A lot of soldiers were coming in with uniforms covered with oil, and the fabric on these uniforms was beginning to fall apart. We didn't know whether the oil was destroying them or whether there was some other chemical attacking them. The oil on the uniforms probably came from the oil well fires that were burning all over the area. When it rained, the rain would be oily. It left an oily coating on everything, and it was almost impossible to clean that off the tents.

When I left the Persian Gulf, I was ill. I was having fevers and had become sensitive to many chemicals. I can't stand to go into any kind of store that sells fertilizer or pesticide. We don't use anything like that on our lawn anymore. I use all natural fibers in my house, and we have taken out the carpets and replaced them by wood floors. I can't wear polyester clothes now because I start swelling if I do, but before I went to the Gulf War, I had no problem wearing polyester.

Rashes are a problem for me now, as for almost all the vets with Gulf War syndrome. The rashes are like small pustules that leave scars. My joints swell up all the time; I participated in a study at the University of Pennsylvania that showed they were all swollen and that I have bursitis and osteoarthritis. The arthritis in my hands is really severe now, particularly in my thumbs and wrists, which are enlarged and constantly inflamed. I have had severe headaches and chronic sinusitis since I returned from the Persian Gulf. I've had my gall bladder removed and a foot of my colon removed because of chronic diverticulitis (a condition I didn't have before the Gulf War). My ovaries and uterus were removed because they were in a precancerous state. I've had stomach polyps and rectal polyps, and I have a slight case of Barrett's esophagitis, which is a precancerous condition of the esophagus that you have to keep an eye on. I have some brain lesions, and I've also developed diabetes this last year.

The VA still doesn't recognize that my autonomic nervous system has been damaged as a result of my service in the Gulf (causing the rapid heart rate and uncontrollable blood pressure fluctuations). When I went to the Navy for those problems, they said it was stress. Fortunately, the National Institute of Health was doing a study on stress and the effects of stress, and they sent me to participate. The researchers there said that I had autonomic nervous system damage—cause unknown. It's hardly surprising that I was the last Gulf War vet they sent over to participate in that study.

After many years of battling with them, I have finally received disability status from the Navy on the basis of autonomic nervous system damage, but they won't recognize the cause. I'm also listed as having chronic fatigue syndrome and post-traumatic stress disorder.

I would still like to know what chemicals I was exposed to at our fleet hospital site in the Gulf. There must have been some reason why those Seabees' shirts turned purple. We've asked the government to analyze those cement pads that they were pouring when the missile exploded, but it's never been done.

After all these years, the VA and DOD still do not recognize Persian Gulf syndrome as an illness with a CDC code. If there is no illness, then of course there cannot be any cause. The DOD has admitted there were some exposures to "industrial pollutants" and chemical weapons, but the latest "studies" by the Navy have shown no side effects from chemical exposures. (These studies were done in military hospitals, not VA hospitals, where those soldiers whose illness is so advanced that they have had to leave the service would be seen.) Most of the time, low chemical exposure does not cause an immediate effect but can cause long-term damage. I'm convinced that the government *does know* the effects of low dose chemical exposure, be it Agent Orange or

Persian Gulf exposures, and yet does not accept responsibility for its part in the medical problems. If they don't accept responsibility, then there is no hope of protecting future military forces or cleaning up our environment.

Sr. Airman Tom Colisimo, U.S. Air Force (Ret.)

On October 3, 2000, Sr. Airman Colisimo submitted the following prepared statement to the Committee on Government Reform, U.S. House of Representatives, in conjunction with his oral testimony at its hearing on the anthrax vaccination program. Slight changes have been made in the capitalization of a few terms. Sr. Airman Colisimo was sent to the Persian Gulf several months after the cease-fire that ended the Gulf War.

I have served proudly in the Air Force for over nine years. I have had no regrets for my service to my country. During this time I have been deployed to the Middle East eight times to include: Kuwait, Saudi Arabia, and classified locations. I also have been to twenty other countries.

My job was a Nondestructive Inspectionalist. I would inspect aircraft by the use of X-ray, ultrasound, eddy current, bond testing, penetrant, magnetic particle, and oil analysis. By these means I could tell what part of an aircraft or engine was bad or was going to go bad and have it fixed or replaced by specialists before it turned into something catastrophic, such as loss of a pilot or damaging the aircraft. This job was very exciting because wherever the jets went, I went. I enjoyed traveling anywhere the Air Force sent me. . . .

When I voiced my concerns about receiving this [anthrax] vaccine, I was told failure to comply was punishable under the Uniformed Code of Military Justice (UCMJ). I was uncomfortable with accepting the vaccination, but I complied and put my faith in the system. I received all four shots at Hill Air Force Base, Utah.

I received my first anthrax shot (lot # 36) on 20 February 1998. I felt a pain in my upper left arm, starting immediately following the injection, confined to the injection site. The day following this immunization, I felt sick, as if a cold were starting. I felt fatigued, lightheaded, and had a headache. A few days later, I developed a cyst on my scalp, which seemed almost insignificant at first, but gradually increased in size. It became noticeable every 2 weeks when getting a hair cut because of the soreness. At the same time a similar lesion developed in the corner of my right eye. At the time, I didn't think much of it and thought they would just go away.

I received my second anthrax shot (lot # 38) on 15 March 1999, over one year later, even though shot protocol is two weeks between shots 1, 2, and 3. Again I felt immediate pain at the injection site. On the day after the injection, I felt like a cold was coming on with coughing, sneezing, running nose, headache, fatigue, and lightheadedness. Also the cysts that I had originally developed from the first anthrax shot multiplied and increased in size.

I received my third anthrax shot (lot # 38) on 29 March 1999. Again I felt immediate pain at the injection site, but this time instead of feeling like a cold was starting, I just felt very tired. I was so tired that I slept about 16 hours a day for two weeks. I had no energy. The only thing I wanted to do was go to bed and sleep. By this time I had 9 cysts on my scalp, the largest one being the size of a half dollar, and 1 at the corner of my right eye. The pain I was experiencing from these cysts was unreal. If I were to rate it on a scale of 1 through 10, it would definitely have been a 10. Every time I bumped my head or got a hair cut, it would bring me to tears.

The pain got so bad that I finally went to the base hospital in July 1999 and made an appointment to have the cysts surgically removed. . . . I didn't relate these symptoms to the anthrax shot until I received my fourth shot.

I received my fourth anthrax shot (lot # 24) on 22 September 1999. This time the pain at the injection site was unbearable. While leaving the hospital, I kept my arm at my side because it hurt to move it. I had to sit down a few times because it was hard to catch my breath from the pain. The following day, I was sick. I was fatigued, lightheaded, sneezing, disoriented, and had a headache. I also started developing a terrible cough that would cause me to gag when I was done and continued until December, when I deployed to Al Jaber, Kuwait and my condition worsened.

Once there, I started to lose weight rapidly. . . . I lost a total of 50 pounds within the next three months. My energy was declining rapidly, the lightheadedness increased to the point of feeling like I was going to pass out. I had night sweats, chills, ear ringing, tremors, and severe fatigue. My sleep alternated from excessive sleeping one week to insomnia the next week. I went to the hospital and spoke with a doctor who was also from Hill Air Force Base. He ordered several tests for me at Camp Doha, an Army base nearby, and told me the results were "normal" and my concerns were dismissed.

I finished the deployment and returned to Hill Air Force Base 8 March 2000. I went to the Base Hospital to disclose my health concerns, which included increased episodes of vertigo, short term memory loss, shortness of breath, mood swings, confusion, tunnel vision, and fatigue. I expressed that my symptoms might be an adverse reaction to receiving the anthrax vaccine. The first doctor I saw said I could have had the cysts before I came in the military, that I was probably allergic to milk, and that I was starving myself accounting for the severe weight loss. I was told I could not be evaluated or treated until my medical records were returned from Kuwait. Two weeks later, my medical records arrived — having been hand carried by the physician who treated me in Kuwait. Once they arrived, I was told they were "confidential" and was not allowed to see them. I saw the same doctor that I had seen in Kuwait; he again minimized my concerns.

I was told I was due for my fifth anthrax shot on 27 March 2000. Because my complaints of malaise were not taken seriously and because I had concerns that all the symptoms I was experiencing were anthrax related, I decided I couldn't risk taking the next shot.

I was told by the doctors at Hill Air Force Base that my illness was not anthrax related and that I "had to take the shot." They tried to convince me that my cysts predated my anthrax series, that the weight loss was a result of a poor diet, and that everything else was psychosomatic. I contacted my Pennsylvania Representative, John Peterson and shot number five was put on hold pending a medical evaluation. Several appointments with area specialists were made, again due to Representative Peterson's intervention.

My condition continued to worsen. I started to experience staring spells. My wife said it took several minutes before I would snap out of it. She said I would have a blank look on my face and talking to me would not help. I was also getting severe abdominal pains when going to the bathroom, shin pains that lasted for days for no apparent reason. My ability to concentrate was declining and forgetfulness was increasing. Memory loss with dizziness was now constant.

The evaluation by several specialists was to no avail, that is—no diagnosis was discerned. The dizziness was soon followed by daily drop attacks and later led to full loss of consciousness. At first the loss of consciousness only lasted for a few minutes, but as time went on, increased in duration from 30 to 45 minutes, resulting in the inability to speak for about 20 minutes. Several of these episodes included respiratory arrests. An overwhelming feeling of tiredness occurred prior to these incidents.

On 30 March 2000 around 1600 hours (4:00 pm), I was at work, pouring water from a pitcher. I blacked-out and fell to the floor. My supervisor immediately called 911 and the paramedics took me to the base hospital. They ran some test and found nothing "out of the norm." My doctor then placed me on a profile stating no driving or working alone and sent me back to work.

The next blackout happened on 4 April 2000. I was sitting in the break room at work. The next thing I remember I was laying on the floor in a different room with paramedics all around me. They took me to the Davis County Hospital where I was seen by a neurologist and sent home. He did some lab work and scheduled me for some tests the next day.

The following day I went to the base hospital for more lab work and to get a halter monitor placed on me. I called a co-worker for a ride and went outside to sit on a bench and wait. Witnesses said I got up from the bench, lost consciousness, and fell to the pavement. I woke to find the paramedics with me again and was admitted to Davis County Hospital overnight for more "tests and observation." My halter monitor recorded the incident and showed my heart rate went up to 198 bpm and down to 40 bpm when I blacked out. The neurologist said what I had was sinus tachycardia and prescribed heart, sleep, and anxiety medication. I was then put on indefinite convalescent leave.

On 8 April 2000, I was home vacuuming the living room and blacked out. When I came to, my downstairs neighbor, who heard me fall, rushed upstairs to help; he and my wife were yelling and shaking me. They said my eyes were rolled back, eyelids were twitching, my complexion was pale, and I stopped breathing. My wife performed rescue breathing until I came to. It is almost incomprehensible for me to admit to you that these "drop attacks" were becoming "almost normal."

The next day my wife and I went on base to visit with a friend who is in the Air Force Reserves. While visiting with him, I started to feel tired and told them I wanted to go home. While we were walking out to the car, I blacked out. I woke up to an oxygen mask on my face and in the back of an ambulance. I was told I fell face first in the gravel, stopped breathing several times, and had rescue breathing performed on me by a Master Sergeant who was nearby, until the paramedics arrived. I was out for a total of 45 minutes. I was admitted again to Davis County Hospital overnight, with more tests to follow.

The next morning I was taken to Colombia Ogden Regional Medical Center for a tilt table test by Dr. Jones (a cardiologist). . . . He diagnosed me with postural orthostatic tachycardia and chronic fatigue syndrome. He gave me an events monitor to wear; this would record what my heart was doing. He stated I would need someone constantly with me because with my loss of consciousness, I would not be able to activate the system. My wife took a family leave of absence from her job to stay with me. I was told I was not allowed to go back to work, drive, or to be alone.

On 6 May 2000, I was out on our balcony. Upon reentering the house, my wife said I looked very pale and disoriented. I had to hold the door to keep myself up and steady. My wife helped me into the recliner and noticed that my eyes were halfway open and were rolled back. She said my breathing was slow and deep at first, but got faster and harder. She noticed that the events monitor that I was wearing showed my heart rate had increased from 62 bpm to 220 bpm in a few seconds. She then ran downstairs to get our neighbor to help, but when she returned my chest was "jumping" as though I was having muscle spasms. She then decided to call 911. At this time I stopped breathing. The operator told my wife to start rescue breathing. On the 10th breath, I started breathing again, and my heart rate had slowed down.

The medics then arrived and put an oxygen mask over my face. They asked if I could hear them and I shook my head "yes." At this time, one of the responders (policeman) walked into the room. He asked my wife if this "was the same guy" they responded to "a few days earlier on Hill Air Force Base." She replied, "yes." He then reached down, grabbed and twisted my nipple and tried to pull me off the floor by it.[1] He told me to sit up, that he "was sick of playing (my) games," that he was "not going to play this game tonight, that (I) was a faker, and that nothing was wrong with (me)." By this time, I was screaming in pain and he dropped me back to the floor. I couldn't speak and I was having trouble catching my breath. He also told my wife that my "doctor at Hill Air

---

[1] Pinching a patient's nipple to check the level of consciousness is a procedure some-times used by medical personnel. Obviously, this emergency responder was using the technique in a totally inappropriate way. The county sheriff reprimanded him and sent a letter of apology to Sr. Airman Colisimo. The author has in her possession a copy of that letter.

Force Base said, (I) was faking it and nothing was wrong with (me)." He repeated this assault again and threatened to repeat it a third time if I didn't respond to him. I was then dragged down three flights of stairs, loaded in an ambulance, taken to the emergency room and kept overnight for observation.

I had 14 more blackouts, most resulting in minor injuries such as scrapes, cuts, scratches, and bruises. Only with the strong influence and intervention from Representative Peterson and my wife's and mother's involvement with the media, did Hill Air Force Base decide to send me to Walter Reed Army Medical Center on 9 May 2000. After 35 days of numerous and extensive tests . . . Walter Reed diagnosed me with neurocardiogenic syncope, chronic fatigue syndrome, obstructed sleep apnea, anxiety disorder, and situational stress. None of these symptoms predated my first anthrax vaccine.

On 13 June 2000, Walter Reed Army Medical Center released me back to Hill Air Force Base with a strong recommendation that I be immediately transferred to Andrews Air Force Base, so I could have intense medical follow up. They also tried to contact my doctors at Hill Air Force Base to establish medical treatment contingency and were repeatedly told "no one was available."

When I returned to Hill Air Force Base, I found out that I had no doctor assigned for my care and no one knew what to do with me. Two weeks went by until I finally met with a doctor who was assigned to me. He told me he was leaving in a few weeks and my "case was too complicated to deal with," so I would "have to wait for another doctor to return from leave." I ended up having no one to accept the responsibility for monitoring my illness and medication regime because it didn't fall within "the norm." Because of this, my condition worsened and I started to develop new symptoms. I was then left with the responsibility of adjusting my own medications.

On 29 June 2000 around 0100, I got out of bed to get a drink of water and on returning collapsed to the floor. With the help from my wife, I got back into bed. She said I appeared delirious and then at approximately 0230 (2:30 a.m.) I got out of bed. I have no recall of where I was going or why. At approximately 0630 (6:30 am), I returned home. All I remembered was waking up in a parking lot covered in blood, vomit, and urine, not knowing how I got there. . . .

Hill Air Force Base then requested a Medical Review Board. The Medical Review Board decided that I was "fit for duty" and to return to work [with several limitations]. . . .

However, my squadron (388th MXS) told me I was still not allowed to return to work and I was to stay at home and wait for orders to Andrews Air Force Base. It was at this time that my vision started to fade in and out as with tunnel vision, causing me to fall down stairs and run into walls. I also started to become overly sensitive to household chemicals that never bothered me before, causing me to have episodes of delirium. My wife said I would get out of bed, usually at night after being around the cat's litter box, oven cleaner or other cleaning products and walk outside and away from our apartment for 6 to 8 hours.[2] She would then call my First Sergeant and the police to help look for me. When I returned or was found, I would go back to bed, wake up the next morning, never remembering a thing.

My wife, my family, and I pleaded with the Air Force that I return to Walter Reed but was denied this again and again. I asked if Hill Air Force Base could at least contact the Walter Reed doctors for advice and possible treatment or testing but was ignored. They promised I would get a doctor at Hill Air Force Base, "soon." I was told weekly that I would be receiving orders "soon" and "it wouldn't be cost effective" to send me sooner if I were getting orders anyway. I used my chain of command including the Base Commander, the Inspector General of the base, the Air Force Inspector General, and the Secretary of the Air Force to no avail. Please be assured, I don't take Congressional advocacy lightly, but I was left with no choice.

Once again with the strong and persistent intervention of Representative Peterson, Senator Santorum, Senator Hatch, and national media exposure caused by my wife and mother, Hill Air Force Base reluctantly returned me to Walter Reed on 8 August 2000, until I got orders to Andrews Air Force Base. I was given less than one days notice and told that I was not allowed to return. It took Hill Air Force Base a total of 10 weeks and my falling over 50 times to be allowed to return for treatment. Since mid March, I have had over 200 falls.

When I arrived at Walter Reed, I was told that they were never notified that I was coming. They admitted me as an inpatient for observation and ran more tests. . . . I received my orders to transfer to Andrews Air Force Base three weeks later on 1 September 2000. I am currently being seen by Walter Reed medical personal on a regular basis.

Because of my increased sensitivity to chemicals and sleep deprivation, I had another episode on Friday, 16 September 2000. My wife said I was delirious, stumbling, had slurred speech, my thought process was unclear, forgetful, and I was in a drunken-like state. She said it was like I had Down's syndrome. By Saturday night my condition worsened. That night, I went to the Base Hospital ER at my family's insistence. They took some urine and blood samples and asked us to wait. Five hours later, the tests results came back "normal" and I was released in the same condition as I arrived, with the recommendation to see my primary physician at Walter Reed Monday morning. This state of delirium lasted until Sunday evening and I don't remember a thing. My doctors at Walter Reed are uncertain what caused this.

While we were at the emergency room, our home was entered by the security police and searched. The neighbors told the police we were at the hospital and they called it in to verify it. Once they knew where we were, the police told the paramedics to wait outside. The cops then entered our home through the back

---

[2] Sr. Airman Colisimo's mother reports that on at least two occasions an exposure to the air freshener in a public restroom has caused her son to black out and fall. On one of these occasions, he got confused and wandered off. His parents found him lying at the bottom of an incline, bruised and bleeding.

door and proceeded to search every drawer, cupboard, closet, and room. They then asked our neighbors if (I) "had a mental problem?" They said "no, he has a medical problem." They asked if (I) "was ever violent with (my) wife?" They also said "no." The police told our neighbors that I "kidnapped (my) wife and was out to hurt her." They also asked if (I) "was on any drugs?" They said that (I) "was on medications." This is clearly harassment and an attempt to discredit my credibility. Ever since I got sick from the anthrax vaccine and acknowledged it as the cause, I have received nothing but hostile retaliation.

Certain Air Force officials who are in charge of reviewing my request for extension and disability have told the doctors at Walter Reed that I am "milking the system" and using my "illness to stay in the military," that I am "a trouble maker" and I "showed it with my mother's and wife's involvement with Congress and the press," that they "were going to make sure any attempts for a medical extension would get denied." My Walter Reed doctors said they needed at least 6 months to do a complete re-evaluation due to the regression that occurred in my health because I received no medical treatment at all from 15 May 2000 through 8 August 2000. They were told by the Air Force two weeks was all they had. My enlistment is up 23 November 2000 and I am being told by my doctors at Walter Reed that I will have to continue taking my current medications for at least a year before they can even consider taking me off of it, even though they are uncertain how I will react without it. I am 28 years old. I was healthy. I had dreams and visions. I did what I was told. I got sick.

I do not understand why the Air Force has abandoned me. Is it because my sickness is associated with the anthrax shot? . . .

I believe the Air Force has taken a retaliatory posture with me for the Congressional advocacy my family sought for my medical care. But it was that or die. . . . The Air Force has only given me the medical care when forced to. Until Representative Peterson intervened, no one listened.

When I mentioned what happened after taking the anthrax vaccination to my Air Force doctors, they got defensive. They repeatedly denied that it could be anthrax. I was even sent to a psychiatrist, but my doctor warned the psychiatrist "be cautious, this patient has questioned the possibility of anthrax induced problems."

I am scared about the future. What effect is this going to have on my wife and will we be able to have healthy kids someday? What will happen in a year from now, when the doctors take me off the medications? Will I be able to work, drive, and support a family? Will I be able to afford medical insurance with this illness? Who will ever hire me with the current symptoms I have described? . . .

I am very afraid to testify before you today for fear of reprisal. But with the strength and encouragement of my wife and family, I am convinced that I needed to come forward and tell you my story. I know of numerous individuals who are ill from the anthrax vaccine that I have seen while I was at Walter Reed, have talked to over the phone, and have received written letters from. They are afraid to come forward for fear of a repetition of the same treatment, or lack of, that I have sustained. They are afraid of losing their job, as well as destroying their career, and not being able to support their families. It sickens me that the military "leaders" have instilled this much fear. I must stand up for what I believe is morally and ethically right. It is for them and others who will soon be sick from this vaccine, that I testify before you today.

Swc. Fred Willoughby, U.S. Navy (Ret.)

I was a Seabee in Naval Mobile Construction Battalion 24, headquartered in Huntsville, Alabama. I remember hearing in 1990 that the Iraqis were causing trouble and some of the reserves might be called up. Well, we were. I received my orders on December 3, 1990, and we were on the way to the Big Sandbox, Saudi. I remember that we landed at night, and it was still very hot then. But we all adapted to the heat pretty fast.

I was assigned to be in charge of the steel yard at the King Azziz Soccer Stadium a couple of miles south of the port of Al Jubayl. Everything went well for quite a few weeks. The SCUD alarms would go off a lot, but we just finally didn't pay any attention to them. At first we went underground in the bunkers, but the SCUDs would pass over on the way south.

On the morning of January 20, 1991, I was standing guard duty during the 10 p.m. to 2 a.m. watch. When our watch was over, I started for our tent and met a friend who was coming back to our area. We put our gear inside the tent and decided to get a cup of coffee and stand outside a while and talk. We had been outside for a while when we heard a loud explosion. Some people said that the sky lit up. We were standing on the south end of the tent so I didn't see the red sky, which was to the north. I did notice that the tents were shaking. We both said, "What the hell was that?" and decided that we had better get our gas masks on. We ran into the tent, yelling to the others who were sleeping to get their gas masks on. But by the time I could get my mask on, my face was numb, just like I had gotten a shot of novocaine from the dentist. By that time, we were told to go to MOPP-4 and were told this wasn't a drill. We all got our MOPP gear on and headed for the bunker. You could hear the chemical alarms going off all around. When we all got in the bunkers, a lot of people were having problems breathing, and their skin was burning in the places where it had not gotten covered up fast enough. Several people said they had seen a mist in the area, but I did not see the mist. I guess I just didn't pay attention to what was in the air. All I remember is that my face, lips, and mouth were still feeling numb.

We were in the bunker for what seemed like a long time. When we finally did get to come out, we were told by the officers and chiefs that it had been a sonic boom. (Yea, sure.) I know that a sonic boom doesn't light up the sky. I have heard lots of sonic booms, and that wasn't one. We were told to shut up and not to talk about it. Later that morning all our MOPP gear we had used the previous night was taken up, and we were issued all new gear. We were told that the gear we turned in had been used and needed to be replaced. But we had been told that the gear would be good for several weeks if it wasn't contaminated. I guess the officers just don't think that the enlisted can think for themselves and figure out that something is definitely wrong here. Especially when we heard a rumor that an enemy plane had been splashed in the Gulf.

We went to the port of Al Jubayl after the January 20 incident, and we saw a fenced-in area containing a lot of dead animals. We were told to get out of the area. First there is an explosion, and then the next morning there are these dead animals. They tried to tell us that our own troops had shot the animals, and they were all taken to this area to be counted. Again, I guess the officers think the enlisted can't think for themselves.

Then there were the oil well fires. We were south of the fires and got oily smoke for several weeks. You could be working outside and just watch the black soot landing on you, and you could taste the oil in the air. It would also get all over the food we were eating, and there was the taste of fuel in the water that we would shower in. Sometimes the smoke was so thick you could not see the sun in the middle of the day. You just went ahead and worked in all this oily smoke and breathed it all day. For several months after I got back home, I would have heavy sweating at night, and the bed sheets and pillow cases on my side of the bed were black from all the stuff coming out of my skin.

Depleted uranium was another thing we were exposed to. I was assigned along with several of the personnel in our detachment to load the ships for the trip home with equipment sent from Iraq and other places. We were told that the equipment was clean and we had nothing to worry about. So we climbed in, over, under, and through the equipment brought in because they said it was clean. I remember one day I was trying to chain down a Iraqi vehicle that was hit with shells. I put the chain in a opening and tried to fasten it down. When I pulled my hand back out of the hole, a human finger came with it that wasn't mine. So how much of the equipment really had been cleaned to remove all the DU that was in the shells? We spent about three weeks on this detail, but we were assured by the DOD that we couldn't get any exposure to DU. That sure didn't make me feel any better either.

Now comes the trip home. We were in the mess hall attending a medical exam. All it consisted of was two things: Question 1—How do you feel? Question 2—Do you have any problems right now? No. OK, you can go home. Some exam, huh? Anyway, we got home, and I didn't have any problems right then. But after I had been home for a few months, I started having continuous diarrhea and headaches. Then I had a tooth just fall out for no reason, and I started to get lightheaded and dizzy. I was continuously tired, and my shoulder and hip joints were aching. I also had a rash (big purple blotches) and was having memory problems. So I signed up with the Desert Storm Registry. That was a hoot also. After spending a few hundred dollars, I was told that I was not supposed to pay for the registry physicals, so I talked to my congressional representative. When I called the VA hospital where I had gone for the exam, they said I had not even been there, even though I had a pile of bills. That was a year and a half after I started going there. I also found out that I wasn't on the Desert Storm Registry, so I had to start all over again. Two years later I still didn't have a report on my health or blood tests or anything else they had tested for. The doctors and the hospital just kept asking for more time. Finally, I got signed up after trying six or seven times. Seems the VA has a problem with losing paperwork.

Anyway, after I finally got signed up, I went for another exam. When that was over, I put in for disability. After many, many months, I decided to check on the status of my claim with the VA. Their reply was, "What claim?" That was in 1994, and I tried submitting a claim again in 1995. Again I checked on my claim. Again they asked, "What claim?" So I thought maybe the third time is the charm. I started to get the paperwork together, but in the meantime I had heart problems. I ended up with a six-bypass open heart surgery, and I still have a leaking valve that has not been fixed. That was September 1997, and I retired in December 1997. I finally got my paperwork together and forwarded it again. That was in 1998, and this time I didn't give them time to lose my paperwork. I kept calling and had senators and representatives help me. I think from 1992 to October of 2000 is long enough for the VA get something done. I did finally get a percentage for chronic fatigue, but nothing for undiagnosed illness.

I have been diagnosed as having blood in my urine and blood in my stools, but I have been told not to worry about it. I finally had a polyp removed from my colon. I have been told by several VA doctors that we sick veterans are all lying and that there is nothing wrong with us. We are just trying to get something out of the government that we are not entitled to. Anyway, all we can do is just try to keep fighting before we all die. My wife and I went to the Fort Mitchell, Virginia, cemetery, which is a new cemetery, about three months ago. We counted almost 40 headstones that said, "Persian Gulf War." Most of them were between 20 and the early 40s. That just isn't right.

Sfc. Terry Dillhyon, USANG (Ret.)

I was in the Marine Corps from 1960 to 1966. When I left the Marine Corps, I got a job with a major railroad company as a steel worker building rail cars. I started a family and earned a college degree by attending classes at night while I worked for the railroad.

In November 1990, I was activated with the Army National Guard unit that I had joined and sent to the Persian Gulf. I served both as a medic and as an intelligence NCO.

Just before we left for the Gulf, we had to spray paint all of our equipment with this CARC paint, which we found out later was a very toxic paint. I had to stay near where the vehicles were being painted, and there were a lot of fumes. They gave us paint and spray guns, and we were painting our generators without all this protective equipment that the guys that painted the vehicles were using. They said because we were out in the open air it didn't matter.

When we had our first SCUD attacks, all the chemical alarms went off. The SCUD attacks came regular near 9, 10, 11, 12 o'clock at night. You could count on them, just like clockwork. Patriot missile batteries would go off, and we would blow them up. But right after they blew up, all the chemical alarms would go off. Some nights you spent all night in MOPP4—your complete chemical suit, gloves, boots. After a while they started telling us the alarms were defective.

We used DEET, which is an insect repellent. The cans we were given were actually supposed to be for large area usage, but the mosquitoes were so bad, people used these cans of repellent anyway. We would coat our clothing down with this DEET, and ourselves. All your guard positions, your bunkers, your machine gun positions, and everything that was enclosed, were constantly sprayed with DEET to keep away the mosquitoes.

Sand, dust, chemicals, shots. Didn't think too much of all that then. I had been a Marine, I was a platoon sergeant, and I became a detachment/senior NCO. I was in good shape. I was 46 when I went over there, for a 46-year-old man I was in real good shape.

The first thing I noticed when I got back, however, was that I had a fatigue that was unbelievable. It was about a month before I was able to go back to work. I worked in an office at the railroad, and I used a lot of numbers in my job. I was doing billing repair, and I knew all the billing repair codes and stuff like that by heart. But I got to where I was messing up real bad in the office, forgetting numbers. I even forgot my own daughter's phone number.

They moved me out of the office, transferred me out to the railyard. And in the railyard, I was falling down for some unknown reason. I'd get like an electrical shock in my ankle, and I'd fall. Fortunately, my friends in the railyard took care of me and kept me working.

Then in January 1993, I could not pass the Army basic physical fitness test and had to retire from the Florida National Guard.

My illness kept getting worse. I went to the VA hospital in Lake City, which has always treated me great. It's the best hospital I've been in. They did some tests and decided to send me to the VA hospital in Washington, D.C. I wound up there six weeks, and they found about 14 things wrong with me. And before the war, I was in great shape, I never even took an aspirin.

While I was in the VA hospital, they found that I had multifocal motor and nerve neuropathy of the upper and lower extremities, and I had demyelination of the nerves in my arms and legs. That means the coating on my nerves is coming off.

Right after they had done these lumbar punctures and tests like that, one night a doctor came into my room, and he said looking over my blood work and everything he had found that I had gone into renal insufficiency. They had been giving me high doses of Motrin. And come to find out I was allergic to what they call nonsteroidal antiinflammatory drugs. Needless to say, they had to do a lot of work on me to get my kidneys back in working order. And right now, to this day, I have a difference in size between my two kidneys, and there are signs of problems with one kidney.

I did not know the extent of my sensitivity to chemicals until I was in the hospital. While I was there, they were taking me to have an MRI, and they were rolling me down the hallway. They went by a room where the floor was being stripped, and they were using a paint stripper. I actually went unconscious and they had to take me to the emergency room and give me oxygen and everything. I'd been around floor strippers plenty of times before, but they didn't knock me down.

After we found out that I had problems with the chemicals, the hospital immediately quit cleaning my room and all the Gulf War veterans' rooms with any type of toxic chemicals. Now when my wife cleans the house, I have to leave the house because I can literally be knocked unconscious from some of these chemicals in household cleaning products that are used for cleaning bathrooms and other things.

I have panic disorder now and phobic symptoms for heights and bridges, but these were all things I was never scared of before the war. When I was in the Marine Corps, I did mountain repelling and helicopter rappelling. Even when

I was in the Army, I went through rappelling. So quite naturally, before I went to the war, I was not scared of heights at all.[1]

After I had been sick a while, I started having trouble driving. One problem was that I was unable to determine distance. I would look and see traffic coming and pull out and then have to swing over. Sometimes the traffic light was green and I saw it was green, but it could change to red and it would still be green to me. I would drive right through it. After the last time I had a near fatal collision, nothing was said. My wife looked at me, I looked at her, we changed sides, and she drove.

When I told a doctor at the VA hospital about my driving problems, he was very concerned and gave me several tests to check my balance and my coordination. I guess it would be sort of like giving someone a field sobriety test, and I could not pass the test.

In 1994, I had to start using two canes, and that worked for about six months. If I happened to smell something like gasoline or perfume, however, it would affect my coordination and I would fall down. Finally the VA gave me a wheelchair, and a couple of years ago they even gave me an electric one because I have a lot of nerve damage in my arms. I can't complain about the medical care the VA has given me. They have paid for my medications and hospitalizations, even though they claim my problems are not service connected. The VA refuses to give me any disability payments, however. I filed my first claim in December of 1992, and everything comes back claim denied. It's been eight years now that I've been trying to get that disability.

Some of the VA doctors who have seen me have admitted to my wife and me that I'm sick from something I got into during the Gulf War. Once when a doctor said that, my wife put her hand on the evaluation form on the desk in front of him and said, "Write that on his form." The doctor replied, "I can't," and he admitted to us that he might lose his job if he wrote something like that on my form.

I have a discharge paper from Washington, D.C., that says I have possible multiple chemical sensitivity, etiology unknown. The doctor told me he had to say "possible" because a lot of doctors don't recognize multiple chemical sensi-

---

[1] For a discussion of the relationship of panic attacks to chemical exposures, see S. Dager et al., "Panic Disorder Precipitated by Exposure to Organic Solvents in the Work Place," *American Journal of Psychiatry* 144, no. 8 (1987):1056-58. See also C. J. Levy, "Agent Orange Exposure and Posttraumatic Stress Disorder," *Journal of Nervous and Mental Disorders* 176, no. 4 (April 1988): 242-45. Levy compared Vietnam veterans who had been exposed to Agent Orange with those who had not and found that "The exposed Vietnam veterans, in contrast to a matched control group of Vietnam veterans, showed a significantly higher rate of posttraumatic stress disorder."

tivity. When I was applying to get Medicare, the Social Security people sent me to one of their doctors. In a casual conversation with the doctor before we started the examination, I mentioned multiple chemical sensitivity. The doctor went crazy, really flew off on me. He said, "I'm going to tell you right now, sir, you just lost all your credibility with me. There's no such thing as that." And sure enough, I got turned down. I don't know what kind of a report he wrote. I haven't got my Medicare yet, but I recently applied for it again. Hopefully I'm going to get to see a different doctor, and I'm not going to mention multiple chemical sensitivity to him.

I had a bad perfume reaction when I went to my granddaughter's kindergarten graduation. We were packed into a room, but I had gotten to the side by a window because if I have a window close by I don't have too much of a problem. Then two or three ladies came in and sat down right behind me. I don't know what kind of perfume they were wearing, but it got to me so bad that before long I was lying on the floor unconscious. Even other people commented on the perfume, "Oh, my God, I smelled them coming."

I can be bothered by something as simple as a perfume ad in a magazine. I hate the way you open a page and it releases a perfume. One time I was just going through a magazine, and it contained a pretty potent perfume that put me immediately into an asthma attack. (I had only been diagnosed with asthma since I had come back from the Gulf War.)

The asthma attack I had kept getting worse even though I used my inhalers. I went to bed anyway, but my breathing got extremely bad, bad enough that my wife had to call for help. They sent a rescue unit to get me, and in the rescue unit, I stopped breathing three times. And they were using what was called a nebulizer, a breathing thing to help me. They took me straight back into the emergency room and continued giving me treatments. About the time they thought I would be all right, I quit breathing again. It took a couple of days to get me back to breathing like I was supposed to, and all because of a dadburned little advertisement for perfume that cost me a couple of days in the hospital.

Just because of this advertisement, I had a $580 rescue bill, I had over $2000 in emergency room bills, and approximately $3000 in hospital bills. I had to pay these bills myself. I can't help thinking that if that doctor the Social Security people sent me to hadn't been so prejudiced against multiple chemical sensitivity, I might have been on Medicare and these bills would have been covered. I'm on a fixed income, so trying to pay $6000 in medical bills is really difficult.

Sp4c. Brad Coats, U.S. Army (Ret.)

My husband Brad was in the 23rd infantry out of Ft. Stewart, Georgia; his unit was one of the first deployed to the Gulf War. He was on the front lines doing the "left hook" procedure that General Schwarzkopf commanded—the one that went way up into Kuwait to fight against the Republican Guards. The Army gave him all the inoculations, and he was made to take the PB pills. He was also exposed to depleted uranium, nerve gas, pesticides, and the smoke from the oil well fires. But what scared us most was that his unit blew up the munitions depot at Khamisiyah. Who knows what all he breathed in or what settled on his skin.

Brad has had most, if not all, of the symptoms associated with Gulf War syndrome: unexplained rashes and terrible itching that covers his whole body, terrible mood swings, and no short-term memory to speak of. He has back, muscle, and joint aches that require countless bottles of medications. He has such severe vertigo that at one point he had to crawl around because he would have fallen over if he had stood upright. He says he can deal with all of this, but what pains him the most is the problems with our two children born after the war.

When our son Christian was three days old, I took him to a local pediatric clinic because he had a slight cold and was turning blue and breathing heavy. The pediatrician explained that newborns don't know that they can breathe out of their mouths, so when their noses are stuffy they don't breathe regularly and will turn slightly blue around their mouths. Christian was four weeks old the fourth time I took him in. This time he saw a different pediatrician, one who listened to me. After getting X-rays of Christian and analyzing them, the pediatrician told me that I needed to take my son to the ER at St. Joseph's Hospital because he had a congenital heart defect—his heart was twisted. I was stunned, but I got directions for the hospital and said I would drop my other two children off at a babysitter's and head right over. The doctor looked at me sternly and said, "I really don't think you understand the seriousness of his condition. He needs to get there immediately." I hurried to the hospital, where my husband met me. I will never forget that day. While I was registering Christian, I told the admitting clerk he was being admitted because his heart was twisted and all they needed to do was to untwist it and he would be okay. I thought we would be in and out in a jiffy. The look in her eyes was priceless. She must have thought I was insane.

After all the testing and waiting in the ER, Christian was admitted to the pediatric intensive care unit. There we saw something amazing as we were entering the unit. To one side there were six or seven mattresses piled one on top of the other and on the top mattress was a small boy about five years old with all these tubes and wires running in and out of him. I shuddered and asked the nurse what was going on. She explained, "Nothing to worry about, your child will never need that. The boy is on ECMO, which is a heart-lung machine that oxygenates his blood because he is having a severe case of asthma and that is the only way to keep him alive." (I later learned he had to be elevated so that his blood would drain into the machine.) They started running tests and basic procedures on Christian. They put an electrode on his big toe that told what his blood oxygen level was. After several quiet discussions and three tests with pulse ox machines, they kept thinking that the machines were malfunctioning since not one of them had even seen a live person with that low a blood oxygen level. Christian's blood oxygen level was 43, while the normal is 98-99. They asked Brad and me to leave the room so they could intubate Christian, put a tube down his throat to get oxygen directly to his lungs.

While I was in the waiting room on the phone to my mother, the nurse interrupted me and said that they needed us to come back to the pediatric ICU immediately because the intubation had not helped. Christian's blood oxygen level had dropped to 32, and they wanted us to sign some papers allowing them to perform emergency surgery on him to place him on ECMO, the same heart/lung machine as that little boy on the mattresses was on. My mom, who is an LPN, later told me that when she heard the nurse tell me what Christian's blood oxygen level was, she packed her black dress and her black nylons and pumps. She thought without a doubt that she was flying out not just to be support for me but to attend Christian's funeral. Christian was on ECMO for three days until they performed his first heart surgery. To date he has had four heart surgeries as well as too many heart catheterization procedures to count. It was soon learned that he has six severe heart defects. The most severe one is that he has only one ventricle and he is missing the artery that takes the blood from his heart to his lungs.

While Christian was on ECMO, my mother and I would sit by his bedside just touching him and talking to him. One day while we were sitting there one of the nurses looked at me and said, "There is only one way he could have this kind of heart defect. It's caused by chemicals, drugs you took while you were pregnant." I was floored. I could not think of anything besides Tylenol that I had taken, no over-the-counter drugs or any kind of recreational drugs, not even alcohol or cigarettes. What chemicals could he have been exposed to?

About a week after Christian had been released from the hospital, there was a story on the front page of our newspaper about a baby who also had just had heart surgery. The baby's father had been in the Gulf War, and he and his wife felt that his exposures in the Gulf had caused their child's heart defects. Of course we wondered if Brad's service in Desert Storm could be the source of Christian's birth defects.

We soon learned that not only did Christian have the six heart defects, but he also had had numerous strokes in several parts of his brain. After extensive testing, he has been labeled as mildly retarded. His neurologist told us we needed to change our way of life—instead of saving for his college education, we needed to save money to take care of him when we were gone. About a year ago, after a severe grand mal seizure, Christian was diagnosed with epilepsy. Not even two months later our daughter Brittany, who was also born after Brad returned from Desert Storm, was diagnosed with epilepsy. She has always been very delayed developmentally.

What is our son's life expectancy? They can't even give us a guess. Did Brad's exposures in the Gulf War cause our children's severe defects? We think they did. Every day my husband faces such horrendous guilt, worrying that he may have inadvertently caused our children's defects by doing his duty as a serviceman, taking those PB pills, blowing up Khamisiyah, getting all those exposures. Doing his duty for God and his country. But who is paying? Our children are. Why should they have to pay such an awful cost for their father just doing his duty, just following orders?

Sgt. James Green, U.S. Air Force (Ret.)

I have Gulf War syndrome, but I never went to the Persian Gulf. I did have the anthrax vaccine, however, and I also took the PB pills that the Gulf War soldiers were given.

When the Gulf War broke out, I was in a mobile unit that was being sent to Germany as part of an antiterrorist team. I knew all my shots were updated because I had just got them the week before, but the sergeant in charge told me I was on the list to get some more shots. I believe this mistake occurred because I had been on a list to go to Saudi Arabia, but I hadn't been home for the deployment.

A day after I received the anthrax vaccine I felt like I had the worst case of the flu that I had ever had. I hurt all over and had a headache from hell. A day later I developed a strange rash. When we arrived in Germany, I was the only one give a packet of PB pills, apparently because my name was still on a list for deployment to the Persian Gulf. At any rate, I took all of them.

When my unit returned from Germany, I felt like I had the flu. I was tired all the time, and I knew something was very wrong when my health didn't improve as the weeks passed. At this time, I had the highest priority clearance to guard aircraft. Every 15 minutes or so, I had to walk around the airplane to be sure everything was OK. In between those patrols, I would sit in a tiny little shack that was heated by a diesel ground heater. The fumes were horrible, and I started getting terrible headaches every day after work. I was also having really bad diarrhea, and that has continued to this day. My joints and muscles ached, and I began having memory problems. Once I left my M-16 rifle and a full clip at a snack shop. My memory is so bad now that I can't even drive on back roads here where I've driven since I was 16 because I forget which way to go.

I also became very sensitive to various chemicals. I couldn't stand being around cleaning chemicals, and diesel fumes or exhaust always gave me horrible headaches. Finally, I just couldn't keep working around all the diesel exposures on the flight line, so I left the Air Force. For a couple of months, I drove a truck for a man who was laying cable for TVs, and that worked out only because he told me where to go and when to turn. The worst thing was that my diarrhea was so bad that we would have to stop every half hour for me to use a bathroom. Of course, after a while I had to quit that job.

By this point, all my symptoms were intensifying, and I couldn't see how I could support my wife and two little children. The VA refused to recognize that I had any real health problems. They kept telling me I was suffering from stress, and they put me on Prozac. Finally, they gave me $119 a month for 20 percent disability related to an old back injury I got the first year I was in the Air Force. Of course, the four of us couldn't live on $119 a month, so we had to give up and go on welfare. After three more years of fighting the VA, I finally obtained 100 percent disability for the back injury because they concluded I could no longer work.

At one point I was hospitalized for a shigella infection, and after that stay in the hospital with all the exposures to disinfectants and strong cleaners, my multiple chemical sensitivity became really intense. Exposures to things like strong cologne or strong cleaners make my eyes water and my nose clog up. I also get a severe headache. Like many Gulf War vets, I'm plagued by night sweats. Soon after the hospital stay I was diagnosed with chronic lung obstruction. I'm so sick now that I have to lie in bed most of the time. Only once in a great while do I have the energy to go outside and toss a football with my ten-year-old son. My seven-year-old daughter draws pictures for me to cheer me up when I'm lying in bed all day. I used to love to read, particularly history, but now I can't remember what I just read. I have to keep going back to read a page over again. It takes me three months to read a little book.

One doctor recommended that I have a SPECT brain scan, which I did. The scan showed compression and diminished activity on the right side of my brain. Another test indicated that my blood clotting level is much higher than it should be. Tests for antinuclear antibodies have come back positive four times. My family doctor says that means I am likely to get an autoimmune disease like lupus. I already have two other autoimmune conditions—Hashimoto's thyroiditis and Sjögren's syndrome. Doctors have told me I have the body of a 60- or 70-year-old man, and I'm only 34.

I repeatedly went to see the VA doctors about a lump in my throat. For over a year I complained to them about this lump, but they ignored it, trying to say I was just having psychological problems. Finally when the lump grew, I was diagnosed with thyroid cancer and I had to have half of my thyroid removed. Then last summer I had to have the rest of it removed.

After all these years, my private doctor and some of the VA doctors are saying I have Gulf War syndrome. They have referred me to the Gulf War syndrome clinic, but even though I received the anthrax vaccine and took the PB pills, the clinic has refused to see me because I was never deployed to the Persian Gulf.

The VA doctors keep saying Gulf War syndrome is stress related, but as I testified to Congress, I didn't even go to the Gulf War and my jobs weren't stressful. But I'm still experiencing the same symptoms as the other sick vets. I think the vaccinations and the PB pills made many of us sick. So much for stress as the cause of Gulf War syndrome.

I wonder now if I will live many more years, and my main concern is worrying about my family. If I die from Gulf War syndrome and the VA hasn't recognized the condition as being service connected, then my family will get only a one-time death benefit of $800.

I gave the government five years of my life, and in return they have destroyed my health and haven't taken responsibility for their actions. It doesn't seem fair.

Major Michael Donnelly, U.S. Air Force (Ret.)

The following interview appeared in the fall 2000 issue of Fairfield Now, the alumni magazine of Fairfield University in Fairfield, Connecticut, from which Major Donnelly graduated in 1981. The interviewer was Barbara D. Kiernan, Director of Pub-lications, and the interview was conducted online.

An initial disclaimer from Michael:
What follows are strictly my personal thoughts and feelings. In no way do I claim to speak for anyone else, either with this disease or any other life altering (threatening) disease.

Why did you agree to this interview?
One reason is a selfish desire on my part, to tell as many people as possible that ALS does exist and that it's virtually a death sentence. I can't help but think that if the right person hears the story, he or she may be the one who can make a difference. The second, and chief, reason is that I have come to believe that God uses all of us, and is using me (if I may be so presumptuous) to help people.

Why is it that this disease still exists?
I have to admit that I knew next to nothing about ALS when I was healthy. I certainly didn't know there was a disease that was 100 percent fatal—a disease that we didn't understand, either its causes or treatments to combat its relentless march toward death. Now, unfortunately, I know too much. I'm afraid it all comes down to money. It's up to those with ALS and their families to raise the money for private researchers to seek treatments. A million dollars in the right hands today, and in six months we could have realistic treatment options.

People who are paralyzed have no feeling in the limbs and organs affected. Do you feel your body even though you cannot move it? Do you experience physical pain, pleasure, or other sensations (like an overstretched muscle, itchy nose, sore throat, stomach ache, etc.)?
Yes, people with ALS can feel everything. I guess the correct way to state it would be to say that people with ALS retain complete sensory function while

losing complete motor function. I've never lost sensation myself, but I think not losing "feeling" is on a very short list of positives about this disease.

Let me give you an exercise to try; it might give you a glimpse of this disease. Find the most comfortable chair in the room. Sit down and get as comfortable as possible. Make sure you can see a clock. A watch won't work since you won't be able to look at it. Now open your hands, fold your thumbs across your palms, then close your hand. This is meant to be a minor irritation, the same kind of irritation anyone with this disease encounters every day. Put your hands down so your knuckles are down. Now, don't move, anything, for ten minutes. I think even a small amount of time like ten minutes can give you a glimpse into the frustration that is so very much a part of this disease.

For an added measure of frustration, try it in a room full of friends. Oh yeah, you can't talk either. I sure hope a hair doesn't fall across your face and tickle your nose. Or a mosquito doesn't buzz in your ear and land on you.

A quick observation: As I sit here banging my head on this button to type this, the keyboard is only two inches from my hand. It may as well be two thousand miles. Either way, I couldn't touch it.

Can you say something about letting go versus giving up?

When I started losing the ability to control my immediate environment, I got very frustrated very quickly. There was so much I couldn't do anymore. To start with, I'm a "Type A" personality (squeeze the toothpaste tube from the bottom, roll it as you go, and put the cap back on). My wife, Susan, on the other hand, is a "Type B" personality (grab toothpaste tube in middle, squeeze until it comes out both ends—What cap?).

I suddenly realized that nobody could do anything as well as I could. To my great dismay, everyone around me was completely incompetent! That's a slight exaggeration, but I did realize that if I were going to "live" with this disease, I'd have to find a way to let go of the non-essentials. Prioritizing was difficult at first, but actually became easier as I got weaker.

Let me stress though, this idea of letting go is in no way related to giving up or quitting. Computers and technology are wonderful things for me now. They allow me to remain connected to life. They give me that all-important control of my life.

What is your sense of time like? Do days drag on— pass quickly—or what?

I have a strange relationship with time now. On the one hand, I know that every passing day brings more losses, more weakness, more challenges for me. On the other hand, I believe that researchers are getting closer and closer to a realistic treatment that will first stop the progression of this disease, and some day reverse it.

Each day I try to find an objective for the day. Something I want to accomplish, something I want to see, somewhere to go. Anything will do, it just has to be enough to give me a reason to get out of bed in the morning. This helps time pass at a more even pace for me.

So you still get out, then?

Yes. I mostly go to family events like my kids' [Erin (13) and Sean (9)] soccer and baseball games. It's a little hard for me to go out in public. I can't swallow too well so I drool a lot. I also choke occasionally. Most people I don't know, don't know how to act toward me. Some people talk very loud to me. Some talk as if I'm not there. It's often quite amusing and I have to admit that I wouldn't have known either. The trick is, just be yourself.

I used to try to get into conversations using my computer but I found that I couldn't keep up. It was just too frustrating. By the time I typed out my response, I was three subjects behind. I miss conversation.

Do you ever think about, "Why me?"

When I was first diagnosed, I asked that question a lot. I was angry with God, and hurt. I would be less than honest if I didn't admit that saying "goodbye cruel world" popped into my head from time to time. There were times when it all just seemed unbearable.

Then one day I saw something written by someone else with ALS. It said "What right do I have to ask 'why me?' Did I ask that question before I got sick?" In other words, did I ask "why me?" when God gave me this wonderful, athletic body that let me play sports? And the great hand-eye coordination that allowed me to fly jets? I don't know if you can understand that, but to me, it makes sense. There are no guarantees in life.

Do you have hope that this illness could change direction and be something less than a death sentence? If not, how do you live without this hope?

In answering this question, I began thinking back to when I was a budding fighter pilot, assigned to fly with a grizzled old lieutenant colonel who had flown in Vietnam. He drilled it into me over and over again, "Never, never, never give up." I, in turn, passed it on to my students when I became an instructor pilot. What that means is: Even when the Bandit is at your 6 o'clock and bearing down on you and it seems all hope is lost, don't give up. You never know, that bandit's guns might be jammed, he may run out of fuel, or have an aircraft malfunction. I carry that training over into my battle with this disease. I keep hope alive by remembering that lesson and by believing that anything is possible.

That is the fighter pilot side of me. The spiritual side of me tells me over and over again that if I believe in God—there's always hope.

When you know that death is near and inevitable, how do you order your life?
I could easily ask you the same question. Death is both near and inevitable for all of us. In fact, I've drastically reduced my exposure to a sudden, unexpected death. I don't drive back and forth to work anymore. I don't fly jet aircraft anymore, and I don't hunt or fish anymore. So you see, I believe in the randomness of life and I expect to live several years.

To say "Live your life as if every day were your last" is just words, and can never even come close to expressing how I feel.

Do you sometimes struggle with 'dark thoughts'?
As I read back through my answers to these questions, I'm struck by the fact that there's also a dark side to this disease. A dark side maybe even to me.

When I was first diagnosed, for example, and the doctors explained what would happen to me, I felt like I had been given a death sentence. Like I had been found guilty of a crime I didn't commit and was now on death row. What rules could possibly pertain to me now? What could the law do to me, since I already had a death sentence?

There are times, even now, when I tend to pass judgment on people. I'll see someone who isn't making the best use of their gift of life. Then I'll barter with God. I'll say things like, "That person is obviously not making the best of their gift. If you'd give it to me, I promise you that I will."

Also, I have a love/hate relationship with my wheelchair. I hate it. I hate the fact that I need it. I hate that I can't even control it anymore. It's my own portable prison. I'd love to kick it to the curb. But it's also my support, my mobility. It makes everything possible for me.

I'm not particularly proud of some of these thoughts, but I'm including them so you'll know how much of a challenge this disease is, not just to the body but to the soul.

What role does faith play in your dealing with this disease?
I remember a sermon I heard a long time ago. While the priest's name and the church I can no longer recall, the story has stayed with me. It seems a family was on vacation and facing a long drive so they decided to take it easy and make frequent stops. When they saw a sign for a cavern up ahead, they all agreed to stop, have some lunch, and explore the cavern a little before getting back on the

road. While they were exploring the cave, they became separated. When they finally got back together, they realized that one of the children was missing. The mother decided to take the other children out and get help while Dad searched for the missing child.

After a half hour or so, the father turned a corner and found his child, alone, scared, and standing on a ledge about four feet above the father's head. Because of the lighting, the father could see his frightened child. But the child could see only black. Though the Dad's voice calmed the scared child, there was no way to reach the ledge. The child would have to jump. What could the father say to the frightened child to reassure the child that he would catch him?

About four years ago, I found myself on that very same ledge. I quickly understood that I couldn't handle this on my own. It was time for me to make that leap of Faith. Since that time many people have praised me for the way I have dealt with this disease. However, I think they've misplaced their praise because without Him, I could not even get out of bed in the morning.

And on a daily basis, what gets you through?

The longer I live, the more I realize the impact of attitude on life. Attitude, to me, is more important than facts. It is more important than the past, than education, than money, than circumstances, than failures, than successes, than what other people think or say or do. It is more important than appearance, giftedness, or skill. It will make or break a company . . . a school . . . a church . . . a home.

The remarkable thing is that we have a choice, every single day, regarding the attitude we will embrace for that day. We cannot change our past. We cannot change the fact that people will act in a certain way. We cannot change the inevitable. The only thing we can do, is play on the one string we have, and that is our attitude.

Capt. Richard Caron, USANG (Ret.)

Before I went to the Gulf War, I had a full-time job as a carpenter. I was also the pastor of a Baptist church and the chaplain of my Army National Guard unit. My health was good before I went to the Persian Gulf.

My unit arrived in Saudi Arabia in early December and soon moved northwest to our desert camp about 15 miles from the border of Iraq. When the air war started, chemical alarms went off many times. This was the point at which we were given the PB pills, an anti–nerve gas medication. Within a few days, I wasn't feeling well; I was fatigued and had headaches and muscle and joint pains. At this time, I was so busy doing lots of different things that I thought my health problems came from being on the go for what seemed like 24 hours a day. Within a few weeks, however, I started noticing that diesel exhaust and the fumes from diesel fuel were making me slightly nauseated, even though I had been around diesel before the war without any problem.

When the ground war started, I went forward with my company to a position only five miles from the Iraqi border. We had one SCUD missile explode about seven or eight miles from us. After Saddam Hussein gave orders to set all the oil wells on fire, the air was so full of smoke that daytime was like nighttime. We were close enough to the fires that we could see the flames and hear the roar of the fires. The smoke started bothering me a lot.

The insect spray we were using was also bothering me. My skin would get red when I used it. By this point, I was often getting short of breath—I didn't know whether that was from the fires or the insect repellent. I had bronchitis several times while I was in the Persian Gulf. Before we left Saudi Arabia, we were given a physical. My blood pressure was really high, 180/104. Before I went to the Gulf War, it had been 120/70.

In June 1991, I was released from active duty. A week later I ended up going to the VA hospital in my state. I was having a hard time breathing, and I had bronchitis again. I told the doctors there about the various other symptoms I was having. By this point I was getting sick from household cleaning products, and going into a store would make me sick. Before the Gulf War, I had only had a couple of migraines, but during the war I started having them very frequently, and they continued when I returned to the States.

Since my health problems continued for a year or two, the local VA hospital finally sent me to the VA hospital in Washington, D.C. There they diagnosed me with chronic fatigue syndrome, asthma, sleep apnea, and brain damage (the brain damage was shown on an MRI). My hands and arms would also sometimes go numb, and they told me I had carpal tunnel syndrome. I'd never had that before the war, however. While I was at the VA hospital in Washington, I met other Gulf War vets who had symptoms similar to mine and were also sensitive to chemicals at this point. Through them, I learned about Dr. Myra Shayevitz, a physician at a VA hospital in North-hampton, Massachusetts, who was very interested in multiple chemical sensitivity. About six months after I left Washington, I entered the North-hampton hospital, where they kept me for three months and I was diagnosed with MCS. They sent me to a VA hospital in Connecticut to have a SPECT scan. It showed damage to my right frontal lobe and right temple, as well as damage to the right side of my thalamus. The results of that brain scan probably explain the memory problems I've had since the war.

I have had to make many adjustments in my life because of the chemical sensitivity I brought back from the Gulf War. I had to give up my job as pastor at my church because I was having a hard time remembering scripture passages that I used to know by heart.

The construction trade was slow when I returned from the war, so I got a job in law enforcement because I had previous experience in the field. I worked for the sheriff's department for a while and also for a city police department. I wasn't able to continue that line of work, however, because I had become very forgetful since my return from the war and would get confused about where I was. There would be times when I'd be out driving on roads that I'd traveled many times before, and sometimes I couldn't remember where I was. I would just have to keep going, and finally I would realize where I was. When I was trying to work in law enforcement, I would get a call to go to a certain location where something was happening, and I couldn't remember where that street was located. So I just had to give up that work.

Before I went to the Gulf War, I used to love to go snowmobiling, but I can't go anymore because the diesel exhaust fumes give me a headache and make me feel nauseated. My sensitivity to chemicals makes life pretty difficult. Perfume bothers me, and so do newspapers and magazines. I get nausea and headaches from the ink, and my nose gets stuffed up. I broke out in rashes while I was in Desert Storm, and I still get rashes today. I have a lot of problem with asthma now, and I didn't have asthma before the war.

MCS also affects your home life a lot. It's hard on my wife to have me be so sensitive to chemicals now. When I left for the war, I was in good health. Now my health is bad, and I never feel like myself, I never feel good. There are many places I can't go because people are wearing perfume. Sometimes I have to wear a mask to go in a store, and people often stare at me when I wear it.

At first I was having a hard time getting compensation from the govern-ment when I filed claims on the basis of different medical conditions I had been diagnosed with. They kept turning me down. Then finally they used some other diagnoses, and I was able to get some disability payments. I'm now getting 100% compensation because I can't work. I had to keep pushing and pushing to get that money. I just wouldn't give up, and the Disabled American Veterans Association helped me out a lot. It took me seven years to get that full disability status from the VA. In the meantime I had applied for Social Security disability in 1996, and I got that in seven months.

I've noticed that the younger servicemen who are Gulf War vets are reluctant to let people know that they're not feeling well. Many of them are still on active duty, and they're afraid that if they let anyone know that they're sick, they will be discharged.

The VA hospitals are still just treating symptoms; they haven't come up with any cure. I think it's a terrible shame the way the Gulf War veterans have been treated, but it's no surprise to me because the Vietnam vets who were exposed to Agent Orange were treated the same way.

Capt. Louise Richard, CAF (Ret.)

I joined the Canadian Armed Forces in 1986 after years of Cadets, Reserves, and obtaining my nursing license. Having been born into a family of great military tradition, this was the only career I had ever wanted. It was in my blood—my father was a lieutenant general. When I went to the Persian Gulf, I was 29 years old, in prime health and in the prime of life. I was already a captain and was at the pinnacle of my career.

The air war had begun before we left Canada. We were welcomed by a SCUD missile that hit the tarmac area just prior to our landing in Al Jubayl in Saudi Arabia. I was part of a team of 42 soldiers composed of physicians, nurses, and medical assistants who were sent out to the desert in support of a British field hospital. Shortly after our arrival, we were inoculated against biological warfare agents, and I had a very bad reaction to the anthrax shot. My arm swelled up and an oozing boil formed where I had been vaccinated. I felt terrible for two days after that shot. We also started taking PB pills soon after we arrived. When I took them, I got flu-like symptoms that got progressively worse. I began experiencing a lot of pulmonary problems which increased to a chronic cough, a runny nose, headaches, diarrhea, abdominal cramps, loss of bladder control, and hypersalivation. I was diagnosed as having bronchial pneumonia, but it was not treated because there were no medications available. All my other symptoms were ignored; we were just told that was the body's reaction to the stress of war and the climate.

We had numerous SCUD alerts during the air and ground wars. During these alerts, we would have to wear our protective clothing. Some other times when the alarms went off, we were just told they were false alarms and we should ignore them.

The field hospital I was deployed with was less than 20 km [12 miles] from the frontline battle areas on Kuwait's border with Iraq. As a result, we had a lot of POW patients. Most of them were very ill with communicable diseases, infested with parasites, and covered with open wounds. As a nurse, I treated these patients daily.

We were also exposed for several weeks to the smoke and toxic fumes of the burning oil wells. That was just one of many toxic exposures. We applied the DEET they issued us against the sand fleas and other desert insects. It remained on our skin for prolonged periods of time and also remained on our clothing.

Another problem was that water used for food preparation and minimal personal hygiene was brought in by oil tankers and was contaminated by residual oil in the tankers.

About three months after I got back from the Gulf, I tested positive for TB and underwent a one-year treatment program for this disease. I suffered many side effects during the following year, but this was only one of the medical problems I was to experience. From 1991 to the present, I have suffered from many different symptoms. I became bald after the war, and my hair has never grown back. I suffer from headaches, blurred vision, muscle and joint pains, tenderness and numbness in my hands and legs, thyroid problems, asthma, abdominal cramping, diarrhea, rectal bleeding, and gynecological bleeding necessitating a hysterectomy—the list goes on and on. I'm very sensitive to chemicals now, so things like perfume, paint, gasoline, household cleaning products, and lawn pesticides will give me symptoms such as headaches, tightness in my throat and chest, vomiting, heart palpitations, or lightheadedness.

I can no longer practice my profession as a nurse, and I have been released from the military because I no longer meet their medical standards and have been declared disabled. Nevertheless, my request for a disabled veteran pension has been denied because they refuse to recognize my illness as service related. All the Gulf War veterans whom I know have had to appeal their claims, and this sends us into a paper-warfare nightmare that we don't understand and are unable to cope with. Canadian veterans have lost trust, faith, respect, and loyalty towards the authoritarian figures involved with our care and our well-being. We have been abandoned and criminally neglected. We are not a priority on anyone's desk. We are just a file, a nuisance, a problem.

All we know is loss of career, loss of income, loss of independence, loss of physical, emotional, and psychological health. The outcome is illness, pain isolation, depression, and dependence. We now exist, we do not live. What hope do we have in the future when our lives consist of surviving through this inflicted slow death that has now become a life sentence? Gulf War veterans have been made to feel like toxic waste that has been dumped into the civilian environment, which is now expected to care for us and understand our needs without any knowledge or direction or support from government officials or agencies. There is nowhere to turn. No one to talk to, just closed doors and walls. The war has lasted over ten years for us. We are sick, we are tired, we are afraid. We want to be welcomed home from the war once and for all.

Appendix

The following materials can be ordered from:

Alison Johnson
MCS Information Exchange
2 Oakland Street
Brunswick, ME 04011

Videos cost $20 each, plus $2 s&h book rate or $4 priority rate. The book listed below can be ordered for $14, plus $2 s&h book rate or $4 priority rate, as can this Gulf War syndrome book. These rates apply to individuals with Gulf War syndrome or MCS or their family and friends. Please write for rates for libraries or other institutions. No phone or credit card orders please.

Multiple Chemical Sensitivity
How Chemical Exposures
May Be Affecting Your Health
90 minutes

This video illustrates the devastating effect that MCS has had on the lives of sixteen patients from various backgrounds. The following national experts also appear in this video: Nicholas Ashford, Ph.D, J.D., Professor of Technology and Policy at MIT; Iris Bell, M.D., Ph.D., Associate Professor at the University of Arizona Health Sciences Center and staff member at the Tucson VA Medical Center; Gunnar Heuser, M.D., Ph.D., a toxicologist in private practice and Assistant Clinical Professor of Medicine at the UCLA School of Medicine; William J. Meggs, M.D., Ph.D., Associate Professor at East Carolina University School of Medicine; Claudia S. Miller, M.D., M.S., Associate Professor at the University of Texas Health Science Center at San Antonio; and Gerald Ross, M.D., the first director of a clinic in Halifax, Nova Scotia, that is the first government sponsored clinic in the world established to evaluate and treat patients with chemical sensitivity.

Also available are Vol. II, *Multiple Chemical Sensitivity: Commentary by Three Experts* (Miller, Ashford, and Bell), and Vol. III, *Multiple Chemical Sensitivity: Commentary by Four Experts* (Ross, Meggs, Heuser, and business executive Will Pape). These two videos consist of long lectures by experts.

Gulf War Syndrome
Aftermath of a Toxic Battlefield
78 minutes

This video contains interviews with thirteen veterans and with experts Mohamed Abou-Donia, Ph.D., Gunnar Heuser, M.D., Ph.D., Claudia Miller, M.D., M.S., William Meggs, M.D., Ph.D., Doug Rokke, Ph.D., Gerald Ross, M.D., and Jim Tuite.

Casualties of Progress
Personal Histories from the
Chemically Sensitive

This book contains the stories of 57 people with chemical sensitivity. These people describe in their own words how they became chronically ill from exposure to the chemicals in substances like new carpet, building materials, paint, cleaning products, fuel oil, or pesticides.

*   *   *   *   *

Also available from the same address are the results of a survey I conducted about the experience of 351 people with multiple chemical sensitivity with 160 different therapies. Therapies surveyed include Neurontin, magnets, ozone, hydrogen peroxide, mercury amalgam removal, macrobiotic diet, sauna detox, juicing, homeopathy, Nambudripad desensitization, Total Body Modification, chelation, massage, transfer factor, biofeedback, melatonin, and Prozac. A nine-page statistical table of the survey results is provided, as well as five booklets giving further information about many of the therapies.

This survey provides information about which treatments are helpful, which ones are potentially dangerous, and which ones may deplete already strained finances with no benefit. Unfortunately, too many of these therapies fall into the latter category. The survey can be ordered for $18 ($14 for those experiencing severe financial difficulty) from the above address. Price includes s&h.

*   *   *   *   *

I am setting up a nonprofit foundation to raise money for medical research into chemical sensitivity and to develop housing for the chemically sensitive in developments with restrictions on pesticides, wood smoke, fabric softener, and other air pollutants. Please contact me if you are interested in contributing to either of these projects.

Index